Joshua Chamberlain

A HERO'S LIFE AND LEGACY

JOHN J. PULLEN

STACKPOLE
BOOKS

Published by
STACKPOLE BOOKS
5067 Ritter Road
Mechanicsburg PA 17055
www.stackpolebooks.com

*The author makes grateful acknowledgment for permission to quote or reproduce material
from the following sources:* Patton: A Genius for War *by Carlo D'Este, reprinted by
permission of HarperCollins Publishers Inc.;* The Hero With a Thousand Faces *by
Joseph Campbell, reprinted by permission of the Princeton University Press; "'Gettysburg'
Film Should Be Applauded" in the June 1998 issue of* The Civil War News, *Turnbridge,
Vermont; "In Memoriam, Joshua Chamberlain" in the February 24, 1996, issue of* The Day,
*New London, Connecticut; Chamberlain and Thomas Brackett Reed Collections, the Bow-
doin College Library, Brunswick, Maine; Chamberlain and Abner R. Small Collections,
the Maine Historical Society, Portland, Maine; Chamberlain and Rutherford B. Hayes
Collections, the Rutherford B. Hayes Presidential Center, Fremont, Ohio; and the
Chamberlain Collection, the Pejepscot Historical Society, Brunswick, Maine.*

Printed in the United States of America

10 9 8 7 6 5

FIRST EDITION

Library of Congress Cataloging-in-Publication Data
Pullen, John J.
    Joshua Chamberlain : a hero's life and legacy / John J. Pullen. —
1st ed.
      p.   cm.
    Includes bibliographical references (p.) and index.
    ISBN 0-8117-0886-1
    1. Chamberlain, Joshua Lawrence, 1828–1914. 2. Generals—United
States—Biography. 3. United States. Army—Biography. 4. Maine—
History—Civil War, 1861–1865. 5. United States. Army. Maine
Infantry Regiment, 20th (1862–1865). 6. Gettysburg (Pa.), Battle of,
1863. I. Title.
E467.1.C47P85   1999
973.7′441092—dc21
    [b]   99-17606
                                           CIP

For Margaret

Contents

Acknowledgments

The author is most fortunate to have had at his side in this work Margaret Rogers Pullen, whose editorial experience and advice, research assistance, and patience in enduring the trials of a writer's wife are deeply appreciated.

Two people must appear near the top of my thank-you list for more than alphabetical reasons: Herbert Adams and Rita C. Bailey. Rita's extensive knowledge of Chamberlain's correspondence, her research in furtherance of the work, and her care and skill in preparation of the manuscript have been of immense help. Herbert, a fine historian and a friend of long standing, has located and suggested the use of much material and has been a valuable consultant in the final stages of writing.

Rosamond Allen, granddaughter of Joshua Chamberlain, graciously gave permission to publish his and other letters of his family. Her friend Jacquelyn M. Beard was most helpful in arranging this permission. Thanks go to Richard Balkin, literary agent, for his guidance and advice; to Pat Wright-Buckley for the photograph of her delightful "Joshua Bear"; to Dwight B. Demeritt Jr. for contributions that will be recognized in the text and notes; to Dr. Thomas A. Desjardin for finding time from a busy life to answer questions; to Fred M. Forsley, president of the Shipyard Brewing Company, and artist Ken Hendricksen for permission to publish the Chamberlain Pale Ale label; to Richard Hede of Stockholm, Maine, for information about New Sweden; to Katherine Jenney for permission to publish part of a Thomas B. Reed letter; to author and historian William B. Jordan Jr. for a creative contribution identified in chapter twelve; to Dr. C. Kenneth McAllister, Colonel, U.S. Army Medical Corps, for his analyses of Joshua Chamberlain's wounds and medical problems; also to urologist Samuel B. Broaddus, M.D., for his help in interpreting medical terms; to Warren Randall for important contributions of material; to David E. Rathbun for his "In Memoriam" notice; and to Edward, James, and Marjorie Spear for permission to publish a letter from the late Abbott Spear's collection.

At a party in the summer of 1994 the author heard from Campbell B. Niven, publisher of *The Times Record* of Brunswick, a story that is a key element of chapter two. Mr. Niven's permission to use this story is greatly appreciated.

Individuals connected with several institutions deserve special thanks. Among them, Susan Ravdin, former assistant curator of Bowdoin College Library Special Collections. Also secretary emeritus of Bowdoin and friend for forty years, Robert M. Cross, whose encyclopedic knowledge of Bowdoin and its alumni and review of the manuscript were most helpful. Special thanks go to Mildred Jones, historian and archivist of the First Parish Church in Brunswick for her assistance. Sylvia J. Sherman, director of archival services at the Maine State Archives in Augusta has been a friend to many authors, and she was a good friend to this one. The privilege of consulting with her is greatly appreciated. Valuable contributions came from Earle G. Shettleworth Jr., director of the Maine Historic Preservation Commission, and Julia Hunt, curator of fine arts, graphic arts, and archives at the Maine State Museum. Craig Freshly, program director of the Maine Development Foundation provided helpful information. Linda R. Mansfield, owner of Chamberlain's former home in Portland, graciously permitted Erik Jorgensen to photograph the house for me. At the Portland Customs House, Jeffrey R. Walgreen, John Foley, John Barrett, and D. Peter Goodridge helped with research and photography.

The library of the Maine Historical Society, in Portland, was a prime resource, with the aid of William David Barry, Don King, Nicholas Noyes, and Stephanie Philbrick. The help of the Military Order of the Loyal Legion of the United States is recognized in the notes to chapter eleven. My sincere thanks to members of the National Park Service, especially Joseph A. Williams, curator at Appomattox National Military Park, and D. Scott Hartwig, supervisory park historian at Gettysburg.

The research center most frequented was the Pejepscot Historical Society, in Brunswick, Maine, where valued support came from several good friends: Erik Jorgensen, executive director 1989–98; Amy L. Poland, the curator; and staff members Jill Wallace and Betty Hyde; and the curator emeritus, Julia Oehmig.

An important photograph was obtained from the Portland Newspapers with the aid of Marcia MacVane. At the Portland Library, Thomas Bennett, Paul A. D'Alessandro, and Thomas Gaffney were most helpful. Nan J. Card, curator of manuscripts at the Rutherford B. Hayes Presidential Center in Fremont, Ohio, responded quickly to requests and sent additional material that was used. Important contributions were made by World Chamberlain Society members, Ted and Welton Chamberlain. Notes to chapter sixteen give the names of visitors to the Chamberlain Museum who offered interesting opinions, as well as those of police sergeant Linda L. Belfiore and of my friend Kenneth Discorfano. Thank you, all.

Prologue

〜〜〜

A cold morning in deep winter, Friday, February 27, 1914: in front of a modest house on Ocean Avenue, Portland, Maine. A hearse is waiting, attended by an honor guard—a sergeant major and five sergeants. Carriages for mourners and honorary pallbearers stand ready to depart.

The door opens; a coffin covered with an American flag is brought out and placed in the hearse. The cortege starts off; it moves north along Ocean Avenue and turns right onto Washington Avenue, proceeding toward downtown Portland. Crossing the bridge that spans the entrance of Back Cove, the cortege is received into a larger formation consisting of four National Guard companies, two companies of naval reserves, a band, and a platoon of policemen. The band strikes up a dirge. The procession continues along Washington Avenue, turns onto Congress Street and enters downtown Portland, where people have gathered on the sidewalks. In spite of the freezing temperature, many of them bare their heads as the cortege passes.

Everyone knows what this is about. The newspapers have been full of it for two days.[1] Gen. Joshua Chamberlain, the hero of Little Round Top, is dead. He died on Tuesday morning—mostly from the effects of a wound he received nearly fifty years previously—attended on his deathbed by his old friend and physician, Dr. Abner O. Shaw. There is an odd thing about that; Shaw as a Civil War surgeon helped put him back together on that summer day at Petersburg, Virginia, when a Confederate marksman sent a bullet ploughing through his body from hip to hip, causing the wound that has now finally killed him or helped to kill him.

The cortege arrives at City Hall. The casket, attended by its honor guard, is carried into the building. An estimated five thousand people have gathered here; fewer than half can get in; the rest wait outside. Dozens of dignitaries attend the services. Maine's governor is there; he has ordered all state flags in Maine to be lowered to half-staff. The governor of Massachusetts has sent a delegation. Many veterans' organizations are represented, including the Grand Army of the Republic and the elite Military Order of the Loyal Legion. A Portland clergyman delivers the funeral oration. The organist plays selections from Grieg and Handel, and Beethoven and Chopin funeral marches.

The service ends with a benediction. A bugler plays Taps; a call not often sounded indoors, its sad notes echo strangely within the great hall. The casket is carried out of City Hall and replaced in the hearse. To the sound of the mournful band music, muffled drums, and the marching feet of military escorts the cortege moves to Union Station, where a special train is waiting to take the funeral party twenty miles or so up the coast to Brunswick, where Chamberlain had spent nearly a third of his life as a student, professor, and president of Bowdoin College and where he had lived while governor of Maine. Throngs of people watch from the sidewalks. An imagined conversation:

"If he was such a great man, what was he doing working in the Portland Customs House?"

"It was a sort of an honorary job—to support him in his old age. After the war he held some important positions, but mostly things went down hill for him. He could have been a U.S. senator, maybe president, but he wouldn't play ball with the politicians."

The train arrives at Brunswick, where all is hushed and silent. Town offices are closed for the afternoon. Classes at Bowdoin College are suspended. More than a thousand people watch the procession as it moves the short distance from the railway station to the First Parish Church near the Bowdoin campus, escorted by veterans from the local post of the Grand Army of the Republic. Also marching along in the column is the Brunswick company of the Maine National Guard. Ideas of national defense change over the years, and now the emphasis along the eastern seaboard is on forts and big guns—this company was infantry a few years ago; now it is officially designated as 10th Company, Coast Artillery Corps, State of Maine National Guard. (The 1st, 2nd, 5th, and 11th Companies had marched with the cortege in Portland.)[2] There is hope that the nation, now united and safe behind the broad Atlantic and its great forts, will never again need armies of foot soldiers like those who fought so desperately under Chamberlain at Gettysburg.

The First Parish Church is filled; inside are the entire Bowdoin student body, dignitaries, and mourners. Dr. William DeWitt Hyde, who had succeeded Chamberlain as president of Bowdoin in 1885, delivers a thoughtful and stirring eulogy replete with praise and honor. A soloist sings "Abide with Me" and "Nearer My God to Thee." For the second time in the day, Chopin's funeral march is heard as the organ plays while the casket is borne from the church.

Now there is only a short way to go—eastward along the Bath Road to the northwest corner of Pine Grove Cemetery, where Chamberlain's wife and two children who died in their infancy are buried. It is getting on in the day; the tall pines standing to the west of the cemetery are beginning to cast deep shadows over the open grave. A squad from the 10th Company is waiting to fire the ceremonial salute. In their brownish, high-collared uniforms and wide-brimmed hats, their appearance is strikingly different from that of the boys in blue that Chamberlain commanded. Angular and dark against the snowy background, they raise their Springfield rifles.[3] Shots shock the winter air. Ejected cartridges fly and shine in the fading light. One of the firing party is Edward H. Snow, a senior at Bowdoin. He will remember it for a lifetime. "They were pretty ragged volleys, but I guess we did our best."[4] Off at some distance another bugler, the second for the day, sounds Taps.

After these grand ceremonies on February 27, 1914, the name of Joshua Chamberlain slips quickly into oblivion. But in the last half of the twentieth century, in large part because of records and writings he entrusted to posterity, he will arise and soar to prominence like a mythological figure returning after banishment to the underworld.

CHAPTER ONE

A Very Perfect Knight

For people who have not heard the story of the fight at Little Round Top on the Gettysburg battlefield—and today there aren't many of these among readers of Civil War literature—it should be stated that it was here, late on July 2, 1863, that Joshua L. Chamberlain arose from the clouds of gunsmoke into the light of fame. Ordered to hold this position—representing the left flank of the entire Union line—at all costs, Chamberlain and the 20th Maine regiment he commanded did more than hold their ground. They fought off repeated massive attacks until, as one participant remembered, "the blood stood in puddles in some places on the rocks,"[1] and the Maine soldiers were nearly out of ammunition; they then fixed bayonets, launched a desperate charge, took many prisoners, and drove the Confederates into a precipitate retreat.

Some said that Joshua Chamberlain and the 20th Maine saved the day at Gettysburg and therefore saved the Union. There were more than 250 other Union regiments at Gettysburg, however, and some of them performed equally well at critical points in the battle. The 137th New York, commanded by Col. David Ireland, held the right (north) end of the Union line on the second day of Gettysburg in a manner comparable to that of the 20th Maine on the left end, with the two regiments suffering losses that were almost identical, yet these New Yorkers have never been given the acclaim accorded Chamberlain and the 20th Maine; in fact, they have scarcely been acclaimed at all.[2]

Consider the 16th Maine on the first day of the battle when the whole Union force was about to be overwhelmed and was falling back. In order to give the rest of its division time to retire, the 16th Maine was ordered "at any cost" to hold a hill—the same command given to the 20th Maine. The 16th held, saving its division, but at the cost of being almost entirely wiped out. Just before that happened the men tore their flag into bits, which they concealed in their clothing. Many of the bits were carried through Southern prison camps. Toward the end of the century the regimental historian wrote, "Today, all over Maine, can be found in albums and frames and breast-pocket-books gold stars and shreds of silk, cherished mementos of that heroic and awful hour."[3]

So, if the 20th Maine saved the day at Gettysburg, they had help. It was a day, as Bruce Catton once remarked, that needed a lot of saving. Yet the action at Little Round Top continues to stand out. A *New York Times* book review stated that "the future of American was decided" here.[4] Maybe, and maybe not. But the fact remains that this was a legendary deed, worthy to be ranked with the famous though less successful stand of the Spartans at Thermopylae.

Going on from Gettysburg, Chamberlain further distinguished himself. Grievously wounded at Petersburg while leading an attack, he was made a brigadier general by Gen. Ulysses S. Grant himself, and after a recuperation of a few months went back to the war to gain more wounds, more acclaim, and a brevet major generalship. So bright were his stars on April 12, 1865, that he was detailed to command the Union troops who received the ceremonial surrender of Gen. Robert E. Lee's infantry at Appomattox Court House.

It was this record that charmed the people of Maine and of the nation—even residents of the South, who heard that Chamberlain had ordered the Union troops to salute the surrendering Confederates when they marched up to lay down their arms. To the public Chamberlain presented a unique persona. Here was a fellow who'd had no military experience before the war, who was an intellectual—a professor—who had left the faculty of Bowdoin College to enter the service. He was also a certified Christian who had graduated from a theological seminary. And a gentleman, polite and compassionate. Yet look at what this scholar-soldier had done on the field of battle!

The surrender ceremony at Appomattox on that April day was a dramatic climax to the fighting between the Army of the Potomac and Gen. Robert E. Lee's Army of Northern Virginia. The momentous meaning of the occasion, Chamberlain said later, impressed him deeply. He thought the defeated soldiers deserved some recognition, not only for their valor at arms but also as a welcome back into the Union, and he ordered this recog-

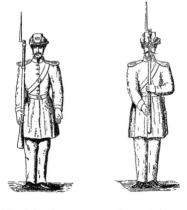

Shoulder Arms   *Present Arms*

nition on his own authority, "well aware of the responsibility assumed and of the criticism that would follow, as the sequel proved."[5] By his instruction, as each Confederate division came up to stack its arms and lay down its colors, a bugle sounded and instantly the whole Union line from right to left, regiment by regiment, came to "shouldered arms," a position of the manual requiring steadiness and silence.

There is some question as to whether or not this was really a salute. In "shouldered arms" as described in Casey's *Infantry Tactics* the musket was held vertically in the right hand and resting in the hollow of the right shoulder. A salute would have required that the piece be held by both hands at "present arms" vertically opposite the center of the body. Many years later Chamberlain said that the men did not "present arms" at Appomattox for "that would have been too much." Nevertheless, it would be generally referred to as a salute, sometimes by Chamberlain himself. For example, in a 1901 interview Chamberlain said, "I instructed my subordinate commanders that as the respective bodies of the Confederates army passed their front they should come to the position of salute in the manual of arms. It was not a 'present' however, which was the highest possible honor to be paid, even to the president, but it was the 'carry,' the musket held in the right hand and perpendicular to the shoulder like a marching salute in review."[6]

Whether or not it was a full-fledged salute, its ordering was an audacious act on Joshua Chamberlain's part, considering the actions and attitude of Congress over the next several years and the widespread grief of thousands of Northern families who had lost fathers, husbands, brothers, and sons as a result of the rebellion. But somehow, in spite of his own suffering in the war, Chamberlain had reached a higher plane, from which he saw the surrendering Southerners as part of the nation he had fought to preserve, and he was welcoming them back into a Union that in his opinion they had never left.

This is what made the "salute" such an enormous, almost appalling gesture. Here at Appomattox Court House Chamberlain had prematurely stepped right into the crux of the Reconstruction dilemma and had given a signal as to which side of the issue he was on. Since the dominant political party in Maine was the Republican party, completely in tune with the Radical Republicans in Washington, this might have been an ill augury for Chamberlain's future. But his popularity as a war hero was so great that the elders of the Republican party in Maine would eagerly adopt him, even as Eisenhower was seized upon after World War II. Chamberlain would serve four one-year terms as governor of Maine. But in spite of his qualifications to go on and become a U.S. senator, ambassador, cabinet member, or holder of some other high office, his would be a slowly falling star, completely adumbrated in February 1914 when he died and his name was virtually forgotten.

Was his bold act at Appomattox Court House the fatal flaw that eventually caused his political demise? By no means. A politician of elementary skill could have brushed this from his garments within a few years. It was rather the character and attitude demonstrated by the episode that held the seeds of his decline. His stubborn insistence on doing whatever he thought to be right, without regard for political pressures or popular opinion, harmed him. It was simply the kind of man he was that would erode his fortunes in the decades of the Gilded Age.

One observer who rightly appraised Chamberlain was Gen. John Brown Gordon, a Confederate commander who was present at Appomattox, leading his surrendering troops. Chamberlain described Gordon's reaction to the "salute," as it was called. "Gordon at the head of the column, riding with heavy spirit and downcast face, catches the sound of shifting arms, looks up, and, taking the meaning, wheels superbly, making with himself and his horse one uplifted figure, with profound salutation as he drops the point of his sword to his boot toe; then facing to his own command, gives word for his successive brigades to pass us with the same position of the manual—honor answering honor."[7]

This sounds like a paragraph from one of the ancient annals of chivalry. It reflects a vision Chamberlain had of himself and an image that the Confederate general readily recognized. Around the turn of the century Gordon was going around the country giving a popular lecture entitled

"Last Days of the Confederacy." In it he described Chamberlain as "that knightly soldier," and he marveled at the ceremony of which he had been part, saying "No scene like it in any age was ever witnessed at the end of a long and bloody war."[8]

The only unfortunate thing about this exercise in magnanimity by Chamberlain, Grant, and others at Appomattox was that it led the Confederates to expect much more generosity than they later received at the hands of a Radical Republican Congress during Reconstruction—a circumstance that would distress both Gordon and Chamberlain.

Up to a point Chamberlain and Gordon were parallel characters. Oddly, both were married to wives named Fanny, and both marriages lasted nearly fifty years. Chamberlain had been a college professor when he went to war and had little practical knowledge of military affairs. Gordon had been a lawyer, journalist, and businessman and was also uneducated in the arts of war. Both were marvels of coolness and courage in combat. Neither was dismayed by the sight of his own blood. Gordon was wounded five times in one battle (Antietam) and left the fight only when the fifth bullet went through his cheek and jaw; Chamberlain received a desperate, nearly fatal wound at Petersburg. Both proved to be exceptional military leaders and rose to the rank of major general, with Gordon commanding a corps at the war's end (he should have been a lieutenant general) and Chamberlain commanding a division. After the war Chamberlain served four years as governor of Maine, Gordon four years as governor of Georgia. Beyond that the resemblance ceases, for Gordon also served in the U.S. Senate and went on to become a nationally known figure as a spokesman for the South and for reconciliation, while Chamberlain ascended no higher than his governorship. One of the reasons is that Gordon displayed a deal of flexibility in dealing with the elements of his constituency—for example, the Ku Klux Klan—but Chamberlain seldom yielded to political expediency. As a human being he had failings, a few of which served him well, while some of the virtues ascribed to him by Gordon were doing him in. Yet he clung to ideas that were those of knighthood—honor, courage, courtesy, and so on—expressed in behavior of a certain grace and words often spoken or written in a high and stately tone. Once in speaking of family lore passed on to him by his father, he said there was "a chivalrous strain of blood in his composition."[9]

Research by Welton C. Chamberlain of the World Chamberlain Society indicates that among the progenitors of the line were the proprietors of Tancarville Castle in Normandy, the ruins of which still stand on a cliff overlooking the lower Seine. According to this research one William, occupant of the castle, was chamberlain (a position of trust and guardianship

Tancarville Castle, as it looked in the fifteenth century.
COURTESY WELTON C. CHAMBERLAIN.

having to do with finances and other affairs of a household or court) to William, duke of Normandy.

When the duke went to England as William the Conqueror, William of Tancarville went with him; and although he returned to Normandy, his descendants remained in England and served as chamberlains to Kings Henry I, Stephen, and Henry II. By the time of Henry II single names were no longer adequate; surnames were coming into use and Henry's man Richard (of the Tancarville line) ceased being "Richard the chamberlain"; he took the name Richard Chamberlain, and the surname became hereditary.[10]

Descent from these people was an idea well rooted in the family of Joshua Chamberlain. This is shown by a letter he wrote to his father from the steamer *England* in the summer of 1878 while going to France to act as U.S. commissioner of education at the Paris Universal Exposition. One sentence read, "It will be a great thing for the children to have the opportunity of seeing Europe with us, & we will try to write you from *Tankerville Castle* [Chamberlain's emphasis] and many other interesting places."[11]

Although documentation of lineal descent going back thirty or more generations would be difficult if not impossible, there is a good chance that Chamberlain's ancestors were participants in events of the age of chivalry. Certainly he seems to have thought so, and that thinking was important.

Some of Chamberlain's lecture notes, written while he was a professor at Bowdoin College before the war, indicate that Chaucer was one of his

Part of the ruins of Tancarville Castle as it looks today.
COURTESY WELTON C. CHAMBERLAIN.

favorite authors. What influence, we may wonder, radiated from the page into his psyche when he read from the general prologue to *The Canterbury Tales:*

> A knyght ther was, and that a worthy man,
> That fro the tyme that he first bigan
> To riden out, he loved chivalrie,
> Trouthe and honour, fredom and curteisie.

And later in the prologue:

> And though that he were worthy, he was wys,
> And of his port as meek as is a mayde;
> He nevere yet no vileynye ne sayde
> In al his lyf unto no maner wight;
> He was a verray parfit gentil knyght.

Physically, Chamberlain looked and acted the part of a knight-errant. A description by one who knew him: "In person General Chamberlain was of medium height, his form was perfectly proportioned, well-knit, neither slender nor stout, and always erect and graceful. His finely shaped head and face of classic features and beauty was nobly borne, with an air well fitting the chivalrous spirit within. His voice was pleasing, strong and resonant and used with perfect art, oftentimes thrilling with tones suited to his utterances."[12] He had blue eyes, which even in old age, as one woman said, "were always snapping right out at you."[13] During the Civil War years his mustache swept back with a winged flair, but this flair disappears in the photographs taken of him in civilian life, subtracting greatly from the wartime impression of elegance and élan. Being in uniform seemed to do more for Chamberlain than alter his appearance; it elevated his spirits.

In one respect, however, he did not quite compare with Chaucer's knight. He was certainly "worthy" and "wys," but he was not "meek as is a mayde." Late in life he wrote an autobiography, which remained in manuscript form until published in part by the college magazine *Bowdoin* in 1991. This account of his life was written in the third person, a form of composition that greatly alleviates any impression of conceit because it eliminates use of the pronoun "I." Also Chamberlain further moderated this impression by dropping in brief interjections of self-disparagement or incidents of failure. Yet he managed to portray himself as an admirable creature and did this so gracefully and unoffendingly that the judicious and charitable reader, considering that he really *was* admirable, must react with mild amusement rather than irritation.

Joshua Chamberlain did not fall victim to a mistake that many people make. He did not set a value upon himself below his real worth. Further, he would have subscribed to the belief: If you want people to know your capabilities, see to it yourself. Do not entrust the task to others. They are likely to be distracted by interests of their own. An episode illustrating this philosophy took place on June 19, 1864, when Chamberlain, then a colonel, was lying shot through the body in a field hospital, and everyone thought he was dying, including Chamberlain himself. This is certain because of a letter he wrote to his wife Fanny on that day telling her that he was mortally wounded and bidding her farewell.[14]

Two generals, Charles J. Griffin and Gouverneur K. Warren, called on Chamberlain and wanted to know if there was anything they could do for him. Result: On the nineteenth Warren sent the following telegram to the army commander:

MAJ GEN MEADE
COL J L CHAMBERLAIN OF THE 20TH MAINE REGT
COMMANDING THE 1ST BRIGADE OF THE 1ST DIVISION
WAS MORTALLY WOUNDED IT IS THOUGHT IN THE

ASSAULT ON THE ENEMY YESTERDAY THE BALL HAV-
ING PASSED THROUGH THE PELVIS AND BLADDER HE
HAS BEEN RECOMMENDED FOR PROMOTION FOR GAL-
LANT AND EFFICIENT CONDUCT ON PREVIOUS OCCA-
SION AND YESTERDAY LED HIS BRIGADE AGAINST THE
ENEMY UNDER MOST DESTRUCTIVE FIRE HE EXPRES-
SES THE WISH THAT HE MAY RECEIVE THE RECOGNI-
TION OF HIS SERVICES BY PROMOTION BEFORE HE DIES
FOR THE GRATIFICATION OF HIS FAMILY AND FRIENDS
AND I BEG THAT IF POSSIBLE THAT IT MAY BE DONE HE
HAS BEEN SENT TO CITY POINT
                          G K WARREN   MAJ GEN[15]

The request was passed on to General Grant, and it resulted in Chamberlain's immediate elevation to the rank of brigadier general. A thought which must spring to mind is that anyone who seeks a higher worldly office when he thinks he is departing from the world is certainly looking toward the perpetuation of his name and fame.

This instinct even entered into Chamberlain's relationship with his wife Fanny. In particular, one artifact surviving in the custody of Bowdoin College provides physical evidence of his seeing her life as revolving around his own. It is a bracelet made principally of yellow gold and diamonds that Chamberlain designed and had manufactured by Tiffany and Company. for Fanny in commemoration of their tenth wedding anniversary on December 7, 1865. On one side of the bracelet is a red Maltese cross (the symbol of the corps in which Chamberlain served) on a white ground. On the opposite side of the bracelet is the insignia of Chamberlain's rank of major general, two silver stars on a bright blue field. The band of the bracelet is formed of twenty-four struts, each bearing the name of a battle in which Chamberlain fought.

This is a beautiful, expensive, and now widely known piece of jewelry; a full-color reproduction of it appears as the frontispiece of Martha Gandy Fales's elegant book *Jewelry in America, 1600–1900* published by the Antique Collectors' Club in 1995. It is a token of Chamberlain's love for his wife and generosity toward her. But it speaks mainly of war, which could not have been a pleasant subject to Fanny. It said nothing about their love, their ten years together, or any of the tender sentiments that should attach to such a wedding anniversary. It was all about Chamberlain and his war record—the sort of jewelry that a knight would have given to his lady to display in his honor as he jousted in a tournament.

In trying to get inside Joshua Chamberlain's handsome head it seems important to recognize that he hungered for an epic life.

It was at Gettysburg that this vision first appeared to him. He had not found much promise of it while correcting papers as a professor at Bowdoin. From an army bivouac in 1862 he had written Fanny, "Let me say no danger and no hardship makes me wish to go back to that college life again. I can't breathe when I think of those last two years. Why, I would spend my whole life in campaigning rather than endure that again. One thing though, I *won't* endure it again. My experience here & the habit of command, will make me less complaisant—will break in upon the notion that certain persons are the natural authorities over me."[16]

Chamberlain experienced his greatest fulfillment in the Civil War, and the military motif continued to be an important part of his life. In a sense he never left the Army of the Potomac—or it never left him. The last official communication from its headquarters, which read "By virtue of special orders, No. 339, current series, from the Adjutant General's office, this army, as an organization, ceases to exist," drew an emotional comment from Chamberlain. He wrote, "Ceases to exist! Are you sure of that? . . . The War Department and the President may cease to give the army orders, may disperse its visible elements, but cannot extinguish them. . . . This army will live, and live on, so long as soul shall answer soul, so long as that flag watches with its stars over fields of mighty memory. . . ."[17]

It is probable that part of Chamberlain's interest in perpetuating his own image was the desire to perpetuate with it the spirit of this army and the patriotism and suffering that saved the Union. As the story of his life is pursued, the impression grows that he thought of himself as more than himself. There were good reasons why the Army of the Potomac remained with him as a mystic presence. One of the first large armies to have its roots in a democracy and an unmilitary society, it had learned the business of war through on-the-job training, a hard method of military education, and had survived much agony to become one of the greatest armies that ever marched. Its members had qualities of intelligence, literacy, courage, and character unlooked-for in soldiery. In going from being an excellent college professor to becoming an outstanding general, Chamberlain may have been remarkable but he was not unique; thousands of men made the same transition from civilian to military excellence. His association with these men and his success in this army had made the military life attractive to Chamberlain to an unusual degree.

Chamberlain was one of the few men who ever publicly stated that Sherman's "War is hell" is an incomplete definition, writing that "In the privations and sufferings endured as well as in the strenuous action of battle, some of the highest qualities of manhood are called forth—courage, self-command, sacrifice of self for the sake of something held higher. . . .[18] Even the fact that he had suffered a nearly mortal wound did not dampen the fascination of battle. This was the wound received while Chamberlain was leading a charge at Petersburg on June 18, 1864. His first reaction, as related in an interview in 1904, was typical of his spirit of honor. "The first pain I felt was in my back and I thought, what will my mother say—her boy shot in the back. Then I saw the blood gushing from my side and I felt better."[19] A bullet had penetrated his body from hip to hip, tearing the bladder and urethra and damaging pelvic bones. After lying on the battlefield several hours, he was carried to a field hospital three miles behind the lines where, after examining him, the surgeons on duty declared his case hopeless and put him aside to die. Not satisfied with this verdict, two regimental surgeons—Dr. Abner O. Shaw of the 20th Maine and Dr. Morris W. Townsend of the 44th New York—who were brought to the hospital by Chamberlain's brother Tom, worked through the night to complete a repair that was improbable under the conditions of that day. In a talk given in 1997, Col. C. Kenneth McAllister, M.D., of the Brooke Army Medical Center, called it "miracle surgery," considering those conditions.

In 1864 surgeons knew nothing about microscopic killers and the need for antiseptic precautions. Usually an internal wound of Chamberlain's sort meant uncontrollable infection and death. Opening an abdomen in surgery only increased the risk of infection. Doctors Shaw and Townsend, working under poor light with primitive equipment, cut out dead tissue, tied off severed blood vessels, removed the bullet, and inserted a urinary catheter, which enabled them to put the urethra back together. According to McAllister, this may have been one of the first times that the urinary catheter, first manufactured in France, was used in America. He pointed out that it preserved the anatomic integrity of the urethra and helped save Chamberlain's life, but the catheter was not the soft, flexible type used today; it was made of metal, and it was left in so long during Chamberlain's recovery that it caused a stricture of the urethra and, probably, the erosion that wore an opening (fistula) half an inch long in the penis just in front of the scrotum.

Dr. McAllister's analysis of the wound indicates that its aftereffects through Chamberlain's lifetime were both painful and embarrassing. There were recurring infections both of the urinary tract and from bone damage. Urine was voided through the fistula. During times of infection there was drainage from the affected tissues and bone. Reconstructive surgery had to be performed four and perhaps five times over the years.

That in spite of this serious physical impairment Chamberlain persisted in leading an active and productive life to the age of eighty-five was a measure of courage comparable to that he displayed on the battlefield. Courage and an unwavering desire to do the right thing were his chief characteristics as he came out of the Civil War a celebrity and entered the life of a nation that the war had changed immensely.

CHAPTER TWO

The Reluctant Republican

Chamberlain was released from the army in August 1865, but was later reinstated so that he could have some needed (and certainly service-related) surgery done. He was finally discharged in January 1866. After the stirring action of the Civil War and his rise to the rank of brevet major general, it was a distinct comedown for Chamberlain to return to a civilian occupation. He had written to his wife Fanny that no hardship of war could make him wish to go back to a college professor's life. But when he returned to his family and home in Brunswick at the war's end, there was really nothing else to do. With his military record and reputation, he could very easily have obtained a commission in the regular army—in fact, one was offered to him in August 1866[1]—but the prospect of being stationed at some dusty, remote western post chasing Indians while still troubled by his wound did not appeal to him, and he declined. It was a wise decision. Within a couple of decades the size of the United States army would decrease to fewer than twenty-seven thousand officers and men.

Chamberlain went back to teaching as a member of the Bowdoin faculty. That summer his position was somewhat elevated when the president of the college resigned and Chamberlain was given his place and his salary until the end of the year, when he left the campus to become governor of Maine. How that happened is easy to understand. Early in 1866, as soon as he returned from the army, Chamberlain began doing a great deal of lecturing around the state, telling people about Little Round Top and other experiences in the Civil War. An attractive man and a good speaker, he caught the eye of Maine's Republican leader, James G. Blaine.

Campaign banner. Joshua L. Chamberlain Museum, Brunswick, Maine.

James G. Blaine was a man who was to hover in the background of Chamberlain's life for many years. Among his fellow U.S. congressmen, he was often referred to as "Blaine of Maine," but he was not from Maine. He was "from away"—from Pennsylvania, where, after graduation from Washington College he had taught school for six or seven years. In 1850 he married a Maine girl, and in 1854 he moved to her native city and Maine's capital, Augusta, where he became editor in chief of the daily *Kennebec Journal* a stalwart organ of the Republican party. He left journalism to go into politics, first in the Maine legislature, where he served as Speaker of the House; next to the U.S. House of Representatives, where he was Speaker for six years; on to the U.S. Senate, from which he resigned to become secretary of state in 1881, also running for the Republican presidential nomination in 1876 and 1880 and as Republican candidate for president in 1884.

Meanwhile, although much occupied in Washington, Blaine continued to be a political czar in Maine. He was chairman of the Republican party in Maine from 1860 until 1881, dictating platforms and candidates, controlling funds, handing out patronage. Maine Democrats compared him to an octopus, with a tentacle in every municipal or county office, a spy in every post office. His opponents attached a suspicion of snakiness to Blaine, mostly because of some dealings he had with a railroad in which, they said, he had used his position as Speaker to profit financially. But no one who reads his addresses or writings can fail to be impressed by the cogency of his thought, the clarity and power of his expression, and the evidence of his having done very thorough homework on any subject he addressed. He was a man of great industry, intelligence, influence, and, by some accounts, of personal warmth and charm.

In discussing his relationship with Chamberlain there is a temptation to portray Blaine as a ruthless political boss who finally became Chamberlain's nemesis. But this disregards certain characteristics of Joshua Chamberlain that Blaine had to reckon with as a political leader. Early in 1866

Blaine saw the general as an ideal candidate for the governorship of Maine. He was a war hero, and one who had risen to his rank not through political influence but by merit. He had been well liked by his men and was sure to be popular with the former boys in blue who now made up such a large part of the voting population. Demographically he was perfect. He had been born and brought up on a farm in Brewer, a small town on the east side of the Penobscot River and therefore representative of northeastern Maine, a largely rural area where people did not always look with favor upon candidates from the more urban southern Maine, which nearly always seemed to get the benefit of governmental dispensations. Popular in all sections of the state, Chamberlain was bound to be a winner.

What Blaine did not know at this time was Chamberlain's political weaknesses. Among these: He did not have the skill necessary to move easily and gracefully out of difficult or embarrassing situations. Although adept at self-promotion in many ways, he would later shrink from initiating and running a political campaign in his own behalf. He lacked the thick, protective, rhinoceros hide that a politician needs. And where matters of principle were concerned, he had little talent for compromise, the art by which most things get done in the political world. He would speak and act according to his own beliefs.

There was also an adverse factor not within Chamberlain's control. He and his family were not within the circle that would facilitate what modern usage describes as "networking." Mid-nineteenth-century Maine was dominated by a group of business and political leaders who were influential not only in the state but in national affairs. Most of the politicians were lawyers who seemed to be clawing one another like tigers in their court appearances, but behind the scenes their rough camaraderie allowed advantageous arrangements to be made. Chamberlain had strong support among the veterans, but in halls where the wheels of real power turned he never had, and never seemed to desire, much acquaintance.

In 1866 these political deficiencies had not surfaced. Some Republicans did, however, have one suspicion concerning Chamberlain. What about that foolish salute he gave the Confederates at Appomattox Court House? Did that betray a secret sympathy for the South? If so, Chamberlain was not their man. The Republican party of Maine was solidly allied with the Radical Republican U.S. Congress, which was entering into a bitter conflict with President Andrew Johnson. Johnson's view, generally reflecting that of Lincoln, was that the Southern states had never ceased to be members of the Union, that they retained their rights under the Constitution, and that they should be brought back into the Union as soon as possible. The Radical

Republicans in control of Congress held that the Southern states by their acts of secession and rebellion had reduced themselves to the status of territories, and it was the responsibility of Congress—using military force if necessary—to bring them into conformity with certain rules, dictated by Congress, before they could return as states. These rules would change the whole political, social, and economic structure of the South.

Clearly the Radical Republicans, true to the reformist traditions of the party, were reaching out to protect blacks from the injustices they were suffering in Southern states and to secure for them the basic liberties they were entitled to under the Bill of Rights. To do this they were preparing to reduce the rights of states and to extend the power of the federal government in an unprecedented way. Further, in their conflict with the president, they were trying to extend the power of Congress in a way that threatened to subvert the Constitution and bring the nation under a parliamentary form of government.

In running for governor on a state platform that was tailored exactly to fit national Republican policy and aims, Joshua Chamberlain as a neophyte politician was stepping into a situation he probably did not fully comprehend.

Many Republicans wondered how strongly Chamberlain was riveted to their policies. One of the principal organs of the party, the Bangor *Whig & Courier* remained neutral on Chamberlain until he made his views on Reconstruction known. Chamberlain obliged with a letter addressed to a prominent pillar of the party in Eastport, wherefrom it was sent to Bangor and appeared in the *Whig & Courier.* Although long and discursive, the letter seemed close to the Republican party line. In accompanying comments the *Whig & Courier* took the letter as an endorsement of "the position and action of Congress upon the question of reconstruction."[2]

In the letter Chamberlain admitted that politics was a new business to him. When he saw congressionally dictated Reconstruction actually at work in the South, his view of it was adverse. The development of this view seems not to have been immediate—if Chamberlain had misgivings when running for governor, he kept them to himself. His attitude seems to have been colored by some personal experience with Reconstruction on a small scale. Immediately after hostilities ceased, his division had been assigned to occupy a region of Virginia where citizens were suffering from marauding stragglers from both armies and lawless bands of freed slaves. Of them he would write:

> The only notion of freedom apparently entertained by these bewildered people was to do as they pleased. That was what they had

reason to suppose white men did. To act according to each one's nature was liberty, contrasted with slavery. Numbers gave them a kind of frenzy. Without accustomed support, without food, or opportunity to work, they not unnaturally banded together; and without any serious organization and probably without much deliberate plotting of evil, they still spread terror over the country. They swarmed through houses and homes demanding food, seizing all goods they could lay their hands on, abusing the weak, terrifying women, and threatening to burn and destroy. This was an evil that had to be met promptly, and we construed our orders to protect the country liberally. . . . In cases of personal violence or outrage, my orders were sharp, and the process more summary than that authorized by courts. There was no other way.[3]

Chamberlain also bent the rules to feed starving civilians in the region; put mills, shops, and stores back into operation; and placed abandoned vehicles, implements, and animals into the hands of those who could use them. And since there were no police or courts functioning, a special court-martial was set up to settle questions of conduct. The records of that court, he thought, did not go to the archives in Washington, nor did he want them to.

The essence of Chamberlain's writings about this period is that while he sympathized with freedmen and understood their plight, he had as much sympathy for the white citizens of the region. "These suffering people," he wrote, "were our own—citizens of our common country we had fought to preserve."[4]

But in 1866 Reconstruction of the South was mostly still in the future. Chamberlain's thoughts on the subject had only begun to crystallize; and if certain Republican leaders had worries about him, their misgivings were not too serious when weighed against his surefire appeal as a vote-getter. In an effort to help his candidacy Republican newspapermen dug into his past and discovered that he had been raised a Democrat but switched to the Republican party in 1856, when he cast his vote for Hannibal Hamlin in the gubernatorial election of that year.[5] A group of Brunswick delegates to the Republican convention in June brought along additional information. In 1864, they said, at the time of the soldier vote, Chamberlain was lying on his back in a hospital at Annapolis, and yet he insisted on being carried to the voting place on a litter, and there he cast what he thought would be the last vote in his life for Abraham Lincoln.[6]

With his loyalty apparently verified, Chamberlain was nominated at the Republican convention (which he did not attend) and the campaign ensued.

In a speech to a Republican mass meeting in Skowhegan, Maine, a few days before the election, Blaine urged support for "our gallant candidate" and explained the platform that Chamberlain supposedly had accepted.[7]

The first two resolutions in the platform urged adoption of the fourteenth amendment to the U.S. Constitution, which Congress had presented to the state legislatures for ratification about a week before Chamberlain was nominated.

The previous amendment (the Thirteenth) had given the slaves their freedom but not much else. A fourteenth would make them citizens. It did not command the Southern states to allow the blacks to vote, but there was sharp encouragement to do so, for if this vote was refused in any state, that state had its basis of representation reduced.

The part of the proposed amendment that bothered Chamberlain most must have been the third section, which stated in effect that any participant in the rebellion who had previous to the war taken an oath of loyalty to the United States could not hold any office, civil or military, under the United States or any state, unless such disability was removed by a two-thirds vote of Congress. This section was obviously aimed at the Southern prewar leadership class. To quiet fears that this might throw the South into chaos under a government controlled by the ignorant and the unprepared, Blaine said in his Skowhegan address, "Careful calculation shows that these disabilities for the civil service will not affect more than fourteen thousand citizens in the entire South, out of the millions that were engaged in insurrection."[8] His calculation did not recognize that leaders in the South represented a much smaller proportion of the population than was the case in the North and that wiping out fourteen thousand might devastate the governmental structure.

This section of the amendment must have disquieted Chamberlain greatly. He would later write of the surrendering Confederates at Appomattox Court House in terms of what he had been thinking at the time and must have continued to think: "Before us in proud humiliation stood the embodiment of manhood: men whom neither toils and sufferings, nor the fact of death, nor disaster, nor hopelessness could bend from their resolve; standing before us now, thin, worn, and famished, but erect, and with eyes looking level into ours, waking memories that bound us together as no other bond;—was not such manhood to be welcomed back into a Union so tested and assured?"[9]

But what kind of welcome was this—a constitutional amendment that barred some of these men from holding office not only under the national government, but also in their own *states*?

If there had been any doubts about Chamberlain among the Republican leaders, there were certainly none among the people when election day arrived on September 8. He won by a large majority—62 percent of the vote cast. Gaining this position of strength may have encouraged Chamberlain to move somewhat out of line as he delivered his first inaugural address in early January 1867. He did his duty by endorsing ratification of the fourteenth amendment, but impressions he left with the public did not convey the spirit that had animated its framers and promoters, as one of the leading Democrat newspapers was quick to observe. This was the *Eastern Argus,* published in Portland. In commenting on the address, the *Argus* said that "upon the constitutional amendment, the message is quite non-committal, leaving us in doubt whether the Governor really desires the ratification of the amendment by the legislature or not."[10]

Another comment by the *Argus*:

> That portion of the message which treats of federal relations reads as though its author really felt that the war was prosecuted on the part of the people, not for the purpose of conquest or subjugation, but to restore the Union with all the dignity, equality and rights of the States unimpaired, and as though he also felt that there are grave dangers menacing our institutions from the usurping, centralizing schemes of reckless demagogues, and yet from personal or party considerations or other cause, he was afraid to speak his mind frankly and boldly on those subjects.[11]

The new governor's discussion of the fourteenth amendment was brief and included a criticism of its implied approval of the right of Southern states to limit or deny black suffrage. In his words: "Imperfect as this was, as hazarding one of the very fruits of our victory by placing it in the power of the South to introduce into the Constitution a disability founded on race and color, still as it was the best wisdom of our Representatives in Congress, and at least a step in the right direction, at the same time that it smoothed the way for the returning South, and especially as it was the declared issue in the recent elections, good faith doubtless requires us to support it."[12]

This was as close as he came to recommending that the Maine legislature ratify the fourteenth amendment. He was in a field, as he admitted elsewhere in the address, "so different from those in which I have hitherto been engaged." Yet he made one wise and prophetic remark about Reconstruction: "The settlement of such momentous issues may well demand the kindly influences of time."[13]

Before Governor Chamberlain was far into his first term the situation worsened considerably. Ratification of the fourteenth amendment was defeated in ten of the former Confederate states. By an act passed in March 1867, over the president's veto, federal military government was imposed on those states. Among most Republicans in Congress, hatred of Andrew Johnson was reaching a boiling point. In the same month they set a trap for him. They passed, over the president's veto, the Tenure of Office Act. This ruled that the president could not dismiss, without Senate approval, an officer who had been appointed with the advice and consent of that body. The particular appointee the radical senators were thinking of was Edwin M. Stanton, the secretary of war, whom they knew Johnson was likely to fire because Stanton, in league with the Radical Republicans, was working against Johnson. If Johnson did fire him, he would have violated the Tenure of Office Act and, its authors thought, could be impeached. Even if he did not fire him, they would have at least protected their coadjutor in the enemy camp. Stanton's control of the nation's military power was well worth having, because wild talk was spreading of the Congress being deposed or the president thrown out of the White House by force.

Johnson did fire Stanton without asking for the Senate's consent. The House of Representatives then drew up articles of impeachment, most of which had to do with Johnson's violation of the probably unconstitutional Tenure of Office Act. Thus the trap was sprung. Taking a wide view of the matter, this was a charade; the stated reasons for impeachment were not the whole story; the trial was brought on by Johnson's opposition to the reconstructive measures of the Radical Republicans expressed in a long series of events leading up to the impeachment. The only flaw in this setup was that the U.S. Senate, before which Johnson would be tried, contained some inconveniently independent people. One of them was William Pitt Fessenden of Maine. He had said, when the Tenure of Office Act was pending before the Senate, "If a cabinet officer should attempt to hold his office for a moment beyond the time when he retains the entire confidence of the President, I would not vote to retain him, nor would I compel the President to have about him in these high positions, a man whom he did not entirely trust both personally and politically."[14] In Johnson's trial, Fessenden would make his judgment on the basis of what the articles of impeachment declared, not on their hidden purpose, and so he would become a key figure in that historic event—and, incidentally, a factor in Joshua Chamberlain's political life.

>─┼─◆>─O─<◆─┼─<

In Chamberlain's description of the "salute" to the surrendering Confederate soldiers at Appomattox his expectation of an adverse reaction in the

North was implied. ("Well aware of the responsibility assumed, and of the criticism that would follow, as the sequel proved. . . .")[15] Who were the critics? It may safely be assumed that the brickbats came from the Radical Republicans. But there were others as well, among them members of the Fessenden family.

Sometimes one gets a glimpse of the past as though seen through a suddenly opened window. In the early 1980s such a window was opened in an experience involving Campbell B. Niven, publisher of *The Times Record*, one of Maine's leading newspapers. The incident had to do with Chamberlain's former home in Brunswick, now the Joshua L. Chamberlain Museum. The building, then in a ruinous state, was about to be torn down—with its space, rumor had it, to be made into a parking lot or occupied by a fast-food dispenser—when it was rescued by the Pejepscot Historical Society, present owner and operator of the museum. Following the purchase the society conducted a fund-raising campaign in 1983–84 to finance the restoration of the Chamberlain house and also the maintenance of another building it owns, the Whittier-Skolfield House. Among the solicitors in this campaign was Campbell Niven. And one of the people he called upon was John L. Baxter, then eighty-seven, a well-to-do citizen of Brunswick.

John Baxter had been a generous and faithful contributor to the Pejepscot Historical Society. He was in the habit of giving $2,000 a year as an unsolicited gift. Niven's words tell the story from here on.

> My visit was simply to ask him if he would be willing to make a pledge of that amount over the next five years. He quickly pointed out that, more than likely, his estate would certainly pay a portion of this gift, but he readily agreed to my request.
>
> I indicated to him that a gift of $10,000 provided him with the opportunity to name a room in either of the buildings. He said that he was not particularly interested in that but he did want to be certain that "not one penny of his contribution went to Chamberlain." I told him that I would make a note to that effect on his pledge card. . . . Before I left I asked if he could tell me why he felt so strongly about General Chamberlain. His answer was very simple and direct. "My mother and Mrs. Chamberlain didn't get along," he said.
>
> When I asked him why, he said that it all went back to that "damn fool salute" that he ordered the Union troops to give to the Confederate soldiers at Appomattox. He said that virtually everyone in the North had lost a father, husband, son, brother or some

other relative in the war and many of them felt that the enemies did not deserve special recognition on that day of their final defeat.[16]

If this attitude could be found in a Northern community 118 years after the event, what must have been the anger of many families of the North when news of the "salute" reached them in April 1865 or shortly thereafter?

If Joshua Chamberlain had entertained any political ambitions at the time, his honoring of the surrendering Confederates would have been the height of folly as far as his relationship with John Baxter's ancestors were concerned.

John Baxter's mother, Mary Baxter, was the daughter of Ellen (Fessenden) Lincoln, a sister of Senator William Pitt Fessenden. And the senator had ample reason for being upset by Chamberlain's action. Besides trying to destroy his beloved nation, the Southerners had killed one of his family and injured others. As he put it, "God gave me four sons. . . . Three of them volunteered and the other volunteered also, but his health broke down, and he was obliged to stay home, much to his regret and sorrow. My youngest fell upon his first field. Another had his arm shattered and his leg shot off. The third was not wounded, but served and fought in twenty battles."[17]

There is evidence that William Pitt Fessenden was no friend of Chamberlain in the years immediately following the Civil War. This is found in letters from the son who had to stay home during the war, William Howard Fessenden, addressed to his father in Washington.[18] William Howard had remained in Portland taking care of the large law practice that William Pitt had established and other family affairs. He made frequent reports to his father. In a letter dated December 11, 1865, William Howard was discussing a vacancy in the office of Portland postmaster—one of the most desirable federal patronage plums in Maine—and he said everyone was talking about Chamberlain as a candidate. As one of the most influential senators in Washington, William Pitt certainly could have arranged this appointment. But he did not. William Howard wrote another letter dated June 23, 1866, following the Republican convention in Bangor that nominated Chamberlain for governor. He said he had gone to Bangor to nominate Chamberlain's opponent, Samuel E. Spring, a wealthy Portland merchant, but it was no use; Chamberlain had too great a hold upon the public. In opposing Chamberlain it is unlikely that William Howard would be acting otherwise than advised by his father.

So matters stood in 1866. But the relationship between Chamberlain and William Pitt Fessenden was to take an ironic twist. It happened during the impeachment trial of President Andrew Johnson in 1868, growing out of the enmity of Congress previously described, when Chamberlain was still governor and William Pitt Fessenden was a United States Senator.

There were fifty-four members of the Senate at that time. In the impeachment trial, a two-thirds vote was necessary for conviction—that meant thirty-six votes. The Democrats had twelve votes; these would certainly be for acquittal. So if seven Republicans also went for acquittal, the Republicans could cast only thirty-five votes and the game would be lost. It became known that some Republicans *were* thinking of voting for acquittal—among them Fessenden, causing great distress among Maine's Republicans.

Up until the time when this rumor circulated it was taken for granted that impeachment was certain. At the end of February all of Maine's U.S. representatives and senators had received a copy of a resolution passed by the Maine legislature approving the expected unanimous vote for conviction. This resolution was voted for by highly respected people, such as Eugene Hale, Nelson Dingley Jr., the great Thomas Brackett Reed, and others who would go on to important posts in Washington.[19] The Republicans of Maine seemed to be solidly for conviction. They were in for a shock.

Fessenden had not voted for the Tenure of Office Act when it was passed. He believed the president should be able to remove any cabinet member he wanted to remove and that the Constitution empowered him to do so. A Maine newspaper reported that in remarks to a secret session of the Senate Fessenden had said thus:

> To depose the constitutional magistrate of a great nation elected by the people on grounds so slight, in my judgement, would be an abuse of the power conferred upon the Senate, which could not be justified to the country or the world. To construe such an act as a high crime or misdemeanor within the meaning of the Constitution would, when the passions of the hour have had time to cool, be looked upon with wonder, if not with derision. Worse than this, it would inflict a wound upon the very structure of our government which time would fail to cure.[20]

Seldom has any public office holder received such pressure to change his mind—urgings from friends, who told him that he would be stepping into his political grave if he voted for acquittal, and letters from constituents who were abusive in the extreme, some of them even threatening assassination.

On the afternoon of May 16, 1868, white in the face but with a determined countenance, Fessenden was the first to vote for Andrew Johnson's acquittal, to be followed by six other Republicans voting "not guilty." In doing so he stepped into the political grave his friends had predicted. And not only his political grave but his actual grave, for he died the following year, a victim, many thought, of the terrible strain that had been placed upon him. In 1955 a brief account of his martyrdom appeared in John F. Kennedy's book *Profiles in Courage*. He was one of the seven who, in Kennedy's words, "may well have preserved for ourselves and posterity constitutional government in the United States."[21]

During this affair what were the attitude and actions of Governor Chamberlain? He evidently did not—as Fessenden was compelled to do by his office and his conscience—throw himself under the wheels of a political juggernaut by making a public declaration. Had he done so there would have been considerably more disturbance than the Maine newspapers of 1868 show. But there is evidence that he was moving into the direction that would eventually make him known as an "anti-machine man."

On Friday May 15, 1868, at seven on the eve of the day that would bring the impeachment vote, Maine Republicans held a mass meeting in Portland—the largest since the Civil War, with the party bigwigs in attendance to beat the drums for President Johnson's destruction. It must not have escaped indignant notice that Governor Chamberlain was not present. At a similar meeting held in Augusta former governor Samuel Cony was called upon to preside; Governor Chamberlain again was not available.[22]

Many years later Edgar O. Achorn, a Bowdoin alumnus and special friend of Chamberlain, asked him what had gone on behind the scenes. He had heard that after the acquittal Republican party leaders wanted Chamberlain to write to Fessenden asking him to resign from the Senate because he no longer represented the people of Maine, and that he had refused to write such a letter. Was that true? Yes, it was, Chamberlain replied; there had been this and other pressure, but he thought that Fessenden was right and approved what he had done.

Finally, at Chamberlain's funeral in 1914 his eulogist, William DeWitt Hyde, the president of Bowdoin College, said this about the chapter in his life that dealt with Reconstruction. "When the leaders of his party advocated the impeachment of the President; the protracted agitation of sectional differences; and immediate suffrage for the emancipated Negroes, he stood firmly, sagaciously, and self-sacrificingly for more moderate and pacific measures—measures which subsequent history has shown to be far more beneficent than those which in the flush of military victory, the heat of party strife, and the fire of personal ambition unfortunately prevailed."[23]

Even though some of the obloquy heaped upon Fessenden's head spilled over onto Chamberlain, there was not enough of it to unseat him in the next election; he was still too popular with the people. But a black mark was placed on his party record, and it would not be forgotten.

This support of William Pitt Fessenden obviously had no mellowing influence upon John Baxter and his mother because they probably never heard of it. But one important member of the family did come to think kindly of Chamberlain. In early 1890 Chamberlain received a letter from Gen. Francis Fessenden, the Fessenden who had lost his right leg in the war. The general had evidently come across a letter written to his father, the senator, on September 8, 1863, by Gen. James Rice highly commending Chamberlain for his courage and skill in the defense of Little Round Top. He was sending Chamberlain this old letter, thinking that he ought to have it.[24] Chamberlain apparently had seen it before. He sent Fessenden a gracious reply, thanking him for the James Rice tribute and adding, "his letter does me more good now than it did then and yours as much as his."[25]

CHAPTER THREE

Dealing with Demon Rum

Joshua Chamberlain was perfectly willing to have a drink now and then. He took one of his most famous swigs, as followers of his Civil War adventures may remember, when wounded in the battle of Quaker Road. On that occasion Col. Ellis Spear of the 20th Maine presented a flask and invited him to take a swallow from it. Chamberlain took more than a swallow; he drank most of the flask, leaving Spear with a "melancholy, martyr-like look on his face." It was a story that Spear used to tell on him, Chamberlain said, "on festive occasions" in later years.[1]

Another bibulous incident took place seven days later, just prior to the arrivals of Grant and Lee at Appomattox Court House and was described by a newspaper reporter who wrote, "A conference of commanding officers on both sides was held. The place of preliminary conference was on the steps of the court house. On our side were Generals Ord, Sheridan, Crook, Gibbon, Griffin, Merritt, Ayres, Bartlett, Chamberlain, Forsyth and Michie. On the enemy's side were Generals Longstreet, Gordon, Heth, Wilcox, Colonel Fairfax and other officers. . . . There were mutual introductions and shaking of hands, and soon was passed about some whiskey (General Ayres furnished the whiskey, and he alleges that it was a first class article,) and mutual healths were drank. . . ."[2] Chamberlain certainly had another drink here; who in the company of these corps and division commanders would have refused?

Another story of Chamberlain's having a drink was told by Edgar O. Achorn, Bowdoin class of 1881. This happened when the general was in his late seventies and was occupying an apartment or hotel room in Portland,

Maine, where he was employed in the Customs House. Achorn was in Portland giving a talk to the Maine Historical Society. Chamberlain was in the audience and after the talk invited Achorn to come to his quarters while he waited a couple of hours for his train to Boston. Just before Achorn was leaving, Chamberlain produced a bottle of whiskey and two glasses. The bottle had been given to him by a friend three or four months before, Chamberlain said, and about a third of it had been consumed. Invited to have a drink with him, Achorn said he would be glad to and would consider it a great honor.[3]

From the evidence of these and other accounts, it is clear that alcohol was no problem to Chamberlain personally, either as an addictive agent or a dreaded smirch on his moral character. But politically it presented an enormous difficulty because as governor of Maine he found himself administering the law of the first state in the nation to prohibit the manufacture, sale, and use of alcoholic drinks.

The emergence of prohibition in Maine followed a trade pattern that existed in the first half of the nineteenth century. Manufactured lumber and products of fisheries were sent to the West Indies from Maine, and the returning vessels brought rum and molasses. The molasses was converted to New England rum in many distilleries operating—some of them day and night—in coastal communities. Their products were dispensed in nearly every grocery store as well as in taverns and public houses. The results were often tragic in terms of increased family disruption, crime, poverty, public brawls and disturbances, and the loss of productive hours in industries, trades, and professions. These economic and social disasters built up to a tidal wave of fear and anger directed against the abuse of alcohol in Maine.

No one alive today can imagine the emotional forces surrounding this issue in the nineteenth century, many of them emanating from women. They may not have had the vote, but they had power. Sylvia J. Sherman, Maine's director of archival services, has spoken of petitions signed in the cause of temperance by women and now still piled up in stacks in the Maine State Archives.[4] Through their pressures on husbands, brothers, and other men they represented a body of opinion to be reckoned with at the polls—added, of course, to the many men who shared their views. The Republican party was strongly identified with this group, which was massed under the banner of "temperance"—rather a misnomer because a temperate use of alcohol was not the idea. It was to be stamped out entirely and its advocates stamped under.

This fervor was not awakened by accident. There was much evil to complain about. Neal Dow, organizer of the Maine Temperance Union and

drafter of the 1851 prohibitory law, in his *Reminiscences* (1898) described
conditions early in the century:

> On one occasion a number of men were injured by the collapse of
> the frame of a church in process of erection, in the town of
> Gorham, about ten miles distant from Portland. The accident was
> due to the drunkenness of one or two of the men engaged in the
> work. Teams came into Portland for doctors to set the broken
> limbs and repair other damages. The "M.D.s" were at some festive
> gathering, it was said, in such a condition from drink as to be
> unable to respond to the call, hence the injured men remained
> without surgical aid until the next day, when some of the Portland
> doctors were sufficiently sober to attend to them. The incident
> fairly illustrates the general habit, and no one lost either social,
> political or, save in extreme cases, religious standing, by such
> excess.[5]

Also, Dow told of walking down a Portland street in his younger days and
seeing a crowd gather in front of a saloon listening to a commotion inside
the building. The wife of a drunkard teamster was in there smashing up
bottles and the bar furniture; she may have been the inspiration for a later
saloon smasher, the famous "Hatchet Carrie."[6]

It all may sound quaintly amusing today, in the tenor of the song "Father,
dear Father, come home with me now" and comic period melodramas. But
there was nothing funny about it to the Maine people who had to deal with
the economic and social results of widespread alcohol abuse. As a proven
master propagandist, Neal Dow, "the Father of Prohibition," undoubtedly
exaggerated at times his tales of depravity, but obviously the people had
become stirred up to the point where they were decided something had to be
done, and they sought a solution in the realm of politics and the law.

The temperance people, according to Benjamin F. Bunker, the author
of *Bunker's Textbook of Political Deviltry,* hovered under the wings of the
Republican party. Bunker, editor of the *Kennebec Democrat,* was known
for his witty and sarcastic remarks about politicians—those of his own
party as well as the others. Bunker went so far as to admire some of the
early Republican promoters of the cause. He observed that in the Republican conventions year after year a good solid temperance plank was inserted
in the platform. And if anyone wanted to get a nomination or an office during the decades when the Republicans held sway, the first stepping-stone
was membership in a temperance organization of some sort. These old

Republican temperance leaders were sincere, but as Bunker put it, "Scheming politicians saw the advantage of having the temperance voters with them, and one after another learned to sing temperance songs by day and drink themselves drunk by night, from a jug behind the bedroom door."[7]

In 1867—the first year of Chamberlain's governorship—the legislature, under severe pressure from the temperance people, considered two amendments to the prohibitory law. One would rule that in all cases the sale of liquor was to be punished by imprisonment. Under existing law judges had been merely imposing a fine for the first offence. Under the amendment a person convicted of selling liquor was not only fined but in addition on first conviction was to be imprisoned in the county jail for thirty days, on second conviction sixty days, and for even longer terms in cases of "common sellers" and "keepers of drinking houses and tippling shops."[8]

The other 1867 amendment provided for a constabulary to enforce the liquor law (it was worded for the enforcement of all laws but was obviously aimed at liquor sellers). This was not exactly the door-smashing type of police employed by the Nazis and other authoritarian powers; its members could not enter a home or place of business without a warrant. But a warrant was easy to get. The constabulary could be called into a town if ten or more legal voters reported that the local authorities were not adequately enforcing the liquor law; when called upon in this manner the constables could move in and take over the functions of the local police.[9] And then the constabulary would be aided by an existing law passed in 1858; under part of this law three persons "competent to be witnesses in a civil court" could state to a justice of the peace or similar magistrate that they believed intoxicating liquors intended for sale were being kept in a certain place, and the magistrate then had to issue an order to search the place, seize any liquor found, and arrest the owner.[10]

Both amendments passed, but during the process Chamberlain strongly opposed the constabulary idea, pointing out that it violated rights and securities guaranteed to United States citizens. This won him the instant hostility of many church organizations, temperance societies, and others.

The Democrats immediately took advantage of the situation. Perceiving that the amendments were not favored by many Maine voters, in the next campaign they used the argument that through them the Republicans had accomplished an invasion of constitutional rights, something that Chamberlain also believed, but he was riding the wrong horse to make an issue of it. He won the governorship again, but Democrats had gained four thousand votes over the previous election. This result frightened the legislators; they feared its augury more than a loss of prohibitionist voters. As the result, the legislature soon repealed the constabulary law and the law requiring prison sentence for a first offence. This, to an extent, was a vindication of Chamberlain's beliefs, but another occurrence worsened his standing with the temperance group.

Each year a large temperance convention was held in the state capital, Augusta, and it had been customary for Republican governors of Maine to preside over these meetings. When Chamberlain was asked to do so, he declined with this letter:

> I have to acknowledge the honor or your invitation to preside over the friends of temperance now assembled in this city. Upon the high and broad grounds which underlie this great cause, I could meet you most cordially, but as I understand the call under which you now meet is to be not so much for the consideration of the subject of temperance generally as to affect particular legislation now pending, it appears to me that the proprieties in the case do not leave me free to participate as I might otherwise in your proceedings.[11]

The letter greatly offended the temperance people. Governor Chamberlain was now in a difficult position. He certainly was in favor of temperance, as he would have been in favor of God and motherhood. There were laws on the books upholding prohibition, and as governor he had to enforce them. The Republican party had to take notice of the prohibition people, or else they might lose the next election; and Chamberlain was a Republican, loyal up to a point. The point was breached when he gave his inaugural address in 1870, the last he would deliver. On the subject of prohibition, he spoke forthrightly and delivered a prescient discourse on the subject of law and society, reproduced here in part:

> For one . . . I do not object to a law's being somewhat in advance of public opinion—that is, more stringent in its provisions than people really like to obey. The requisitions of even an impossible virtue may avail for good. Its broad, high aspects may strengthen and hold up some that would otherwise fall before the influence of bad surroundings, and the terrors of its penalty might cool the recklessness of some who would not be restrained by milder persuasives. But when a law is widely different from the people's judgment, and provokingly contrary to their wishes; then, instead of expecting it to go on crushing its way like an unrelenting law of

the universe, it would be better to look for one that takes some cognizance of human conditions, and reach out a hand that will meet half way the trembling instincts of good.

These are questions which go to the foundations of society. Indeed it may be said that wisdom consists in seeing the practical points of contact between the abstract and the human right. For the human law is not as the divine. That declares the ways of absolute Justice and the inexorable Right. But the object of human law is to protect individual rights so that every man may be free according to his own conscience to work out his obedience to the high. Any law, therefore, which proposes to abridge personal rights, should be ventured upon with the utmost caution and administered with the widest charity.

There are other things to be thought of besides restraining men from the use of intoxicating drinks, though this be the parent of crime, and begets monsters from which all the good avert their faces and seek to save their fellows, yet we must not expect that it can be wholly subdued and driven from among men. The laws against intoxicating liquors are as well executed and obeyed as the laws against profanity, theft, unchastity or murder. Even if they are executed, they will not avail to extinguish crime, nor banish evil from the hearts of wicked men. We must consider what can be done. Restrain and intimidate as much as you can by law; it is only by the Gospel still that men can be converted from evil.[12]

Prohibition was one of the foundation stones of the Republican party in Maine, and chipping at it was not the way to get ahead in Maine politics. The way to deal with Demon Rum—many politicians would have advised— was to drink it in private, damn it in public, and not bother with social complexities and all that intellectual stuff.

CHAPTER FOUR

The Hanging of
Clifton Harris

On the night of January 16–17, 1867, a blizzard descended on southern Maine, depositing a heavy snowfall. At a place called Young's Corner, about three miles from Auburn, the roads were not passable until Saturday, January 19, and a visitor to the home of a widow, Susannah Kinsley, and her elderly companion, Polly Caswell, observed that no smoke was coming from the chimney of her house, and there was no answer when he repeatedly knocked upon the door. He later returned with another man, and when the two entered the house they found the human wreckage of what a judge called "one of the most diabolical murders known to the annals of criminal jurisprudence."[1] A *Lewiston Journal* reporter described it as the most horrible scene that could be imagined. "The bodies cut, bruised and mangled in almost every part, covered with blood, the hair disheveled and bloody, the painful expression of the countenance indicating even in death the fearful struggle for life, and then the bodies and limbs frozen stiff—all made up a scene from which we recoiled even on the succeeding day when some of the evidence of the struggle had been removed.[2]

A coroner's inquest was held and the bodies were examined. Mrs. Kinsley's throat had been cut, and because of the marks of a violent struggle on her body it was decided that there had also been a rape or attempted rape. Polly Caswell had been killed by blows to the head. A search for the rapist-murder, animated by great anger and excitement, immediately began. On suspicion authorities arrested and jailed Charles Fretchie, or Fritchie, a wandering Frenchman of horrible appearance and disgusting language who wandered around asking housewives for food, often frightening them half to death. It was supposed that he had called at Kinsley's house seeking shelter from the storm and, finding two unprotected women there, had committed the crime. Many people thought that he ought to be strung up without benefit of judge or jury.

Fritchie's neck was saved when a professional detective named Blake, summoned by local authorities, arrived from New York. Detective Blake studied the scene of the crime, visited many people, and asked many questions. His investigation showed that there was insufficient evidence against Fritchie, who was released. His general conclusion was that robbery had been one of the motives. Blake reasoned that the criminal was someone in the neighborhood who was familiar with the Kinsley house and who had heard that Mrs. Kinsley had money—a fact well known or suspected locally, which would not have been known to a stranger.

In the meantime a deputy sheriff named Keene had been conducting a separate investigation, which directed him to a black man, in some accounts a mulatto, named Harris, or Harus as he spelled it. Harris was nineteen and stood about five feet two inches. He had come to Maine from Virginia six or seven months previously. He said he had spent time in military service in the war. He appeared to be semiliterate, being able to read and write with some difficulty.

One thing that drew attention to Harris was the knowledge that some time before the murder he had been charged with entering a home and trying to gain access to a room in which two young women were sleeping. Now people had noticed that he had what appeared to be bloodstains on his clothing and boots. After examining Harris and catching him in several untruths with regard to the origin of the stains, Deputy Keene arrested him and had him lodged in the Auburn jail.

Here he was questioned by Detective Blake, the county attorney, and other officials who exposed additional falsehoods related to the crime. Finally Harris broke down and said, "I'll tell you about it."[3]

The confession was a horrid and pathetic story, as a few parts of it as published in the *Daily Eastern Argus* of Portland will illustrate.

> I went there for money. . . . Mrs. Kinsley, I think did not wake till I got into her room. I laid my hands on her before she waked. It was dark and I had nothing in my hands. When I put my hands upon her she hollered "Polly" and got up. I struck her with a chair, and she fell back. I then hunted for money; was there, I should think, three-fourths of an hour; struck her several times. I used my jack knife on her neck.

. . . before I used the knife on her neck, I got upon the bed and tried to have intercourse with her, but didn't succeed. She resisted right hard. . . . After trying to have intercourse with her I got off the bed. She raised up and I struck her with the chair again.

. . . I heard Polly coming out and took a chair and struck her. She fell near the stove.[4]

In his confession Harris implicated a white man, Luther P. Verrill, a laborer who lived and worked in West Auburn. He said that Verrill had been with him and had participated in the crime. In July 1867 Harris was tried, convicted, and sentenced to die on the gallows. Verrill, although protesting his innocence, was also tried, convicted, and held in prison on the basis of Harris's confession. While instructing the jury the presiding judge stated that "the facts alone, independent of the Negro's testimony, and without it, were of a very weak and inconclusive character, scarcely sufficient to create a well founded suspicion."[5]

Then the case took a sudden turn. On July 29 Harris swore that he had committed the murders alone, signing an affidavit to that effect. He also made a confession before a clergyman and a sheriff saying, "The truth is, gentlemen, Verrill was not there that night and knew nothing about it at all. I did the whole myself—everything—and that is true, so help me God." He would say the same, Harris declared, if he was standing on the gallows at the bar of God.[6]

Verrill was granted a new trial and was discharged. The judge who heard the motion of this new trial and granted it wrote a long opinion in which he observed that "ordinary confessions are among the least reliable species of testimony,"[7] but he found reasons to believe Harris's second confession. Among his reflections was the thought that Harris was under sentence of death solely upon his own confession, and if the law believed his confession of murder the court ought to give him credit when he confessed that he had committed perjury to divide the guilt or escape punishment.

In his opinion the judge also reviewed some testimony about Harris that had come out during his trial and de-emphasized the robbery aspect of the crime while expanding that of sex. It portrayed Harris as certainly not a desirable person to have around the neighborhood. Early on the evening of January 16, 1867, he had gone to Lewiston to see a female who either was not at home or who had rejected his advances. The judge wrote:

He spent the first part of the evening in an unsuccessful attempt to gratify a sensual appetite, which had been cultivated from the early age of fifteen, and had repeatedly impelled him to enter the houses of his neighbors clandestinely, and conceal himself in the sleeping apartments of unsuspecting females. He had that evening failed in the attempt to gratify his lust. He first thought of going to Mrs. Kinsley's as he passed by her house that night, with this passion still upon him. He was familiar with the premises, and knew that none but females resided there. He returned for the avowed purpose of gratifying his insatiate lust. Having entered the house, he stealthily went to Mrs. Kinsley's apartment. She did not awake and "he put his hand on her shoulder and asked her to turn over." She immediately rose up in bed. He told her to lie down and keep quiet; she refused to do so, and he attempted to force her down. A desperate struggle ensues; Mrs. Kinsley calling out loudly for "Polly." Unable to master Mrs. Kinsley, he gets off the bed and strikes her with a chair. Polly appearing he deals her a blow, and fells her to the floor, and beats Mrs. K. until she is quiet.

He then accomplishes his fiendish purpose. . . . He makes but a slight search in the darkness for money, and then goes back home.[8]

The atrocity of the crime reignited a controversy about capital punishment that had been going on in Maine for thirty years. And this put Chamberlain into the middle of a situation that several preceding governors had found to be intolerable and that subjected Chamberlain to one of the most trying and unpleasant experiences of his life. A brief review of capital punishment in the state of Maine will put this event into context.

When Maine separated from Massachusetts and became a state in 1820 it established laws requiring the death penalty for several crimes, including murder and rape. In 1829 the penalty for rape, burglary, and robbery was reduced to life imprisonment. In 1837 came a change that put Maine governors into a difficult position; a new law required that a person convicted of murder remain in prison for one year from the date of sentencing. Any time after that the governor was supposed to sign an execution warrant and have it delivered to the hangman. The effect was that a murderer might be sentenced to death, but since the court fixed no time limit within which the penalty had to be inflicted, the governor had to be a judge instead of an executive. He was faced with two decisions: Was the criminal to live or die? If he was to die, when?

Chamberlain and governors before him urged the legislature either to abolish capital punishment altogether or to change the law to fix a certain day after the year of grace upon which the criminal was to be executed. In that way the execution would not be left to the governor's discretion; it would be laid upon him as a duty.

So intense and active was the sentiment against the death penalty in Maine that a series of governors preceding Chamberlain had simply avoided the issue by neglecting to sign death warrants. In the thirty years since the 1837 death penalty law was passed only one person had been executed, which resulted in a large backlog of murderers on death row. In his address to the legislature in January 1868 Chamberlain asserted that he considered it his duty to dispose of these cases and would either see that the law was executed or would commute sentences to life imprisonment.

Clifton Harris was sentenced to death in July 1867. His year of grace expired in July 1868. After that the decision as to his fate rested upon Chamberlain—and so did the weight of the argument about capital punishment that, with its time-worn pros and cons, had been raging in Maine for three decades. The controversy was highly divisive. Even the religious community, which, one might think, would be wholly against capital punishment, was sharply divided. For example, Congregationalists and Baptists held to the view expressed in the Old Testament, as in Numbers, chapter 35, with several verses describing killings and ending with "and the murderer shall surely be put to death," while the Universalists, Quakers, and others were inclined to favor the New Testament's emphasis on repentance and forgiveness of sins, that is, life imprisonment. No matter which way Chamberlain decided the Harris case he would anger large groups of people, religious and otherwise.

William P. Frye, then Maine's attorney general, quite unexpectedly opposed Harris's execution, and he and Chamberlain came to blows verbally. This was unfortunate as far as Chamberlain's political future was concerned for Frye—an accomplished orator and a favorite of James G. Blaine—would go on to become a member and president of the U.S. Senate and a power in Washington. Frye began the exchange with this passage in his annual report at the end of 1868.

> While I fully sustain the position of the Governor, I do not think that justice requires the execution of Harris. To use a common expression, "he turned State's evidence," and the record does not exhibit an instance where an accomplice taking this course has paid the full penalty of the violated law. Again, it seems to me that some considerations, in determining the question, should be given to the birth, the early life and training, and the circumstances of this man Knight [referring to George Knight, one of the men on

death row whose sentences Chamberlain commuted to life impris-
onment]. Born in New England, educated in our schools, a man
intelligent, successful in business, in the full maturity of his powers, murders the wife of his bosom, designedly, deliberately, and
escapes the extreme penalty, while, Harris, born on a Southern
plantation, educated only as to his brutal instincts, compelled into
ignorance and degradation, and a subserviency to a white man by
force of law itself, almost in his legal infancy influenced by a
white companion, commits a murder and is executed. The proposition does not commend itself to my sense of justice.[9]

In this statement there were traces of guilt lingering from the sentiments of abolitionists in the years before the Civil War—and reflections of
what a number of people were saying. What would be gained, they asked,
by hanging this poor ignorant Negro who, in his days of slavery, had doubtless been whipped and abused and whose mother probably had been violated? Also, shouldn't his extreme youth be a reason for mitigating the
penalty?

In preparing his reply to Attorney General Frye, Chamberlain had a
considerable advantage. The governor and other officers of the state made
annual reports, and these reports were published together each year in a
volume entitled *Public Documents of Maine.* Frye and other officers had to
have their reports in well before the end of the year. Chamberlain had considerably more time; his report was delivered as an address to the legislature early in January. Frye signed and presumably submitted his report on
December 10, 1868. Thus Chamberlain had at least three weeks to look it
over and frame his counterattack, which, when delivered, must have made
Frye feel that his argument had been taken apart with lawyerlike skill. Frye
had no chance to strike back before his report and Chamberlain's rather
devastating answer went to the printer and were presented to the citizens
and the press in the *Public Documents.*

Part of Chamberlain's address follows. (By the time it was delivered,
in early January 1869, he had ordered Harris's execution.)

In accordance with my expressed intention I have executed the
duties devolving upon me in reference to convicts under the sentence of death. These cases have been thoroughly considered.
Wherever there has been a mitigating circumstance of any
moment, the convict has had the benefit of it. In two cases the sentence has been commuted to imprisonment for life; in another not

admitting of lenity, the prisoner died before the warrant was to be issued; while in a case of peculiar atrocity and aggravation the sentence has been ordered to be carried into execution.

I should have contented myself with this simple statement of my action without comment, but it has pleased the Attorney General in his official report to protest against this execution, although candidly admitting that it is the Governor's duty to execute this law; and as his careful official statement must be taken as the best expression of dissent which can be made, I may be warranted in giving you the reasons why I am not influenced by that kind of argument.

It is urged by the distinguished attorney that Harris should not be executed because he "turned State's evidence." This means, I suppose—for it will not be pretended that a mere confession of his own guilt after arrest comes within the meaning of this term—that there was some promise or obligation, expressed or implied, that if Harris should succeed in implicating an accomplice, he should escape the penalty of his crime.

I am not learned in the rules of evidence, and I remark upon this no further than to say that if guilt can thus find a scape-goat; if a person can be convicted of capital crime by evidence given under the pressure of this consummate hope of reward, then the altar of justice is no longer the asylum of innocence, and life and liberty must seek some other defence. But, if was so, let those who made the promise keep it—let them see that their witness has his reward while the case is still in their hands. But did the Attorney General avail himself of this privilege, and withdraw any portion of the indictment in token of service rendered? Did the jury in their verdict, or the judge after sentence, recommend to the mercy of the Executive? Nothing of the kind.

Now one of two things: In turning State's evidence Harris must have implicated either a guilty party or an innocent one. If an innocent, then he endeavored to add a *third* murder to the former two; if a guilty, then in afterward contradicting the statement with equal vehemence he virtually shielded the guilty from justice in either case but adding another to his horrible list of crimes, and crowning the whole with perjury. I fail to see the extenuating force of any such State's evidence in this.

It is said that the fact of Harris's early life—the degrading influences of slavery, and the development of his brutal passion alone, and his being almost in his legal infancy, should have been considered. They were considered, and at their full value. They were a relieving element in the case; they were ground of gratitude that no man nursed of woman was left to do these horrors— and of congratulation that this precocity of guilt was nipped in its "legal infancy," before its blossom and full fruits had come. But they did not appear sufficient to entitle him to special grace. "Previous good character" is a plea in mitigation—but to plead a "previous bad character" is a novelty in jurisprudence.[10]

In continuing his address Chamberlain pointed out that neither his own views on the death penalty nor the state of public opinion—whatever it was—could affect his duty to execute the existing law. And the law itself had not been changed. The last legislature, he said, had been confronted with a bill to abolish capital punishment and had refused to abolish it by a vote of nearly two to one. That having occurred, he declared, "It would be an extraordinary presumption in me to take the responsibility of abolishing it myself."

An act to abolish the death penalty and incidentally to save Clifton Harris had been introduced in the Maine House of Representatives unsuccessfully on February 28, 1868. It was brief and to the point. *Section 1: In all cases where by law the punishment of crime is death, the punishment hereafter shall be imprisonment for life. Section 2: The governor shall not issue his warrant for execution of any person now under sentence of death.*[11]

The proposed act had been reported from the Committee on the Judiciary by Thomas Bracket Reed, one of the strongest and most active foes of capital punishment. Chamberlain had a talent for getting on the contrary side, in the infancy of their careers, of political giants who later would be in a position to do or not to do him immense good. One of these, of course, was William P. Frye, whom he had publicly done in, as just related. An even greater figure was Thomas Brackett Reed, then just starting his career in the Maine legislature, later to become famous as a powerful Speaker of the House in the U.S. Congress. Reed was indeed a giant, standing six feet two inches, weighing more than 250 pounds, and possessed of great wisdom and wit—the latter usually suppressed by politicians, who believe that the public takes it as a sign of hidden villainy. Heedless of this belief, Reed would say such things as—in speaking of a few fellow Congressmen—"They never open their mouths without subtracting from the sum of human knowledge."[12]

In the discussions and debates having to do with capital punishment, Reed's eloquent and persuasive speaking against the death penalty stood out, even though it was unsuccessful. It was a demonstration of his abilities that did much to further his political career.

Chamberlain spoke just as forcefully in favor of capital punishment. His Civil War experience may have hardened him in this regard. Most people who say they favor the death penalty would not be able to carry out an execution or even to watch one. But in the war Chamberlain had seen too many good men die to be overly horrified at the extinction of a bad one. In his January 1869 inaugural address he said he thought capital punishment should continue in Maine. He spoke of the beneficial effect in a rape case. "The punishment is imprisonment for life. If the offender sees no higher penalty before him, he has a powerful motive to dispose of the principal witness against him. He has everything to gain and nothing to lose by adding the crime of murder."[13] In more general terms he observed: "It is urged that we be merciful. But to whom? I ask. To the violator of all sanctities—the pitiless despoiler of the peace and good order of society—or to the innocent, the good, the peaceful and well-doing, who rely upon the protection of the state? . . ."[14]

Chamberlain had set the execution date for March 12, 1869. While awaiting the doomful day that winter he was subjected to so much abuse that the Cumberland Association of Congregational Ministers felt impelled to come to his support. Taking the Old Testament view of the matter, members of the association published a statement declaring that they believed Chamberlain's decision to be "consonant with the revealed will of the Supreme Ruler of the world."

Along with this manifestation of one brand of religious thought, the opinion of Civil War veterans was thought to be influential. Thomas Brackett Reed wrote to a friend, "The whole soldier element is strongly for hanging, whether naturally or following Chamberlain I do not know."[15] Cumberland County, he thought, would also be strongly for it. Of one man who based his advocacy of hanging on the Bible, he wrote that he "considers any one who desires to abolish strangulation as 'trying to be wiser than God,' which remark he regards as closing the whole question. Against such inner light it is no use to burn the farthing candles of human reason."[16] On March 4, 1869, an amendment he introduced in the Maine House of Representatives that would have saved Harris's life went down in defeat ninety-five votes to forty-five.[17]

The execution took place in the prison yard of the state prison at Thomaston. According to an account in the *Easton Argus* published on the following day, a chaplain had been with Harris from time to time for several days, and in one of their sessions, Harris again reversed himself about

Verrill. As he neared execution he again stated that Verrill had participated in the crime.

In his talks and writings Thomas B. Reed often, for added rhetorical effect, referred to hangings as strangulations, and unfortunately this would describe the fate of Clifton Harris. According to the *Argus* account the hangman bungled the job, possibly from having had so little experience. Only one man had ever been hanged at the state prison—five years previously—the Mr. Spencer mentioned in the newspaper report.

There were present some fifty people. A few buildings commanding a view of the scene were well occupied by spectators and there was quite a crowd outside. Some among those on the house tops cried and hooted at the condemned. Harris stood erect upon the drop. The Sheriff stepped forward and pinioned him with some light but strong cords. Then the clergymen prayed and one of them read from the 51st Psalm, by desire of Harris, the words being expressive of his feelings. A final prayer, and just as the white cap was to be drawn over his face, the Sheriff asked if he had anything to say. Harris in a low but firm voice replied nothing, except this—"What I stated as to Verrill at the first trial and in my last confession is absolutely true. I have good will to everybody."

The cap was drawn down, and so well timed were the services that precisely as 12 o'clock the Sheriff placed his foot upon the spring. There was a sharp bang from the falling trap and the body of the man shot straight downward about eight feet. It hung motionless for the space of ten seconds and all supposed the neck broken and the man dead, as in the case of Spencer, last executed on the same gallows, but the silence was only from the shock. The hands began to twitch convulsively and there was an effort to pull them from the cords which bound them. The knees were drawn up and the body spun around and around. It was evident that the man was dying from strangulation. The struggle continued some two minutes and then the body hung motionless, with the exception of an occasional mighty effort of the chest. In three minutes the pulse had run down to forty. In five minutes life was just perceptible, with on occasional convulsive movement. At seven minutes life ceased. The body hung twenty-five minutes. It was then lowered into the coffin and Clifton Harris was no more.[18]

Then came the closing paragraph, which must stand as one of the most flagrant cases on record of a writer contradicting his own account: "Everything was conducted in an excellent manner, the only thing occurring to disturb the solemnity of the scene being the shouts from the crowd outside of the yard."[19]

The protesters shouting outside the gates of the prison and people of the same persuasion continued to hound Chamberlain long after the execution. Writing to his mother three months later, he mentioned the many threats he was receiving. But, he assured her, he had upheld the law and carried out the sentence of the court; he had done his duty and no one was going to scare him.[20]

Critics might have pointed out that Chamberlain's unyielding stand on the Harris case was greatly at odds with his leniency in granting pardons. He pardoned nineteen convicts in 1868 and sixteen in 1869. That was about twice as many, the state prison's warden pointed out, as the largest number ever pardoned in one year from the state prison in Massachusetts. The crimes for which these convicts had been imprisoned included assault to kill, assault to ravish (this convict's age, sixteen), rape, larceny, robbing the mail, arson, manslaughter, mayhem, bigamy, adultery, filing a false pension claim, and malicious mischief.

Chamberlain was especially soft on war veterans. He said as much in his 1869 inaugural address: "Many of these cases are of soldiers, who in the extravagance of satisfaction at their safe return home carried their frolics to the extent of crime."

Chamberlain's role in Maine's criminal justice system inevitably did him great harm politically, although it can be said that in the case of Clifton Harris the performance of the whole system, including governor, courts, attorneys, and legislature, left questions to be answered. For example, Harris may have been mentally or emotionally impaired. Should not more time have been taken to evaluate Harris's testimony and mental condition, investigate the circumstances, and get to the bottom of Verrill's alleged involvement in the crime? With Harris erased from the equation there was no further chance of solving that problem.

Within the precedent set by previous governors, Chamberlain could justifiably have left Harris to serve a life term in prison. If he had done that he certainly would have been abused, but probably not by as many people as abused him following the young convict's hideous execution. Not that abuse meant much to Chamberlain; he was determined to do what he thought was his duty. The best that can be said was that he became entangled in a problem for which there was no satisfactory solution; he did what the law required as punishment for an atrocious crime; and the resulting disturbance helped bring matters to a head. The Harris controversy kept fierce debate alive, and eighteen years later capital punishment was abolished in Maine.

Being governor, Chamberlain had found, was sometimes a beastly business. When he had turned to it in preference to continuing an academic or a military career, he thought that it would open up a new channel for service of great distinction. But the governorship had turned out to offer little reward for bravery, creative thinking, and forthright speaking; it was more onerous than honoring. When he was nearing the end of his fourth one-year term, he wrote an astonishing letter to the king of Prussia, tendering his services "in the war now opening in Europe"[21] and offering to resign the governorship on being accepted. What happened as a result of this letter is unknown; it is not even certain that it was posted. But its existence is ample evidence of Chamberlain's longing to return to the remembered drama, action, and glories of military life as he had known it—a longing that would remain with him to the end of his days.

CHAPTER FIVE

Maine As Maine Should Be

When Joshua Chamberlain was governor of Maine (1867–70) two important movements were beginning to affect the state. One was the great influx of "summer folks" attracted by the incomparable beauty and variety of the Maine coast. The other was an exodus of Maine people looking for a way to earn a better living. It distressed Chamberlain enormously to observe, "It is a serious matter to have five thousand a year in excess of the number we receive from abroad, and of the most valuable portion of our population, emigrate from the state."[1] The census at the end of the seventies would reveal that Maine was the only state in the nation, except for New Hampshire, that had lost population since 1860.

Chamberlain sponsored and encouraged one effort to increase the population that proved to be a notable success. Even before the Civil War there was the idea that Maine ought to obtain an immigration of Swedes, who were recognized as a hardy, honest, and industrious people culturally compatible with those already living in the state. Further, it was observed that many Swedish immigrants were showing a preference for the colder climates of America, settling in the northern range of states—Wisconsin, Minnesota, Michigan, and so on. A previous governor, in 1861, had briefly presented the idea of diverting some of this Scandinavian flow into Maine, but nothing happened. A "Foreign Immigration" society tried a scheme, and it failed. Then the idea was taken hold of by William Widgery Thomas Jr., a man who during the Civil War had spent three years as Lincoln's war counsel in Gothenburg, Sweden, where he had learned the language and became acquainted with the people.

Thomas conceived of a plan. He envisioned sending a commissioner (himself) to Sweden. There he would recruit a selected group of young farmers with their wives and children. He would bring this group, all in one ship, to America. He would lead them to a location in northern Maine, where the state would give each family one hundred acres of woodland along with temporary shelter, food, tools, and other help they needed to get started on settlement. Thomas predicted that soon this state aid could be discontinued, because before long the Swedes would be taking care of themselves.

This was a scheme so bold in its conception that it might have drawn instant rejection from a more cautious governor. But Chamberlain liked to be part of bold actions. He urged the scheme upon the legislature, where an act was passed authorizing its implementation. Everything worked out just as planned. In 1870 Thomas went to Sweden and returned with fifty-one people, including a baby who died on the way up the St. John River. The fifty who made it literally carved the farmland town of New Sweden out of the forest. The Swedes had paid for their own passages to Maine, and within a couple of years they were self-sufficient. No further state aid was needed. By the fall of 1873 the settlement of fifty had increased to six hundred, and outside of New Sweden lived many Swedes who had been drawn to Maine by the colony. By 1895 Thomas estimated that there were more than three thousand Swedes in Maine as result of the initial immigration.

While William Widgery Thomas was the prime mover in all this, he gave full credit to Chamberlain for his support and encouragement. Chamberlain was among the several dignitaries who attended a celebration in New Sweden on the tenth anniversary of the colony's founding. In introducing him as one of the speakers, Thomas called him "the constant and chivalric friend of this enterprise from its inception; one, who in fact stood by and rocked the cradle of New Sweden."[2] "The colony," as it is still called, consists of three towns—New Sweden, Westmanland, and Stockholm, plus parts of several surrounding towns (Caribou, Woodland, Perham)—but the total effect of the settlement is much greater, for Swedes from the original stock have moved out into Maine towns near and far to become a valuable part of the state's population.

As for the affluent people coming into the state from the south, they did little for the population head count, because their residence was mostly seasonal, but they had a pronounced cultural effect. These people were mainly the beneficiaries of the great wealth spawned by the industrial revolution that followed the Civil War, and their travel to Maine was facilitated by the corresponding improvements in transportation by rail and steamboat.

They purchased, at prices that were phenomenal to the natives but bargains to them, much of the most beautiful Maine seacoast. Many of the farmers and fishermen of southern Maine were to suffer a fate similar to that of the Native Americans—their land would be taken away and they would be converted in popular literature to fabulous creatures—paragons of old-fashioned virtue or at another extreme comic characters in stories told over Philadelphia Main Line or Manhattan dinner tables.

From the viewpoint of Maine residents in the rural inland areas, the people from away seemed a different race. They had more money, better education, better clothing, better teeth. And they had *leisure*. That was the thing. To most of the inlanders the word vacation meant nothing; they might leave their work for a few days' fishing or go on a trip to see the relatives, but a definitely scheduled and named vacation was an extreme rarity. The idea of sending a child to "summer camp" would be absurd. The sight of grown-ups lolling on the beach or playing games in midsummer while the hinterlander sweated in a sawmill, hayfield, or forest often excited envy, derision, and some resentment.

There already was a rift between the people of inland Maine and those of southern Maine. The urban areas were in the south. So was the bulk of Maine's economic and political power, and these powers were sometimes, it was thought by the northlanders, unfairly used. The advent of the summer people only served to widen the rift. Today in the north there is even talk of secession and "Two Maines" dominates conversations throughout the state.[3] This concept would have grieved Chamberlain, not only because he had served and suffered in a war to prevent the *nation* from splitting apart, but because he had a foot in both Maines. He had been born and brought up on a farm in Brewer, a town well back from the seashore, almost on the edge of the vast northern forest, and his father and mother still lived there. From Brewer he had stepped over into the more cultured and urban Maine on entering Bowdoin College. The disunion of Maine was an idea not yet visible, however, and Chamberlain had other things to worry about as governor. His goal, he decided, was a Maine economy that would encourage young natives to remain in the state and would attract Maine's share of the immigrants then pouring into the United States from Europe.

The summer people, as it would happen, would contribute to a very large share of that economy, particularly when augmented by tourists later brought by the automobile.[4] Should Chamberlain have foreseen that? He was remarkably prescient in most matters. He was familiar with the pleasure of the Maine coast—having a summer place on the shore himself and a boat big enough to be styled a yacht. Yet he never mentioned the summer

*The two Maines, based on a map in an August 1997
issue of* Down East, the Magazine of Maine.

dwellers and tourists in relation to the economy. This may have been a
reflection of his own backcountry origin; the jobs created by the tourists
and the summer residents were, or would be, largely in the coastal area. But
the evidence seems to show that he was aiming at the sort of economy that
would correct the basic trouble, which was that most of Maine was exporting raw materials and depleting its natural resources instead of creating
products through the ingenuity and skill of its inhabitants, or, by the same
means, adding value to materials by exporting them in a finished rather
than a raw state—a much more profitable path to follow. "Look at England," Chamberlain urged, "not much larger than our own State and with
far inferior natural facilities. See what a system of industry has made of
her."[5] As for the state that relies solely on the sale of her products, "when
they are gone, she is gone,"[6] he declared.

Chamberlain's vision for Maine encompassed many small and varied
industries in locations all over the state. "It does not appear to me," he said,
"that the only manufactures we should long for are the great ones which
bring in crowds of foreign operatives who do not understand our institutions, and who do not enter into our social life and well-being."[7]

The governor had some very definite ideas for attracting and supporting industrial enterprises. One was to send out well-printed reports through
New England and the middle states acquainting capitalists with Maine's
remarkable waterpower resources. In his 1867 inaugural address he asked

Illustration from The Water Power of Maine, *which reported results of the hydrographic survey initiated by Joshua Chamberlain.*

the legislature to make an appropriation for conducting a hydrographic survey of the state.

The resulting survey and reports present an amazing picture of hundreds of sites where dams, waterwheels, and turbines were capturing power to drive the machinery of sawmills, gristmills, woolen mills, carding mills, and other operations, together with statistics on the various lake and river systems: areas and capacities of storage basins, rates of flow, volumes of water, heights of falls or "heads," and other information. Nontechnical as well as technical language is used. For example, Maine's rivers could produce power "equivalent to the working energy of over 34,000,000 men, laboring without intermission from year's end to year's end."[8] Meteorological conditions are stated. Also geological—for example, the availability of granite and other stone for building dams at different sites. Not only the principal lake and river systems are covered, but also Maine's tidal power resources, underdeveloped now, the report states, but perhaps a great source of energy someday, and when that day comes it will be worth remembering that the mean rise and fall of tide along the total Maine shoreline is about twelve feet compared with less than six feet for the rest of the East Coast.

Almost as amazing as the contents of the books was the time in which the survey and publication were completed—less than three years. And the cost was low. Walter Wells, the superintendent, and his staff simply sent out circulars and questionnaires to town, city, and plantation officials, engineers and agents of waterpower companies, and so on, and everyone cooperated with enthusiasm.

Determining the exact economic impact of this hydrographic survey would require a study well beyond this work's scope. But it is known that by the turn of the century waterpower plants were scattered all over the state, and some of them were beginning to belt electricity generators to their waterwheels. In Wells's reports published in 1868 and 1869 there is no trace of any awareness that waterpower would soon be used for the generation of electricity and that small hydroelectric companies growing up around waterpower sites would serve as stepping-stones to large utilities. But the survey and reports initiated by Chamberlain were so basic to this source of power that they continue to be useful and still represent one of the best presentations ever made by a state of its industrial inducements. With the failure of nuclear power in Maine and the existence of many undeveloped hydroelectric sites, the generation of electricity from Maine's waterpower could still be what Chamberlain thought it was—a great provider of jobs and income.[9]

Another recommendation made by Chamberlain had to do with education, which he saw as a prime ingredient in the plan to bring limited industrialization to Maine. It would be of no use, it was implied, to invite manufacturers to a state if they saw that its people were lacking the knowledge and skill necessary to operate their enterprises. "We must begin at the bottom and build up," Chamberlain said, "rather than begin at the top and build down. Institutions of learning of high grade doubtless have an important influence on the community, but the hundreds of modest little schools in every nook and corner of the state are the real fountains of knowledge and power."[10] Many of the rural schools of that day could be taught by almost anyone who could read and write. Chamberlain urged more training for teachers through normal schools.

At the upper level of education Maine had just established at Orono what Chamberlain referred to in his 1867 inaugural address as the Agricultural College. He urged that it be expanded into a College of Industrial Arts. Its curricula would grow into the Colleges of Agriculture, Technology, and Arts and Science, and it would become the University of Maine in 1897.

Another inducement for industry that Chamberlain encouraged had already been authorized by a Maine law enacted in 1864. It allowed manufacturers of a certain capitalization to be exempted from taxation for ten years if the cities or towns where they were located or proposed to locate would consent. In his 1867 inaugural address Chamberlain pointed to some Maine cities where this offering had borne fruit; he then went even beyond this plan (and beyond the Maine Constitution) by suggesting that limited state aid be given to manufacturers. This proposition was not accepted by the legislature.

It would be pleasant to report that today Maine is buzzing with activity, as it was when Chamberlain was a boy and lumbering and shipbuilding were at their height, with its young people staying in the state and its population and industry growing. But according to census figures released in March 1998 its growth was insignificant between 1990 and 1997—except in coastal Maine, where sizable increases further defined the "Two Maines." Meanwhile many traditional Maine industries, including shoe manufacturers, fish processors, lumber and papermaking factories, have closed or moved out of the state, leaving behind low-skilled workers without even their old minimum-wage jobs, and what will take the place of the old industries and old jobs is still uncertain. Education, although above the nation's average at the high school level, is below that average in the production of bachelor and graduate degrees.[11]

At this writing in 1998, Maine has a leader in Gov. Angus S. King Jr., who seems to be animated by the spirit of Joshua Chamberlain. In fact, if reincarnation is possible he may *be* Joshua Chamberlain. He rather looks like him. He lives in Brunswick and commutes to his office in Augusta, as Chamberlain did. And his house is on Potter Street, where Chamberlain lived.

In Governor King's "State of the State" address on February 2, 1998, there are echoes of Chamberlain's inaugural speeches, altered by awareness of the term "Two Maines," which King said he hated (as would have Chamberlain). But, he continued, something would have to be done about the disparity that had spawned the term. He declared, "I said last year that my ultimate goal as Governor was to make it so that none of our children would have to leave Maine to find a decent job. I'm modifying that tonight; our young people shouldn't have to leave Rumford, Houlton or Machias, either, for a chance at a good job and a decent life for their families . . . and so tonight, I'm announcing *One Maine* [King's emphasis], a comprehensive initiative to rebuild the economies of rural Maine. . . ."

Some of Chamberlain's ideas had parallels in key elements of King's *One Maine.* Examples:

Chamberlain's water power survey. King's proposal: "Invest in research, science, and technology to unlock the secrets of the sea and to develop valuable new products from our forest."

Chamberlain's proposal to increase state aid to manufacturers. King: "Let's put some money where our mouth is—we've got a program now called ETIF where the state returns back to new businesses a percentage of their state income tax withholding for new jobs created. The percentage is currently 30% in low unemployment areas and 50% in areas of higher than average unemployment. Since these are new jobs we're not counting on for revenues, I propose that the percentage refund be increased to 75% where the local unemployment rate is more than twice the state average."

Chamberlain's emphasis on education. King: "Focus the resources of the Technical Colleges and the University of Maine system—which have campuses strategically located in the very areas we are talking about—on supporting the local economies."

Chamberlain's same idea about education has a life-or-death importance today: On the basis of muscle power and simple manual skills there are many states and countries where people will work for less and draw industries away from Maine. But when brainpower is the criterion—as it is more and more as technology advances—the work goes to the places where educated people abound. Telecommunication has begun to erase the disadvantage of Maine's rather remote geographical location. A sound basis was established in 1996 with the enactment of an Internet telecommunications law providing funds to assure Internet access for Maine's schools, libraries, and museums by supplying the necessary equipment, software, and training.

So who knows what may happen? It may soon not be necessary for natives to leave the state and work long years so that they can come back home and enjoy life as it should be. As Gov. Joshua Chamberlain once said, "We have been too long content with the doubtful compliment that 'Maine is a good state to go from.' She must be made a good state to come to, and stay in."[12] This vision, amplified and carried forward by state and community leaders, may yet become a reality.

CHAPTER SIX

Reveille for Bowdoin

With his fourth and final one-year term as governor of Maine having come to an end, early in 1871 Chamberlain was informed by the governing boards of Bowdoin that their current president had given notice—he was resigning to become a professor at Yale—and they would like to consider him for the post. When the former governor responded favorably he was unanimously elected to this executive position in the academic world which, he hoped, would be quieter, pleasanter, and less troublesome than the one he had just left behind.

Settled in Brunswick with his wife Fanny and their two children, Grace and Wyllys, he bought a twenty-six-foot sloop and intended to spend many hours cruising over the sparkling blue waters and among the green islands of Casco Bay. During the summer and fall he carried out an exuberant plan for improving his living quarters. While he was governor of Maine, commuting to Augusta and living in temporary quarters in the capital city when duties called him there, he had maintained his home in Brunswick. Located first on Potter Street and then, moved to the corner of Potter and Maine Streets, the house had also been lived in by Henry Wadsworth Longfellow when he was a newly married professor at Bowdoin.

The improvement that Chamberlain engineered involved actually raising the old house and building a more stately mansion underneath it. The new first floor had an impressive entrance hall with a spiral stairway ascending to the upper story, a spacious drawing room, a library, and a dining room, all elegantly fitted out with fine woodwork, beautiful wallpaper, and—in the drawing room, also called the ballroom—ornate ceiling

A. *In 1871 Chamberlain constructed this house (top) by raising the house shown below and building an entirely new first story beneath it. It is now the Joshua L. Chamberlain Museum.* COURTESY DOUGLAS RICHMOND ARCHITECTS.
B. *This is the house originally purchased on Potter Street, Brunswick, in 1859. Chamberlain relocated it to the corner of Potter and Main Streets in 1867.* COURTESY DOUGLAS RICHMOND ARCHITECTS.

decoration and a fireplace with windows on both sides of the chimney, which enabled one, in winter, to watch the snowflakes fall and the fire burn in one field of vision. A little more than a century later when, after decades of neglect, the house was sinking toward decay, it was acquired by the Pejepscot Historical Society, and in the process of restoration some interesting structural problems were encountered. "Joshua Chamberlain was a great man, but he was no architect," is an opinion once voiced by Erik Jorgensen, executive director of the society (1989–98).

The rationale for this way of putting a house together—creative to the point of being eccentric—has never been found in any written record. Why wasn't the old house simply dismantled and a new one built on the site? It could be that Chamberlain thought that the old rooms would provide cozy and comfortable living quarters. Or he might have wished to retain the old dwelling because of its association with Longfellow, for whom he had great affection and regard. When in 1875 Longfellow returned to Bruswick for the fiftieth reunion of his Bowdoin class and Chamberlain took him upstairs to show him his old home, tears came to the old poet's eyes.

The downstairs rooms clearly were for entertaining. Obviously Chamberlain was thinking of old friends among Civil War generals who would be visiting him, as many of them did, and of figures from the academic, political, and business world who should be received in appropriate surroundings. As president of Bowdoin College he wanted a home equal to his position. He could, of course, have gone to live in Bowdoin's official president's residence, a large, square Federal-style house located on Federal Street, but that was a house where presidents would come and go. It would not be a house where people would say, "This is where Joshua Chamberlain lived." He wanted a house that would express his personality. One thinks of the Mark Twain house in Hartford, which some people think, rightly or wrongly, enfolds in its architecture and furnishings elements of a Mississippi steamboat and other reminders of the great author's life. The Chamberlain house, now a museum, has a comparable effect. Entering it a visitor can understand why anyone who ever sat with Joshua Chamberlain in his library could never forget him as he looked in this setting. Around him, on walls or in corners, were swords, pistols, stacked muskets, and other memorabilia of the Civil War, and overhead was a giant American flag covering the ceiling. Here on display was the image of himself he saw and others saw, that of the military hero and civilian patriot.

Now, in 1871, Chamberlain was about to begin a campaign as president of Bowdoin, and what he planned to do to the college was somewhat analogous to what he did to the old house in giving it a lift.

Chartered in 1794 and opened in 1802, Bowdoin in its early days had, in common with most colleges, strong religious affiliations. It was founded basically as a college of the "standing order," or the Congregationalists, some of whom considered themselves to be a cut above the Methodists, the Baptists, and other upstart denominations. Moreover, its early trustees were mostly Federalists at a time when the members of the prevailing party in Maine were the closer-to-earth and socially less delectable Jeffersonian Democrats.

In an issue of the *Bowdoin Orient*, the student newspaper, published in 1873, could be found this statement: "There is probably no college in the land, with such limited means, that has been so lavishly honored by the names of the great men it has educated."[1]

The statement was well justified.

By the middle of the nineteenth century Bowdoin men were prominent in every occupation. Franklin Pierce (Class of 1824) was elected president of the United States in 1852. Henry Wadsworth Longfellow (Class of 1825) was second only to Tennyson among the leading poets of the English-speaking world. Nathaniel Hawthorne (also '25), who would have a shorter life but a more durable reputation, saw his novel *The Scarlet Letter* published in 1850.

Famous people were glad to be recognized by Bowdoin. The college gave Jefferson Davis an honorary degree in 1858 and in spite of criticism during the Civil War period refused to withdraw it. Ulysses S. Grant came to Bowdoin to receive an honorary Doctor of Laws in 1865 and while in Brunswick visited Chamberlain at his home on Potter Street.

Yet all was not well with the college as the 1870s began. Bowdoin has always been thought of as an elite institution. In Maine, particularly in the first half of the twentieth century, Bowdoin was the college attended by sons of the better-off families in town, and there they expected to meet the best class of boys from other states. It is now difficult to believe that when Chamberlain became president in 1871 the status of the college was far less enviable. In fact, Bowdoin was at a low point in its history. It was under-populated. Classes were smaller than they had been in the late 1830s.[2] It was underfunded. And its curriculum was out-of-date. Like so many other colleges then, Bowdoin offered courses of study that were heavily oriented toward the education of clergymen, with a strong emphasis on Latin, Greek, Hebrew, and other subjects bearing upon the ministry. This seems to have had no predominant effect upon the total body of alumni. Robert M. Cross, secretary of Bowdoin College emeritus, has said, "My own feeling is that Bowdoin has turned out more lawyers and doctors than professors and ministers, despite the 19th century curriculum." What seems to have bothered Chamberlain most was Bowdoin's sequestered nature and its spirit. As he put it, "Something had come between the college and the life of the people. . . . the times had shot past the college."[3]

The whole situation demanded changes, and Joshua Chamberlain was the right man to accomplish them. He had the ability to look around the corner into the future and see what was coming—and then to take action to meet the challenge. He had demonstrated that sort of creativity in battle and as governor of Maine. But in 1871 there was no need to look around a corner. The signs of momentous changes were all around—overwhelmingly so. The economic demands of the Civil War and exploding technology had spurred or spawned hundreds of new enterprises—new industries, amazing inventions, big corporations, great money-making schemes. During Chamberlain's presidency, 1871–1883, Alexander Bell was speaking over his telephone. Thomas Edison was playing his phonograph, developing his incandescent lamp, and starting the operation of electric power companies. Manufacture of the internal combustion engine was beginning, opening the road for the "gasoline carriage," a machine that could utilize the great underground reservoirs of petroleum discovered in 1859. From the same resource John D. Rockefeller and a group of other capitalists were forming the Standard Oil Company. Andrew Carnegie and another group of moneymen were building a mighty steel mill. Railroads were expanding into a network that reached every settled section of the nation.

Great changes were either present or sensibly just over the horizon when Chamberlain took office as president of Bowdoin, so he quickly concluded that his college had to do more than create learned professors and ministers of the Gospel if it was to survive. Many of the postwar alumni who had gone out into the new world agreed with him. In his inaugural address on "The New Education" Chamberlain put forth his ideas for reform. It was, in the words of historian Charles C. Calhoun, "perhaps the best inaugural the College has ever heard in terms of a new president's willingness to express a vision in very concrete terms."[4]

In his address he talked about Bowdoin as though it were already a fragment of the past, and he did not spare the sensibilities of those connected with the college who were still living in bygone days. "It was the cloister spirit, after all," he said, "that made most mischief with the old college. Its tendency was away from life; the natural affections rebuked; the social instincts chilled; the body despised and so dishonored; women banished and hence degraded, so that even to admit her to a place in the higher education is thought to degrade a college. The inmates separate, secluded, grown abnormal and provincial, came out into the world strangers to it. . . ."[5] One can imagine some of his older hearers shifting angrily in their seats and reddening under their whiskers. It was almost the equivalent of Chamberlain's charge down the slopes of Little Round Top. In a speech that was otherwise graceful, logical, and full of affection for old Bowdoin, his words contained a considerable amount of shock tactics.

The changes in curriculum that took place under Chamberlain were abrupt and, for the Bowdoin of that day, dramatic. Bowdoin was then under the management of two boards consisting of the trustees, given primary responsibility, and the overseers, who had to approve the actions of the trustees. Most members of these boards seem to have liked and respected Chamberlain, and they quickly approved his recommendations. In July 1871 the boards authorized the establishment of a scientific department; in July 1872 a Department of Military Tactics and Science (something Chamberlain had not mentioned in his inaugural address and, as it turned out, a ticking time bomb); and also in July 1872 the hiring of a professor of civil engineering, George L. Vose, who was to teach an engineering course.[6]

Machiavelli, that noted fifteenth-century adviser to rulers, once said that "there is nothing more difficult to carry out, nor more doubtful of success, nor more dangerous to handle than to initiate a new order of things. For the reformer has enemies in all who would profit by the old order, and only lukewarm defenders in those who would profit by the new order. . . ."[7] Apparently somewhere among the members of the faculty, governing boards, and alumni simmered difficulties such as Machiavelli had foretold, for in July 1873 the overseers felt it necessary to voice the following:

> Resolved that the Board of Overseers of Bowdoin College after listening to the statements of the President in the convention feel bound to express our cordial approbation of the President's course in endeavoring to carry out in good faith the new measures authorized by previous actions of the Boards, enlarging and improving the College curriculum.
>
> Resolved that while engaged in this grand experiment to meet the public demand for a more liberal course of College instruction, the President and Faculty are entitled to the moral support of the guardians and friends of the College until such time as the Boards authorize the discontinuance of the experiment.[8]

Reading between the lines it can be seen that the overseers were trying to rally troops in which some lack of confidence had been perceived; also the Overseers were not too confident themselves, since they were regarding Chamberlain's program as an "experiment." Their doubts, very likely, had less to do with the merits of the program than with finances. Equipment and faculty needed for the new courses were much more expensive than those of the old curriculum. Nowhere was the financial strain more keenly felt than in the engineering course. In November 1873 the governing boards received a letter from its only professor, George Vose.[9] He wrote that he had twenty to twenty-five students, some of them very promising. The department was sorely in need of an endowment, Vose said, pointing out that Latin, Greek, or mathematics could be taught using only books, but apparatus was needed for engineering, and his department had only a single transit and a level. Further, he had no library except his own private collection. Professors of engineering in other colleges, he reminded the boards, received $2,000 to $4,000 a year for working from two to four hours a day, and they had one or two assistants. He worked seven hours a day six days a week with no assistant and received only $1,600 a year. He couldn't continue at Bowdoin without going into debt.

In 1875 Vose and other Bowdoin professors received a raise from $1,600 to $1,700 a year, and Vose got an extra $700 "in lieu of assistance." But the professors didn't get another raise until 1882, when some went to $1,800. Chamberlain was hired as president at $2,900 a year but because of the financial condition of the college he annually relinquished $300 of it until 1880, when the full $2,900 was restored.[10]

The college was trying to support itself mainly on tuition. A few donations drifted in but they were small by today's standards. Typical of these was $10,000 from the Edward Little Institute for establishing a professor of mental and moral philosophy. Chamberlain took on the duties of this professorship for five years without accepting pay for it.[11]

Chamberlain had encountered the reality that money has much to do with the quality of a college. Some sizable donations were needed. For example, he figured that the scientific department needed an endowment of at least $250,000. Early in his administration the governing boards authorized a fund drive, and as his part of it, Chamberlain solicited many people he had known personally or officially.

One of the prospective donors Chamberlain wrote to was James G. Blaine, who was an overseer of Bowdoin from 1866 to 1873, although not a very active one. Blaine's reply, from his congressional office in Washington, said that one of the misfortunes of his life was that people thought he had money, and so he was always being expected to give what he gladly would give if he were wealthy, but he was not wealthy. Bowdoin was not enriched by this solicitation.

Another person Chamberlain wrote to was Adelbert Ames, who had been his friend and mentor as the first commander of the 20th Maine. Ames had married into a wealthy family in becoming the husband of Blanche Butler, daughter of Gen. Benjamin F. Butler, and Reconstruction had taken him into a strange byway. When Congress imposed military government on the South and divided it into five military districts, Ames, after holding various positions in the fifth district (Mississippi and Arkansas), went into politics. In their brief day at the polls, blacks, for whom he was a courageous advocate, helped to elect him U.S. senator and then governor of Mississippi. Replying to Chamberlain's appeal from the state's executive office in Jackson, he wrote affectionately of their old army days together and briefed Chamberlain on the racial situation in the South but failed to enclose a check. He had engaged in some speculation, he said, and was $15,000 in debt.[12]

In various exchanges of correspondence having to do with donations, one of the most significant was that with Abner Coburn, who seemingly could not have been improved upon as a prospect. He and his brother Philander had taken advantage of a time when vast areas of northern Maine consisted of cheap land covered with valuable forest. Buying up this land and lumbering the huge pine and spruce trees, the Coburns made an enormous fortune, which led to investments in other enterprises such as banks and railroads. The Coburn brothers eventually owned more than seven hundred square miles of timberland in Maine plus large tracts in the western part of the United States, as well as steamboats, hotels, and all manner of money-making property. In the early days, when there was little ready money in Maine, it was said that their notes, signed "A & P Coburn," were often used as currency. They were people of absolute integrity and notable generosity. Abner Coburn was interested in promoting higher education, although he had never had any of it himself. Further, he must have thought well of the new Bowdoin president; he had been governor of Maine in 1863, the year of glory for Chamberlain at Gettysburg, and he had had much correspondence with him about affairs of the 20th Maine in which he must have been impressed with Chamberlain's good sense and sound judgment.

In a letter written to Abner Coburn in January 1873 Chamberlain sought to interest him in Bowdoin's new science department—something that might appeal to a self-made, hard-headed businessman. He wrote, in part:

> I took this place, as you must know, simply because I thought I could here soonest and best try the experiment of *liberal course of study which should tend to the widest practical use in life.* The great demand of the times is that knowledge, instead of being turned inward, and shut up in the cloister, should face outward toward the work of life.
>
> I have tried to meet that demand here and have organized a Scientific Department, separate from the college course, and vigorous and effective in itself. Many students have come in and even

in the brief space of time, and many more—a very large number
in fact—are to join us next term.

Indeed the effort is a thorough success, and has attracted
attention all over the country and been recognized in a substantial
manner by the Scientific Department of the Government of the
United States. Letters of inquiry and congratulation are coming in
from nearly ever state in the Union, and if I am enabled to carry
the work on as I have begun, it will have a National reputation.[13]

Chamberlain offered to name the new department after Coburn if he would
provide the needed endowment. It would be known as the Coburn School
of Science and Art.

In a rather disjointed letter Coburn commented on how expensive academic institutions were getting to be, explained that his properties took a
lot of expenditure to develop, so he didn't have much loose cash, and wondered if it would be appropriate for him, an outsider, to do something this
big for Bowdoin—shouldn't that distinction go to someone in the large and
wealthy denomination controlling the college? He had to decline the
honor.[14]

There is no record of any endowment at Bowdoin bearing Coburn's
name. But he was a trustee of Colby College in Waterville, Maine, and one
of its greatest benefactors. There was—before Colby moved in the late
1930s from its old location literally on the wrong side of the railroad tracks
to beautiful Mayflower Hill, two miles away—a Coburn Hall on its campus, built as a result of Coburn generosity. (There is a Louise Coburn Hall
on the new campus, a residence building, named for a member of the same
prominent family.) Abner Coburn was also responsible, through a matching
grant, for the endowment of three academies to serve as fitting schools for
Colby, one of them named Coburn Classical Institute. Later they were to be
joined by a fourth academy, completing a satellite system of great importance in Maine education.[15]

The Coburn correspondence underlines the fact that while Bowdoin,
with its Congregationalist association dominated higher education in Maine
in the first half of the nineteenth century, by the time Chamberlain took over
as president there was strong competition from the institutions now known
as Colby College (then Baptist-affiliated), Bates College (founded by a
Freewill Baptist minister), and the University of Maine (nondenominational).

These state of Maine institutions were not just in place as general con-
tenders—their curricula also were competing with the sort of progress
Chamberlain was trying to introduce at Bowdoin. The Coburn Hall at Colby

just mentioned was devoted to the sciences. Bates was well up with the times; founded in 1855, it didn't have much old baggage to dispose of. And the University of Maine, then known as the State College of Agriculture and the Mechanic Arts, was offering courses in agriculture, civil engineering, mechanical engineering, and other forward-looking studies.

In trying to introduce changes at Bowdoin, Chamberlain was not trying to make it a trade school. His idea of what college education ought to be was clearly stated in a letter to another Bowdoin man in 1858: "My idea of a college course is that it should afford a *liberal education*—not a special or professional one, nor in any way one-sided. It cannot be a *finished* education, but should be, I think, a general outline of a symmetrical development, involving such acquaintance with all the departments of knowledge & culture—proportionate to their several values—as shall give one insight into the principles & powers by which thought passes into life—together with such practice & exercise in each of the great fields of study that the student may experience himself a little in all."[16] It would be hard to find a better credo for a college like Bowdoin, and there is no evidence that Chamberlain ever changed his belief. If there was a change it was to be found in his trying to broaden the offering of the college and make it more relevant to the life of the times.

In addition to curriculum changes, Chamberlain had another idea that was not to be realized until after three more generations had passed. In his inaugural address he said that women ought to be part of the college "because in this sphere of things her 'rights,' her capacities, her offices, her destiny, are equal to those of men." In 1872, shortly after he began his presidency, an alumnus, Dr. Cyrus Fogg Brackett, handed Chamberlain a letter he had received from a girl who wanted to know if she might be admitted to Bowdoin's medical school, the Medical School of Maine. Chamberlain immediately wrote her: "I perceive the reasonableness of your proposition and regret that not having contemplated such applications we cannot make such arrangements as would be fit & proper in this case. I am sure that with the high character & earnest purpose you evince, women will soon find those 'equal terms' they so justly desire, either by building up new colleges or by raising up the old ones."[17]

The idea, of course, was not new. A few women's colleges had existed since 1821, and coeducation had been established at Antioch and Oberlin by midcentury, while in Maine the first women were admitted to Bates in 1865, to Colby in 1871, and to the University of Maine in 1872. But it was not until 1971 that Bowdoin opened its gates to members of the supposedly weaker sex. Among the earliest was one who confounded that supposition—Joan Benoit Samuelson, who became the gold medalist in the first women's Olympic marathon.

The drive for donations during Chamberlain's administration was productive. By 1876 he could report to the governing boards that the college funds had nearly doubled. But there was still not enough to meet the expense of new equipment, the salaries of added faculty members, and the competition from the science-oriented University of Maine and the giant Massachusetts Institute of Technology. In 1880 Chamberlain's scientific department—as a distinct element—was abolished.

Chamberlain's attempt to update the curriculum at Bowdoin had been a failure. Yet many people who have studied Bowdoin's history agree that with his presidency the greatly respected Bowdoin College of today really began, for under his successor, the vigorous William DeWitt Hyde, many of his ideas bore fruit: The curriculum was modernized, the faculty was enlarged, methods of study were liberalized, and other changes were made that brought the college into the twentieth century as an institution in tune with the times. Some thirty years after Chamberlain's presidency Hyde said that "he advocated the very reforms, using often the very phrases, that are now commonplaces of progressive education discussions. Modern languages, science, classics in translation, political and social science, research, individual instruction: all these were included on the program of the professor of 1859 and the president in 1872. He had the misfortune, or rather the glory, to advocate these expensive reforms before the college had the funds to make them completely effective."[18]

Looking back at all this at the turn of the century Chamberlain might have seen himself as having been a Moses on Mount Nebo, looking at the Promised Land but destined never to set foot upon it.

CHAPTER SEVEN

Mutiny of the Bowdoin Cadets

By the mid-1870s about twenty colleges, with the help and encouragement of the U.S. government, had established military departments employing instructors, arms, and equipment provided by the War Department. It is easy to imagine some of the officers in that department—Civil War veterans—saying to one another, "For God's sake, let's not get caught in another big war without national conscription, civilians trained as officers, and every other civilian component we can get." They had seen, in the Civil War, the inadequacy of the regular force in trying to meet the manpower requirements of a major conflict and were correctly anticipating similar inadequacies in future wars calling for great masses of people: World War I, nearly five million; World War II, more than sixteen million; Korean War, nearly six million; Vietnam War, nearly nine million. No standing army could meet demands like these unless it were so large that it would be intolerable to the citizenry. Hence this reaching out to the colleges, where it was hoped, the essentials of military leadership could be taught.

Nothing could have been more appealing to Chamberlain as president of Bowdoin than having this program on his campus. He had seen the need for such training at first hand—fighting a war in which Union casualties had exceeded the whole 1860 population of the state of Maine. The unnecessary injuries and deaths, the suffering and grief resulting from the ignorance of men suddenly converted from farmers, lawyers, clerks, teachers, and other civilian occupations and called upon to lead equally ignorant soldiers into battle had been all too apparent to Chamberlain, even though his own performance as a scholar turned soldier had been a remarkable exception.

With the hearty approval of the governing boards the Department of Military Tactics and Science was established at Bowdoin in 1872.[1] It represented one of the earliest stages of the student training in America that eventually led to the Reserve Officers Training Corps forty-four years later, and so it is understandable that the program was not very well thought out, either by the War Department or by Bowdoin. There was no promise of commissions, no financial aid, no rewards of any specific kind. In fact, it cost the students extra money in paying for their own uniforms. According to the student paper, *The Bowdoin Orient,* the very slim advantages offered were three: "1st, physical training, 2nd, acquaintance with military tactics and discipline; 3rd, that dignity of bearing and spirit of obedience and self-possession so necessary to the constitution of the thorough man."[2]

Bowdoin was extremely fortunate in the War Department's detailing of Maj. Joseph P. Sanger to serve as the organizer and instructor of the military unit. He later became a general officer in the army and a noted military educator. After leaving Bowdoin he accompanied Gen. Emory Upton (author of an army book of tactics used at the time) on a two-year trip around the world studying military organizations in Europe and Asia, and upon Upton's death, he wrote or edited important reports imparting lessons of war to his countrymen. Whether he ever wrote of his experiences at Bowdoin is not known, but he probably never forgot them.

As so often happens in military matters, all went thrillingly at first. The faculty and boards were solidly behind the program. The students were excited. In a retrospective article written a few years later, *The Bowdoin Orient* described the beginning:

> In the first part of the academical year '72, our college was on the *qui vive* for the coming of the military drill. It was to be something new; it would give an opportunity for show, and it promised a pleasurable relief from the monotony of regular studies. The idea of imbibing a military education in our leisure moments, and becoming, without effort or cost of any kind, trained soldiers, while we steadily pursued our way toward law, theology, or medicine, was very captivating to the student, even as it had taken the fancy of college authorities. So when at last the officer detailed by the Government had come, and the Juniors had begun their drill in the south wing of the Chapel, we underclassmen waited impatiently for the time when we too should be allowed to participate in the exercise. What better circumstances could be desired for its trial?[3]

But soon some of the horrors of war—or of preparing for war—appeared. In September 1872 an eight-page manual signed by President Chamberlain was issued under the title, *Regulations for the Interior Police and Discipline of the Bowdoin Cadets.*[4]

The manual almost made it seem that Bowdoin was to become a little West Point. The students were to be organized into a battalion of four companies with the men of each company quartered together as far as practicable. Muskets, bayonets, bayonet scabbards, and cartridge boxes were to be issued—the arms kept in arms racks, as in an army barrack. Whenever the cadets turned out in uniform under arms, they were to wear white gloves. The tone of the manual is illustrated by excerpting five of the forty regulations:

> 6. There will be a military exercise for instruction every day when the weather is favorable; Saturdays and Sundays excepted. Each exercise will continue at least one hour, and shall not exceed an hour and a half.
>
> 7. There will be Guard Mounting and Dress Parade daily, when the weather permits, according to the forms prescribed in Upton's Infantry Tactics.
>
> 8. There will be an inspection of the Battalion under arms on Sunday morning, whenever the weather permits, according to the form prescribed in Upton's Infantry Tactics.
>
> 9. No cadet shall be absent from any military duty whatever without the permission of the President, unless excused by a Surgeon, in consequence of sickness or disease.
>
> 10. Hours for Daily Duties
>
> Reveille
>
> Guard Mounting. 2 P.M. Daily
>
> Drill. 1½ hours before sunset
>
> Retreat. Sunset
>
> Sunday Inspection. 9 o'clock A.M.

The *Orient* complained that this document imitated "the severity of Prussian discipline."[5] It appears that it was considerably modified by college authorities or disregarded by students in the months that followed.

Hostility to the program was apparent as soon as the drills got well under way. The chief point of contention had to do with the uniform prescribed by the manual, which was denounced as a symbol of oppression and needless cost. But in a letter written to the governing boards in 1874, Major Sanger disputed student claims to that effect.

> The truth is briefly this: it was not thought advisable to submit the question of uniform at the outset, so, early in 1872, the students were called together in the chapel, the subject was discussed, committees were appointed to test the sentiment of the classes, and at an adjourned meeting held the following day, the committees reported in favor of the West Point Cadet uniform, at a cost of $28.00 for each suit. The Faculty knew nothing of these actions, and neither gave nor withheld consent. No pressure was brought to bear on the students, whose action in adopting and purchasing the uniform was deliberate and voluntary. But as there were a number of students who could ill-afford the expenditure, and the necessity for a uniform becoming more apparent, the Faculty, early in the Fall of 1873, adopted the blue flannel blouse and made its purchase compulsory by those who had not the gray uniform. The entire outfit of cap, blouse, belt and gloves cost less than $6.00, which is within the reach of every student in the institution. Further than this, many students habitually wear the cap and blouse and thus economize in the purchase of more expensive clothing.[6]

Fortunately, the grounds for one complaint had been eliminated. In winter weather the students did not have to drill outside in the snow. One of the buildings available for this training was Memorial Hall, which had encountered a halt in construction and consisted only of wall, roof, and window openings for the most part for several years. The alumni owned the building, and they rented the empty inside space to the college for a gymnasium and the military training.[7]

During 1873 some students liked the drill or remained indifferent; some tried to avoid it in every way possible; but the majority grumbled while they drilled. The troops, to take a phrase from the earlier Book of Joshua, "murmured against their leaders." Toward the end of the year the students determined that they would draw up a petition to the governing boards asking that the military department be abolished. This was done in an orderly and reasonable manner. The gist of the petition was that the military program was scaring prospective students away from Bowdoin; that the college had facilities for "more popular and profitable exercise"; that they were purchasing otherwise useless clothing; that too much time was being taken away from regular studies; and that the program was intensely unpopular. The petition was signed by 126 of the 133 students constituting the three upper classes.[8]

A. G. Bradstreet, a respected member of the senior class, presented the petition to a committee appointed by the boards and argued the case of the students at some length. According to the *Orient* he was told that a decision upon the matter would be deferred until the next meeting of the boards and was also advised that a written statement of the case should be prepared and presented at that time.

Still according to the *Orient*—at the time of the next meeting of the boards (which may have been during vacation) Bradstreet was out of town but did write offering to appear if needed; he was not called for, however, and that was the end of the petition.

If the reports of the *Orient* are correct, this rejection or neglect on the part of the boards ignited the fuse that set off the rebellion. In the week beginning May 17, 1874, the revolt exploded. On Tuesday the nineteenth there was much shouting and profanity as the students dispersed from artillery drill, and the next day Major Sanger warned against any recurrence. On May 22—a fateful Friday—the greater part of the sophomore and freshman classes refused to report for duty. On the same day it became known that a majority of the junior, sophomore, and freshman classes had signed an agreement to resist the drill at all hazards. Members of the Bowdoin faculty investigated, talked with many of the disaffected students, and tried to persuade them to desist in their insubordination. The students held firm in their resolve not to drill. Here then was General Chamberlain confronted with what was probably the most traumatic event in Bowdoin's history.

How had it happened? Chamberlain by peaceful means had quieted a mutiny of a large group of soldiers—replacements coming to his 20th Maine regiment just before the battle of Gettysburg. How had he allowed this situation at Bowdoin to get out of hand? It could be said that the situation at Gettysburg was considerably different. The mutineers delivered to the 20th Maine were virtually under a death sentence; Chamberlain was instructed to shoot them if they did not return to duty. These were desperate times, with the fate of the nation at stake. Patriotism, fear of a disgraceful death, and Chamberlain's fair treatment and persuasive words were enough to return these men to duty with decisive effect at Gettysburg.[9]

The Bowdoin cadets were in a much stronger position. What could Chamberlain do? Expel them? Constituting as they did three-fourths of the college, that would be the ruination of Bowdoin. If this was the thought of the Bowdoin mutineers they perhaps had forgotten that they were dealing with the man who had led the desperate charge against overwhelming odds down the slopes of Little Round Top—and won. Chamberlain made many courageous decisions during his lifetime, rarely counting on the probable cost, and now he was about to make one of them. He sent home nearly every man who refused to drill, quickly followed by a letter to his parents that explained all that had happened, and then made this offer.

> If your son will sign the enclosed blank, renewing in good faith and without reservation his matriculation pledge of obedience to the Laws and Regulations of the College, and forward it to the President within ten days from date, he will be allowed to return and resume his place in his class, and this he will be expected to do without further delay. If he does not do this, he must consider himself by the act of refusal as expelled from college at the expiration of the ten days. If he concludes to return to his duty, and his objections to the drill are not removed he can at the end of his term but not before, receive an honorable dismission and go to some other college.[10]

All but three of the students returned to Bowdoin within the time limit Chamberlain had given them, and these three eventually came back and were accepted. Chamberlain had won the battle but lost the war. The governing boards voted to make the military drill optional, although they continued their support and urged the students to enroll in it until near the end of Chamberlain's administration. By May 1878, only twenty-five men were drilling. Finally, in 1882, Bowdoin's military department was shut down.[11]

How could an idea so well received at first end so badly? There are possible reasons. Discipline is the backbone of a military unit; Chamberlain wanted the student-soldiers to learn that. But the "Prussian severity," as the *Orient* put it, with which it was established may have been too big a dose for the youngsters to swallow suddenly. Another possibility: Chamberlain was unable to stay close enough to the trainees to exercise the personal leadership he was famous for; his duties as college president may have been too demanding. But the most likely reason was that the program was too rigorous for its reward—too much like West Point or one of today's army officer candidate schools without offering commissions or anything else. And this may have been due to the same weakness that afflicted other departments: lack of funds that might have provided free uniforms and scholarship assistance.

In summarizing the ill-fated attempt to introduce military training at Bowdoin it could be said that here again Chamberlain was ahead of his time. He certainly would have thought so if, a couple of years after his death, he could have returned to see the ROTC in operation at many colleges. And he would have chuckled ruefully—had he been alive during World War II—at seeing students in uniform again marching across the Bowdoin campus.

CHAPTER EIGHT

Maine on the Brink of Civil War

In late December 1879 and early January 1880 the state of Maine, in whose precincts all the good old New England civic virtues are supposed to dwell, almost became a banana republic, with gangs of armed men trying to seize control of the government and the streets of its capital about to be stained by rivulets of blood.

If Joshua Chamberlain, sitting in his quiet presidential office at Bowdoin College, was occasionally daydreaming of participating in one more epic event, one more chance to face a monumental challenge, this was it, for quite unexpectedly he was about to be drawn into the vortex of chaotic happenings in Augusta.

Although somewhat secluded in the academic world, Chamberlain had been watching the events leading up to this crisis. Under the chairmanship of James G. Blaine the Maine Republican party had enjoyed more than two decades of domination at the polls until 1878, when they lost the gubernatorial election because of two circumstances. One was the difference between the words "plurality" (more votes than anyone else) and "majority" (more than half the votes). Under the Maine constitution the person with a plurality might not win. The constitution said that if none of the candidates had a majority, the house of representatives would, by ballot, choose two from the four candidates having the highest number of votes, and then the senate would elect one of the two governor.

The other circumstance was the entry of the Greenback Party, a party advocating the issue and widespread circulation and use of paper money, into Maine politics. The federal government had done this, out of necessity, during the Civil War; millions of "greenbacks" had been issued, backed not by a specie but *promises* to pay the face value. Members of the Greenback Party believed that wartime money was good in peacetime, too; it would bring about great business activity and prosperity. Opponents pointed out that paper money of this kind always depreciates; it is good for debtors but bad for creditors; it throws the whole economic system out of whack. In the annual election of 1878 there was a Greenback candidate as well as a Democrat and a Republican candidate for governor. When the votes were counted it was found that the Republican had a plurality but no candidate had a majority. In the legislature combined Greenbackers and Democrats controlled the house of representatives but the Republicans still dominated the senate, which had the final choice between two candidates selected by the house. These were a Greenbacker and a Democrat, and the senators picked what they thought was the lesser of two evils, the Democrat, Dr. Alonzo Garcelon of Lewiston.

A Bowdoin graduate in the class of 1836, Garcelon was sixty-five when he became governor. Behind him was a life of conspicuous public service. He had been Civil War surgeon general of Maine, and in that capacity he had done such a good job caring for wounded soldiers both in Maine hospitals and at the front that he had built up a large constituency of grateful veterans. Similarly, as a founder, promoter, or benefactor of institutions and industries in Lewiston, including the *Lewiston Journal,* Bates College, the library, hospital, and so on, he had attained a well-deserved popularity. He had been a mayor of Lewiston. In his politics Garcelon had been a Whig and a Free-Soiler before the Civil War, a Republican during the Civil War, and then, disgusted with Radical Reconstructionists, he had switched to being a Democrat. In Joshua Chamberlain's bosom there may have lurked a secret affection for him.

In the election of 1879 Garcelon ran again as the Democratic candidate. The 1878 Greenbacker, Joseph L. Smith, also ran again despite being a very odd candidate. One plank of the Greenback platform expressed hostility to the issue of government bonds, declaring that they should all be paid off or canceled. Yet their candidate Smith was a wealthy man who owned stacks of bonds. The Republican candidate was Daniel F. Davis, a thirty-six-year-old lawyer. Davis met one of the day's most important tests for political acceptance; he was a veteran of "the war"—a private in a cavalry regiment. Also, he had served in the Maine legislature for eight years.

The 1879 election was considered highly important, not only in Maine but all across the country. Maine was being watched for the usual reason: The outcome of its early September 8 election might foreshadow national results.

But this year it was being watched more intently than usual. Politicians had at least three big questions. Would the Democrats once again break into the "solid North?" Would "soft money" make further penetration? And how strong was James G. Blaine in his own home state? Blaine was being talked of as a candidate for president of the United States in 1880, and although he was not on the ballot in Maine, the overall Republican performance in the state would redound to his credit or discredit among national party leaders.

The Republican party threw a great deal of weight into its campaign that summer. Important speakers bearing big names in the Republican party came into the state to whip up enthusiasm, including two future presidents, James A. Garfield and William McKinley; Maine congressmen, Thomas B. Reed and William P. Frye; and, of course, its senator, James G. Blaine. In Maine the Republican organization, known to Democrats as the Blaine ring, or machine, worked overtime amid widespread charges of corruption. During and after the campaign some Democrat newspapers charged the Republicans with buying votes and forcing minor officials to contribute to party campaign funds. The *Boston Globe* asserted that "evidence gleaned from all sections of the state . . . shows that this system of purchase and pressure was general all over the commonwealth, and had its origin in the headquarters of the party, and in a certain head of the organization."[1] According to the *Portland Eastern Argus* even in church one was not safe from the tentacles of James G. Blaine; speaking of a certain Sunday school teacher in Androscoggin County the *Argus* reported, "His class was taken away from him for no other reason than that he was a Democrat."[2]

Although September 8, 1879, was a rainy day there was a big turnout, the largest ever in Maine. Results showed the Republicans to be in the same situation that thwarted them in 1878. Their gubernatorial candidate had a plurality but had missed getting a majority of the votes by a narrow margin.[3] They had triumphed in elections of state senators and representatives, however, so they felt absolutely certain that a Republican governor would be chosen when the election went into the legislature.

Although the Democrats and Greenbackers had nominated separate candidates for governor, in contests for legislatures and county offices they were practically united and were known as the "Fusion" group, or party. On that basis the voters had elected the following members of the legislature.[4]

	Senate	House
Republicans	19	90
Fusionists	12	61

With these majorities in the legislature guaranteeing election of their governor, Republicans were elated. And the victory in Maine was an enormous boost for James G. Blaine's chances to become president of the United States. Campaigning in Ohio in October, he was greeted by encouraging banners: "We go for Blaine in 1880," "Blaine for the White House," and so on. The *New York Times* reported that "Blaine of Maine is on everybody's lips, and at every railway station the people gather to catch a glimpse of him."[5]

But soon, on the verge of these sunny Republican skies, a cloud appeared. It arose from the way in which the returns of the votes had to be handled according to the Maine constitution. In meetings open to the public, selectmen were to sort, count, and declare the votes cast; then the town clerks were to make lists of the persons voted for, with the number of votes against each name. (Similar rules applied to plantations and cities.)

Copies of these lists, attested by the town clerks and selectmen were then to be sealed in open meetings and sent to the Maine secretary of state at least thirty days before the first Wednesday in January, the day when members of the elected government were to take office. Then, at least twenty days before the first Wednesday in January, the governor and his council were to complete an examination of the returned lists and issue summonses to all persons who appeared to be elected. Governor Garcelon and his council met and ordered their committee on election returns to begin examining the returns on October 28, which gave them more than seven weeks to get the job done. Their early start may have aroused suspicions.

Before the examination began ominous rumors were circulating. The *Bangor Whig & Courier* reported that a surreptitious scheme was afoot to throw out a number of Republican returns as being "fatally defective"[6] and thus steal control of the senate and house. One rumor had it that the governor and council had voiced the intention to wipe out the Republican majority as with a sponge. Later investigation seemed to show that Garcelon had little to do with the work of the council on the returns—that he had turned the examination of the lists over to the committee on election returns and had accepted the results with little scrutiny.

Somehow the Republicans learned that a tabulation would be reported in the meeting of the governor and council taking place on November 17, and their leaders gathered in Augusta. The meeting was scheduled for four o'clock. At about half past three Nelson Dingley Jr., former governor of Maine, appeared in Garcelon's office, which adjoined the council chamber, with two other Republicans, the three of them representing a committee of sixteen waiting elsewhere. Dingley asked to see the election returns. In the course of the subsequent discussions, Garcelon told Dingley that he was not going to place the returns "in the hands of a mob."[7] Later he explained that this was only a figurative expression: He had not meant to characterize Dingley and his committee as a mob. But the statement proved to be highly inflammatory; it was translated by one Republican newspaper into the assertion that Garcelon regarded the citizens of Maine as "a rabble." Garcelon might impress one as a nice old gentleman who, not altogether aware of the consequences, was moving or being moved one step at a time toward utter chaos. He and his council decided that no one outside their circle could see the returns until December 1, and then only until December 13 could candidates claiming irregularities appear before them. The committee on election returns continued its work.

Through the last half of November and well into December a great deal of premonitory clamor appeared in Republican newspapers. Typical was a headline in the *Whig & Courier:*

The Conspiracy!

Revolution Actually Afoot!

Only Awaiting the Final Act!

Will They Dare Commit the Monstrous Crime?[8]

By now Augusta was a focal point for journalists from all over the country, many of them visiting Maine, many others commenting from afar. The *Boston Traveller* referred to sources in Washington stating that "The Democratic conspiracy to get control of Maine during the next year is the outgrowth of a consultation among Democratic managers from all sections of the country" and that some of the ablest legal minds in the nation had been advising Governor Garcelon.[9]

On December 1 prominent Republicans from all over the state gathered in Augusta with five former governors including Chamberlain meeting in the Blaine house, across the street from the state capitol. (It was not at that time the governor's residence, as it is today.) On that day Chamberlain and his fellow Republicans were allowed to see the returns from one county and promised further examinations. But expectations of redress—if there were any—were short-lived. The bomb burst in mid-December.

The list of persons certified as being elected revealed that many Republicans had been disqualified and that their majorities in the house and senate, seemingly established by the September election, had been reversed.

The Republican *Whig & Courier* announced on December 16 that the results were:

	Senate	House
Fusionists	20	78
Republicans	11	58

Results as reported by the Democrat *Eastern Argus* were slightly different but showed large Fusion majorities in both Senate and House, predicting the election by the legislature of a Democrat or Greenback governor.

It was evident that the council's committee on election returns had done a very craftsmanlike piece of work. Technicalities based on laws, court decisions, and the Maine constitution were cited and used to "count out" various candidates. Later an investigating committee dominated by Republicans charged that there also had been erasures, alterations, and forgeries upon the lists.

An example of a technical knockout was seen in the voting district composed of two towns, Garland and Exeter. The September results were as follows, using the names of two brothers as they appeared on the returns:

	Names on Garland Returns	Garland Votes
Republican	George S. Hill	211
Fusionist	Francis W. Hill	114

	Names on Exeter Returns	Exeter Votes
Republican	G. S. Hill	132
Fusionist	F. W. Hill	220

	Total Votes
George S. and G. S. Hill	343
Francis W. and F. W. Hill	334

Assuming George S. Hill and G. S. Hill were the same person, which in fact was the case, this represented a 343 to 334 victory for the Republican. But the committee on election returns counted the candidates as four different people, and this gave the win to the Fusionist with F. W. Hill's 220 votes. (The constitution allowed legislators to win with pluralities.)

In another case John T. Wallace Jr. was counted as separate from John T. Wallace to the advantage of the Fusionists. When testifying before a special investigating committee on March 12, 1880, former governor Garcelon defended this rather cleverly. He said, "For example there is a Nelson Dingley and a Nelson Dingley, Jr., two gentlemen living in my place [Lewiston]; one of them, Nelson Dingley, Jr., has been voted for governor and elected, and the other, quite as respectable and worthy, is named Nelson Dingley. There is no possible way of counting these two votes as one."[10]

More serious was the disenfranchisement of five cities: Portland, Lewiston, Saco, Bath, and Rockland, a group that together paid about a quarter of the taxes in Maine and sent twelve representatives to the legislature. Portland had elected five Republican representatives by a sizable margin of 629 votes, but on the return 143 votes were listed as "scattering," so all votes were thrown out, even though it could be demonstrated that not in any case would the scattering votes destroy the plurality of a winner. Adding to Republican outrage was refusal by the governor's council to allow a new election.

In the cases of the other four cities all the votes were thrown out because only three aldermen had signed the election returns, and the governor and council said four should have signed. This decision was particularly galling to Republicans because the official form for reporting the returns, sent out by the secretary of state, in the signature area had only three lines for the aldermen.

When the full extent of the destruction became evident, screams of Republican rage echoed across the state of Maine. Scoundrels! Thieves! Villains! were words common to the public discourse. At moments when they could control themselves long enough to express articulate statements, Republicans pointed to a number of what they considered to be suspicious circumstances. The governor and council said that everything had been done legally, but Republicans charged that they had refused to allow new elections and other measures countenanced by law whereby any errors could have been corrected, and not one Democrat or Greenbacker elected to the senate or house had been disqualified. A few Fusionist towns had been counted out to produce a semblance of fairness, Republicans said, but these were cleverly selected so as not to affect the outcome.

James G. Blaine, to whom the Maine election was so crucial as he made his second run at the U.S. presidency, had arisen from his seat in the Senate and rushed back to Maine. Now that the Fusionists had made their move, he was desperately intent on heading it off by any available means. The other U.S. senator, Hannibal Hamlin, also left his post in Washington and returned home to aid in the rescue.

"Indignation meetings" were held, among them one in Augusta on December 19, another in Bangor on December 20, with citizens hurrying over the snow to pack the meeting halls. The venerable Hamlin, speaking at the Bangor meeting, said that never had he returned to his native state "with the mantling blush of shame upon my face and humiliation in my heart until now." How, he asked, could this infamy have happened in a state "so honored in the past by the virtue, intelligence, and patriotism of her sons?"[11] Speaking of the governor and his seven councillors, he intoned that he did not believe that eight men outside the walls of a penitentiary could be found who would do what they had done.

C. A. Boutelle, editor of the *Bangor Whig & Courier* and Blaine's righthand man on the state committee, pointed to some of the dangers ahead if the usurpation was allowed to stand. In 1880 a U.S. president and a U.S. congressman were to be elected and "of what avail are your votes if they go into the hands of these men to be counted?" He clearly suggested an uprising. "If this action is allowed to go on it is not the beginning of the end, gentlemen, it is the end. This gross outrage is not against Daniel F. Davis, but against the will of the people who are the sovereignty in this state. The people alone have the power to right it and they must right it. They must rise like the heroes of Bunker Hill and say this must not be!"[12]

The Rev. George W. Field, D.D., came forward and "with breathless silence settling over the large audience" invoked divine intervention. At one point he harked back to the Pilgrim fathers and to patriots who had fought against oppression, and he cried, "Trusting in the God of battles, they went forth to war, and Thou didst give them victory."[13]

One of the last speakers on the program, Paul R. Seavey, Esq., spoke in a serious and deadly tone: "I thank God that I am not too old to carry a musket. . . . I am not a man of means, nor of widely extended influence, but I have the right to vote, and when I have voted, I have a right that my vote should be counted, and I shall not submit to having this right wrested from me. There are thousands of old soldiers in our state who will lead the men of our state to maintain their rights, even if they thus have to shed their life's blood for it."[14]

James G. Blaine himself spoke at the Augusta meeting. He added substantial fuel to the fire by pointing out that if the Fusionists were allowed to take office they would be in office until January 1883, because the state was changing from annual to biennial elections.

> Within that time they could apportion the state into legislative and congressional districts to suit themselves, gerrymandering at will, appointing the valuation commissioners who would punish certain sections of the state by an undue and unfair share of taxation and generally run riot after the reckless style of administration already inaugurated.

This is the treat to which the people of Maine are invited. This is the burden for which they are asked to bend their backs. This is the degradation to which they are asked to submit. A great and popular uprising will avert these evils and restore honest government to Maine, and the people are already moving.[15]

"The people are already moving," had an ominous sound, as did "a great and popular uprising," unless Blaine simply meant hordes of people marching on the capitol waving placards and singing hymns, an interpretation that seemed unlikely. To the average Republican the "count-out" really was an enormous insult and provocation—denying a man his vote and in effect cutting him off from his citizenship. It was an incitement to white-hot anger—blind rage arising so swiftly there was little time for reason or reflection. Yet reason was urgently needed.

Joshua Chamberlain thought he saw the makings of gunfire and bloodshed in the talk of Blaine and others. He did not like the sound of it. He heard that armed men were preparing to move into Augusta. Blaine had arranged for "indignation meetings" in Gardiner, Portland, and other places. He wrote to Chamberlain asking him to hold one in Brunswick. This is Chamberlain's reply:

Hon. James G. Blaine:

My dear Sir:—I telegraphed Governor Garcelon the day Governor Morrill's letter appeared, urging him as earnestly as I could to submit the disputed questions to the Court. I afterwards wrote him a letter to the same effect.

As to the indignation meeting proposed here, it was my opinion that demonstrations of that sort had already been sufficient to impress upon the Governor the state of public feeling; and that what we now need to do is not to add to popular excitement which is likely to result in disorder and violence, but to aid in keeping the peace by inducing our friends to speak and act as sober and law abiding citizens.

In my opinion there is danger that our friends may take some step which would put them in the wrong. That would be very bad. If wrong is to be done, let the responsibility of it rest with those who do it, and do not let those who are aggrieved seek redress in a way to shift upon themselves the burden of wrongdoing.

I deprecate all suggestions of bloodshed in the settlement of the question. Not only would that resort be deplorable, but the suggestion of it is demoralizing. I cannot bear to think of our fair and orderly state plunged into the horrors of a civil war.

I hope you can do all you can to stop the incendiary talk which proposes violent measures, and is doing great harm to our people. I cannot believe that you sympathize with this, and I am sure your great influence can be made to avail much now to preserve peace and respect for the law.

Pardon me for this, but I think the circumstances demand of me to make these suggestions.

> Very respectfully yours,
> Joshua L. Chamberlain[16]

These are not the words of a fainthearted man. Chamberlain had not only refused to do what Blaine wanted him to do—he had slapped Blaine's wrists and had annoyed if not offended one of the most powerful politicians in the nation.

At the beginning of his letter Chamberlain had referred to a former governor of Maine, Lot Morrill. Just before Christmas Morrill had suggested to Garcelon that he submit to the Maine Supreme Court questions bearing upon the men who were entitled to be seated in the legislature. By that time loud and widespread public clamor had made Garcelon very nervous, and Morrill framed his suggestion shrewdly by saying that quiet might be restored and the public mind pacified by this measure. After an initial refusal and some delay Garcelon did have a list of questions drawn up and sent to the court.

Ever since mid-November Garcelon had become increasingly alarmed by newspaper accounts of fiery Republican speeches and private reports of possible assaults by armed men on the capitol. He thought it best to make preparations for defense. He attempted to have arms and ammunition moved to the capitol from a state arsenal in Bangor. What happened is succinctly told in a *Bangor Whig & Courier* running headline.

Bullets and Bayonets!
Arming to Overawe the People!
Gov. Garcelon Collecting Arms at Augusta
Attempted Removal of Guns and
Ammunition from the Bangor Arsenal!
A Two-Horse Load of Guns!
And Thirty Four Thousand Rounds of Ball Cartridge

Hauled Through our Streets
The Teams Stopped on Kenduskeag Bridge
By a Great Throng of Indignant People![17]

This load of arms, which was headed toward the Maine Central railroad depot for shipment to Augusta, was turned back by a thousand or more Bangor people and returned to the arsenal, but later it was transported to the capitol without attracting public attention.

With threats of civil unrest increasing, Governor Garcelon was urged by his associates to call out the militia, an action that probably would have precipitated open warfare. He was discouraged by Charles E. Nash, the mayor of Augusta, who warned the governor that presence of the militia would only provoke the introduction of opposing armed forces. He assured Garcelon that Augusta was ready with two hundred trained policemen who could keep the peace at the capitol or elsewhere in the city.

Garcelon was suspicious of both the militia and the police. He later said that around December 31 he had a report that a regular military company had left Dexter "or one of those towns," headed for Augusta and, "I had good reason to believe that a very considerable portion of the military was not disposed to obey the Governor."[18] This implied another dimension to the mess that was building up—internecine warfare in Maine's militia.

As for the police, he saw that as a plot, believing that the Augusta police force was all appointed by the Republican party, and the Republicans were introducing them in order to get possession of the statehouse.

These and other fears led Garcelon to do something extremely unwise. He had his superintendent of public buildings assemble a group of about a hundred men and station them in the capitol under the command of one Captain R. W. Black. These men were referred to as state police, but there was no legal authority for such a force; they had no civilian or military status. Later it was charged by the Republicans that eleven of the group were alumni of county jails or state prison—one pardoned from state prison by Governor Garcelon. It was planned to equip them with the arms and ammunition that had finally arrived from the Bangor arsenal.

By January 5, 1880, Garcelon received the opinions of the Maine Supreme Court on the questions he had submitted toward the end of 1879. The opinions were nearly all adverse to the interests of the Fusionists. Most damaging was an opinion concluding that the five cities that were counted out ought to be counted back in. The governor and council declined to do so. Garcelon explaining later, "As an independent body I did not regard the opinions of the Court as a matter to be followed, unless I chose."[19] The crisis advanced a step nearer; there seemed to be nothing left to do but fight.

On January 5 the lawful date for seating of the legislature and governor was two days away. Two competing groups were heading for the statehouse —one including the legislators elected on September 8, 1879, constituting at that time a Republican majority; the other including the men named to be legislators after the "count-out," constituting a Fusion majority.

Garcelon's "state policemen" were holding the capitol. Armed men from both sides were gathering to storm or defend the citadel. It was likely that the dispute would not be settled within the next two days and that the seated government would cease to exist at midnight on January 7, leaving no one in its place.

Maine was on the brink of chaos and civil war. And many in Maine knew what civil war meant. They had been around long enough to remember the pain and sorrow suffered in the 1860s—and in thousands of cases destined for last for a lifetime.

*The gallant Joshua Chamberlain,
Civil War hero.*
MAINE STATE ARCHIVES, AUGUSTA, MAINE.

The civilian Joshua Chamberlain, governor of Maine.
PEJEPSCOT HISTORICAL SOCIETY, BRUNSWICK, MAINE.

Detail of Dr. Abner O. Shaw,
surgeon of the 20th Maine.

Detail of Dr. Abner O. Shaw
in old age; he died in 1934.

Joshua Chamberlain near the turn of the century.
PHOTO COURTESY OF PORTLAND PRESS HERALD/MAINE SUNDAY TELEGRAM.

The bracelet Chamberlain gave to his wife, Fanny, on their tenth wedding anniversary. SPECIAL COLLECTIONS, BOWDOIN COLLEGE LIBRARY, BRUNSWICK, MAINE.

Detail of the Maine State House in a photograph taken in late December 1887. The militia troops are participating in funeral services for Gov. Joseph R. Bodwell, who died in office; they have no connection with the "count-out" crisis, but the winter setting and the State House are the same as they were in January 1880 when Chamberlain's actions here saved the state from civil war. COURTESY OF THE MAINE STATE MUSEUM, AUGUSTA, MAINE.

*Chamberlain's
friend and one of his
favorite presidents,
Rutherford B. Hayes.*
RUTHERFORD B. HAYES PRESIDENTIAL
CENTER, SPIEGEL GROVE, FREMONT, OHIO.

*Alonzo Garcelon,
governor of Maine in
1879, the year when a
disputed election nearly
led to armed conflict.*
MAINE STATE ARCHIVES,
AUGUSTA, MAINE.

Funeral procession of Ulysses S. Grant in New York on August 8, 1885. Joshua Chamberlain rode in one of the carriages near the head of the procession. Museum of the City of New York.

*Main room of the Portland, Maine, Customs House. Chamberlain served
in this building as Surveyor of the Port from 1900 until his death in 1914.*
PHOTOGRAPH BY ERIK C. JORGENSEN.

The Portland Customs House staff when it included Joshua Chamberlain, shown holding his hat. The man at his left is Charles M. Moses, Collector of the Port. COLLECTIONS OF MAINE HISTORICAL SOCIETY, PORTLAND, MAINE.

Joshua Chamberlain at age eighty-four, looking haggard and ill, is number 24 in this group of state commissioners attending a conference at Gettysburg on May 16–17, 1913, in preparation for the fiftieth anniversary of the battle. He was in such poor condition that he brought his physician with him—Dr. Abner O. Shaw, numbered 45 in the back row.

FROM *PENNSYLVANIA AT GETTYSBURG: FIFTIETH ANNIVERSARY OF THE BATTLE OF GETTYSBURG, REPORT OF THE COMMISSIONERS,* VOL. III (HARRISBURG, 1914).

Label of Chamberlain Pale Ale, which was created by the Shipyard Brewing Company of Portland, Maine, to commemorate Joshua Chamberlain. As described, its "classic English style is enhanced by its golden copper hue and creamy white head. It is dry and crisp upfront with an aromatic hoppy finish."

In addition to mementos of the usual gift shop variety and quality, Joshua Chamberlain has inspired works of art. This is one of them: a "Joshua Bear" created by Pat Wright-Buckley of Kennebunk, Maine. The original teddy bear was evoked by Theodore Roosevelt and was created two months after he and Chamberlain met in Portland, Maine, in 1902.

COURTESY OF PAT WRIGHT-BUCKLEY, BUCKLEY BEAR CO.

GENERAL CHAMBERLAIN FUNERAL

FUNERAL PROCESSION OF GENERAL CHAMBERLAIN LEAVING CITY HALL.

GENERAL CHAMBERLAIN'S FUNERAL ESCORT ENTERING CITY OVER WASHINGTON AVENUE.

Photos in the Portland Evening Express, *February 28, 1914, showing Chamberlain's funeral procession leaving City Hall (top) and entering downtown Portland (bottom).*

Joshua Chamberlain's house on Ocean Avenue in Portland, Maine, as it looked in 1998. Photograph by Erik C. Jorgensen.

Joshua Chamberlain visiting Little Round Top at Gettysburg on October 2, 1889. MAINE HISTORICAL PRESERVATION COMMISSION, AUGUSTA, MAINE.

The Late General Joshua L. Chamberlain
Seated at His Desk in the Custom House

Photo in the Portland Daily News, *February 28, 1914, showing General Chamberlain at his desk in the Customs House.*

Part of the tent camp set up to house the veterans attending the fiftieth anniversary of the battle of Gettysburg, July 1–4, 1913. As Maine's member of the national planning commission, Joshua Chamberlain helped arrange this event, despite his struggles with old age and illness.

Even in his old age Joshua Chamberlain was a figure suggestive of the gallantry that earned him a Medal of Honor in the Civil War. Perhaps it was his appearance riding in this Portland, Maine, parade that moved a newspaperman to write later at his death in 1914, "He was a lion to the last." COURTESY OF THE PEJEPSCOT HISTORICAL SOCIETY, BRUNSWICK, MAINE.

CHAPTER NINE

Another Round Top

There were few people singing "Happy New Year" in Maine as 1879 ended. Things were rapidly getting out of hand. Garcelon was receiving daily threats of violence, and he feared for his life. He wrote a personal letter to Joshua Chamberlain asking him to come to Augusta and take charge of the state's militia.

Basically, the militia was then simply that part of the male population between certain ages that was legally obligated to military service if needed and that was required to be enrolled and listed as such by local authorities. After the Civil War the militia had sunk into its usual peacetime desuetude—underfunded, undertrained, and existing more on paper than in uniform. If it had a patron saint and protector, it was Chamberlain, although as a college president he had little time for soldiering. In 1872 he was placed in charge of the so-called volunteer militia, volunteer meaning somewhat organized, and a First Division was established to formalize the organization. Some training took place; a few encampments were held. But governmental neglect of the militia worsened. Maine legislatures refused to appropriate money for uniforms. Some units drilled but did so without pay. In protest Chamberlain resigned in February 1878, and the law establishing the First Division was revoked. But early in 1879 the legislature elected him major general and assigned him again to command of the volunteer militia. Chamberlain declined. As he told the *Lewiston Journal* toward the end of the year as the "count-out" crisis was coming to a head, "I never accepted, although I might and can qualify at any time. I did not wish to throw the honor back on the legislature, but I was equally adverse to taking command of a body of men with such a lamentable lack of proper organization, so I have never been signed to command."[1]

Obviously Garcelon's call for help compelled Chamberlain to put aside his reservations. He appeared in Augusta on January 2, 1880, and was qualified for command by being sworn in before a justice of the peace. On January 6 the adjutant general issued a general order combining the militia of all counties into a First Division, the proper command for a major general, and placing Chamberlain in charge of it. This was accompanied by a special order from the governor authorizing and directing Chamberlain to "protect the public property and institutions of the State until my successor is duly qualified."

The words "and institutions of the state" had great significance. Chamberlain would take them to mean more than guarding of the buildings and other physical properties. He would understand them to call for the protection of incorporeal institutions, including the establishment of government through a fair electoral process, and this interpretation, whether intended by Governor Garcelon or not, would thrust him into the middle of a controversy overhung by the threat of violence and bloodshed.

There are enough questions about this situation to mystify the inquiring mind. Garcelon knew that he and the current members of the legislature were within a few days of ending their terms. After that, unless the controversy was settled and new officeholders were installed, which seemed unlikely, there would be no government at all. And Chamberlain would be in effect military governor of Maine, able to exert influence upon the choice of the new governor and legislature.

Why did Garcelon, a Democrat, decide to put Chamberlain, a Republican, in such a commanding position?

Did Garcelon believe that Chamberlain was really more of a Democrat than a Republican? He surely remembered that after Chamberlain's governorship, some Maine Democrats wanted to run him for governor; he had turned down the offer on the grounds that it would be inappropriate. Did he think that Chamberlain, as a known antimachine man, had Greenbacker tendencies or sympathy for that cause? The *Eastern Argus* had reported that his father belonged to the Greenback party. And as recorded in *Bunker's Textbook of Political Deviltry,* "'The Greenback craze,' as it was termed by the badly frightened Republican organs and political leaders, was nothing more or less than an uprising of the voters in both parties against political bosses in the Republican party. . . . The voters were disgusted and sick of boss rule and corruption, and were ready to rally about any standard, no matter how absurd the principles or claims of the color-bearers or leaders."[2]

An even more challenging question: Why did Chamberlain accept this assignment after having previously declined all responsibility for the militia? He was not stupid, and he had had enough political experience to know what was bound to happen. He did not favor the inflammatory tactics of the Republicans, and they would crucify him for not supporting them. As for the Democrat governor, perhaps he did not know it, but Chamberlain had no intention of calling out the militia if it could be avoided, and what would Garcelon say to that? He would not favor either party, with the result that both parties would abuse him and forever blacken his name.

Why then did he go to Augusta?

Much evidence suggests that the answer is found in one sentence of his December 29 letter to James G. Blaine: "*I cannot bear to think of our fair and orderly state plunged into the horror of a civil war.*"

Beyond these questions are many others as to what happened in Augusta in January 1880. According to Chamberlain some records of the adjutant general turned up missing after the affair was over. In February and March of that year a joint committee of the Maine legislature conducted an investigation, but its scope was limited; it was dominated by Republicans seven to three, with the three Fusionist members filing a minority report; and Joshua Chamberlain was not called as a witness—an extremely significant vacuity, because Chamberlain's role was central to the whole affair. In the early 1950s a niece of General Chamberlain, one whose mother was very close to him, was heard to say that if what happened in Augusta was known to the public "it would blow the dome off the state house."[3] Unfortunately, the meaning of the remark was not pursued, and this affair is as deep, complicated, and difficult to penetrate as anything that ever happened in Maine.

Therefore, very much in order here is a reprise of a theme often occurring in Joshua Chamberlain's life history—his employment of the written word to tell his side of a story and project himself into the future. Winston Churchill once said he was sure that history would treat him kindly because he intended to write it. Chamberlain's writings and his recorded speeches served the same purpose.

Chamberlain's memories of the count-out crisis are contained in a twenty-six-page publication that appeared in 1906. It is entitled *The Twelve Days at Augusta,* which refers to the days from January 5 to January 17, 1880, the interregnum described. It was published by the Chamberlain Association of America, which no longer exists, being superseded by the World Chamberlain Society. No author is named, but scholars who have read it agree that Chamberlain either wrote it or was closely associated with the writing because it contains information only he could have been privy to. Throughout this narrative Chamberlain is referred to as "the General," duplicating a technique of writing about himself in the third person that he used in composing his autobiography.

Another description is found in *The Life and Times of Nelson Dingley, Jr.* (governor of Maine 1874–75, later an important U.S. congressman) by his son, Edward Nelson Dingley, published in 1902. A few passages invite dubiety because they reproduce conversations at scenes where neither Nelson Dingley Jr. nor his son could have been present, and no other listener-recorder is identified—a fault to be found with many historians, including Josephus. Nevertheless the substance seems to conform with Chamberlain's account and the book appears to be a reliable source if its Republican shading can be somewhat discounted.

What follows is derived mostly from these two sources. Edward Dingley tells what happened when Chamberlain arrived at the state capitol:

> He found the building barricaded with heavy planks, and arms and ammunition in evidence.
>
> "This is not an arsenal," said General Chamberlain to the Governor, "and you have one hundred and twenty or thirty fellows about here armed as if for a fight. I don't like the looks of these men."
>
> The governor had sworn these men in as a special body guard. Said he to the General, "I swore these men in because of the threatened insurrection."
>
> "But," replied the General, "if there is any bloodshed, governor, you are in danger of landing in jail. These men are disturbing the peace and you will be responsible for their acts."
>
> "But these Republicans threaten to take possession of this house and senate," argued the governor.
>
> "That would not be so disastrous as bloodshed," replied the General. "We have no right to keep these armed ruffians here, and I shall not remain if they are not sent away within half an hour."
>
> The governor's armed bodyguard was immediately dismissed, and at midnight the Bangor arms were sent away, General Chamberlain taking the precaution of notifying the authorities at every station to see that there was no interference. The mayor of the city placed one hundred and fifty policemen at his command, and the general wrote a letter to Mr. Blaine, counseling no violence.[4]

There were now three camps in Augusta: the Republicans with headquarters in the Blaine House, the Fusionist leaders gathered in a downtown hotel, and Chamberlain with Mayor Nash in a small office at the statehouse. Chamberlain was ready to summon the militia but only if absolutely necessary. He had alerted certain units within striking distance of the capitol and had made special arrangements for railroad and telegraph services. But what his emergency plan was he did not reveal.

Much of Chamberlain's reluctance to get the militia involved may have been due to the condition and situation of Maine's citizen-soldiers at that time. The whole force of organized militia numbered only about seven hundred soldiers, and they were in a poor state of both organization and readiness. The effectiveness of these men, as well as the possibility of divided political loyalties among them, was something to be concerned about.

And that was not the only worry. In addition to the organized militia there were twenty-eight independent militia companies, with about forty men each, scattered around the state. These men had armed and equipped themselves at their own expense, like the militia companies of old. They did not come under Chamberlain's command because they had no connection with the organized militia but were authorized under a special statue that allowed them to parade under arms in public. Chamberlain, or anyone familiar with the situation, could see the possibility of a company whose members were mainly Fusionist having a go at a predominately Republican company. These fellows were dangerous; any one of them, no matter to which party he belonged, could sincerely believe that his rights as a citizen had been violated—that this was Lexington and Concord all over again and it was time to take down the musket from its hangers over the fireplace. Thus, calling out the organized militia, even though its loyalty to its commander might be assured, could provoke uprisings of hundreds of armed men over whom Chamberlain had no control. The militia card was better for bluffing than for play, and Chamberlain was not showing his hand.

When the current officials came to the end of their term Chamberlain found himself in the position of being military governor of the state. As such he tried to keep himself clear of civil functions, locked up the rooms of the governor and council, placed other rooms under guard, and had important papers and documents stored in the treasury vaults. Meanwhile two legislatures, the counted in and the counted out, were meeting inside and outside the capitol, by night and by day, in secret and in the open, each claiming to establish a legal government. Chamberlain was in a peculiar position. He did not have the authority to decide which one was legal. But he had the responsibility of being sure the legislature and governor *were* legal before he turned the government over to them. He was urging everyone to submit the issue to the Maine Supreme Court.

Then arose the problem of who was entitled to submit to the court the questions for which answers were sought. Chamberlain was asked to do this and refused, saying that as a military officer he had no right to perform this function. Finally, on January 12 the counted-out, or Republican, legislature completed and sent to the court a set of questions. Considering the origin of the questions and the probable nature of the court after twenty years and more of Republican domination in Maine, the Fusionists must not have been greatly reassured. And, strangely enough, the militant Republicans were not quieted. It appeared to Chamberlain that their leader Blaine was directing a two-level attack: one through an appeal to the court, the other through a popular uprising leading to use of the state's or even the federal government's military force if necessary. Pressure on Chamberlain from both sides to recognize them as legal governments continued. Threats to persons and property and promises of violence intensified.

Mayor Nash's detectives discovered a plot to assassinate Blaine. Chamberlain had the leaders arrested. In Brunswick, town officers placed a guard around Chamberlain's house after hearing of threats against his family. When Fusionists and a supposed governor-elect, Greenbacker Joseph L. Smith, gathered in the statehouse Republicans planned an attack. They picked Thomas W. Hyde, future founder of the Bath Iron Works, to inform Chamberlain because the two were friends. Thomas Hyde had a distinguished Civil War record—coming out of the war as a brevet brigadier general. His admiration of Chamberlain would be expressed artistically; he would give Bowdoin a bust of the general. When he told Chamberlain that the Republicans had decided to "pitch the Fusionists out of the window" his old friend said to him (according to Edward Dingley's book), "Tom, you are as dear to me as my own son. But I will permit you to do nothing of the kind. I am going to preserve the peace. There is to be no fighting. I want you and Mr. Blaine and the others to keep away from the building."[5] This account is confirmed by that in *The Twelve Days,* which adds, "His reply effectually stopped the movement and greatly increased the animosity against him."[6]

The "governor" elected by the Fusionist legislature, Joseph L. Smith, believing he was legitimate, also came at Chamberlain from the opposite direction. Smith was "an able and sensible man," in Chamberlain's view, but he refused to recognize him as governor. Smith then tried to remove Chamberlain and attempted to arrest him when he refused to go. The attempt was not successful. Chamberlain simply stayed put and nothing happened.

Another confrontation took place when a Fusionist legislature organized and elected a president, James B. Lamson. The constitution granted that if the office of governor became vacant for any reason the president of the senate would act as governor until another governor was duly qualified. Lamson came to Chamberlain and asked to be recognized as such. The general liked Lamson, thinking of him as "a sincere and honorable man." But he refused, telling Lamson that he had been elected by a legislature that included members who, it was charged, were not themselves elected. Another would-be governor, Joseph A. Locke, whom the Republicans had elected president of the senate, received about the same treatment when he approached Chamberlain; he also was told that he could not be recognized until the Maine Supreme Court settled the matter.

Powerful inducements were reportedly offered. According to *The Twelve Days,* two top-ranking members of the Democrat and Greenback parties came to Chamberlain and one of them said, in effect, "Look, Blaine and his gang are the worst enemies you have."[7] And they offered to combine and elect him U.S. senator if he would recognize the Fusionists as legally elected.

Also according to *The Twelve Days,* at about this time Republican former governor Lot Morrill came to him and said: "Mr. Blaine said he will give way, and leave the way clear for you to go to the Senate if you will recognize the Republican organization of the two Houses."[8] This account says that Chamberlain declined, in talking with the representatives of both factions, to use his position of trust for personal gain.

Meanwhile tempers had been growing hotter. It seemed to Chamberlain now that the issue of which party was legal and which was not had become secondary. Both parties, he thought, were mainly concerned with trying to get rid of Chamberlain. Another passage from *The Twelve Days:*

At about this time he observed that when he left the State House, (which was seldom), a squad of policemen preceded and followed him. Upon inquiry he was told that this was by the Mayor's order, who had reason to believe some plot was afoot to make way with him. He hardly gave credence to this, but stood more upon his guard when obliged to appear upon the streets.

There was a well-laid plot to kidnap him by night, and take him off to an obscure town in the "back country," and hold him until the game was over. This plot was awkwardly managed. He got word of it and foiled it by changing rooms at night, and also accepting the attentions of his son, who brought as part of his outfit two pistols that had been well tested in the "civil" war—having, in fact, been captured in a hot moment of battle—and quite used to their business.[9]

Another incident could have inspired the script for a splendid little melodrama. The version of it appearing in *The Twelve Days at Augusta* (corroborated but not so thrillingly told by Edward Nelson Dingley's book) goes as follows:

On one of the most frenzied days at the capitol, one of his staff rushed into his office from the rotunda with the outburst: "General, you are lost! There is a blood-thirsty crowd out there swearing they are sent to kill you and are going to do it!" The General buttoned up his coat, stepped out in front of the crowd—twenty-five or thirty of them, evidently charged and maddened for their deed—mounted two steps up the stairs and faced them.

"Men, you wish to kill me, I hear. Killing is no new thing to me. I have offered myself to be killed many times, when I no more deserved it than I do now. Some of you, I think, have been with me in those days. You understand what you want, do you? I am here to preserve the peace and honor of this State, until the rightful government is seated—whichever it may be, it is not for me to say. But it is for me to see that the laws of this State are put into effect, without fraud, without force, but with calm thought and sincere purpose. I am here for that, and I shall do it. If anybody wants to kill me for it, here I am. Let him kill!"

Here he threw open his coat, looking them in the eyes.

"By God, old General, the first man that dares to lay a hand on you, I'll kill him on the spot!" shouted a grisly old veteran, pushing through them to the front,—a soldier still, in heart. A broken wave ran through the crowd, and it melted away, with various mutterings.[10]

A great moment! Chamberlain must have gone back to his office with his blood tingling as it never had since the Civil War. There is much to suggest that Chamberlain was exhilarated by being in this cockpit of history, with danger all around, the eye of the nation upon him, great issues at stake, and everything contingent upon his courage and cool head. He was confronted by a challenge that might result in one of the greatest achievements of his life, equal to his triumph on the rocky little hill at Gettysburg that made him famous. And he was well aware of that fact, as evidenced by a letter he wrote to his wife on January 15.

My dear Fanny,

Yesterday was another Round Top; although few knew of it. The bitter attack on me in the Bangor Commercial calling me a traitor, & calling on the people to send me speedily to a traitor's doom, created a great excitement.

There were threats all the morning of overpowering the police & throwing me out the window, & the ugly looking crowd seemed like men who could be brought to do it (or to try it).

Excited men were calling on me—some threatening fire & blood & some begging me to call out the militia at once. But I stood it firmly through, feeling sure of my arrangements & of my command of the situation.

In the afternoon the tune changed. The plan was to arrest me for treason, which not being a bailable offence, I should be kept in prison while they inaugurated a reign of terror & blood. They foamed & fumed away at that all evening. Mr. Lamson kindly came to see me & said he would be the one to take out a writ of habeas corpus & have me set at liberty again.

That plan failed.

At about 11 P.M. one of the citizens came & told me I was to be kidnapped, overpowered & carried away, & detained out of people's knowledge, so that the rebels could carry on their work. I had the strange sense again of sleeping inside a picket guard.

In the night Gen'l Hyde of Bath came up with 300 men & Col. Heath of Waterville with 50 men: sent for by Republicans I suppose & greatly annoying to me & embarrassing too.

I wish Mr. Blaine & others would have more confidence in my military ability. There are too many men here afraid for their precious little pink skins.

I shall have to protect them of course: but my main object is to keep the peace & give opportunity for the laws to be fairly executed.

Do not worry about my safety. Make yourself as comfortable as you can at home.

If you are afraid, send word to the selectmen, or to Mr. Thos. U. Eaton to have the police keep an eye on you & the house.

But I don't believe anybody will think of troubling you.

Somebody else besides Auntie ought to be in the house with you. Don't worry about me.

Yours aff.

J.L.C.[11]

As suggested in the letter, James G. Blaine was getting very nervous. He wrote to Chamberlain from the Blaine House on January 14 urging him to call out the militia. He wrote again at noon on the sixteenth saying that since Smith had been elected governor by the Fusionists they were going to occupy the statehouse unless Chamberlain seized it first with a strong military force sufficient to repel all attacks. This show of force would prevent bloodshed, Blaine urged.

Chamberlain's reply:

First Division Militia of Maine
Assistant Adjutant General's Office
Augusta, January 16, 1880, Three P.M.

My Dear Mr. Blaine,

I pay great deference to your judgment as to the imminence of peril.

A storm is raging around me in the State House, & I have no doubt of the designs of wicked men inside of this building as well as outside.

But I do assure you, my dear sir, with the utmost deference to your opinion & also to your wishes that I can guarantee peace with the dispositions I have made, & which I hardly dare to make generally known, lest the bad elements get wind of it and thwart my plans. But do be assured that the position shall be held & that all rights and privileges shall be yet fairly and lawfully vindicated. Neither force nor treachery nor trick shall get the mastery of the situation out of my hands.

I have the means of knowing all that is going on all over the State, & shall be ahead if force is resorted to.

But, my dear sir, as to ordering out the Militia, I want to save the moral issue for our people if *possible* that in this State right shall be vindicated by peaceful measures & not by force, and I shall resort to that only in the last moment when everything else has failed.

Whoever first says "take arms!" has a fearful responsibility on him, & I don't mean it shall be me who does that.

Pardon the haste and nervousness of this; but the pressure & whirl here is enough to distract a man. I beg you to put confidence in me now, & do not think you will be disappointed.

Respectfully yours,
J. L. Chamberlain

I have had to write this by snatches for the last 2 hours.[12]

On that same day the Maine Supreme Court came to the rescue, issuing answers to the questions propounded by the counted-out Republican-dominated legislature on January 12 and opining that this was the legally elected body.

On January 17, Republican Daniel Davis wrote to Chamberlain informing him that he had been legally elected governor and commander in chief and enclosing the court's opinion to prove it. Chamberlain immediately resigned his post. There was still a threat of violence from the Fusionists, so Davis asked Chamberlain to stay on. But the general learned that the new commander in chief had decided to call to Augusta a militia force—two companies of infantry along with a detachment of artillery with a Gatling gun to command the approaches to the capitol, and he found reasons to get out of town and out of the state. On January 28 the Fusionists held a final meeting; there was talk of fighting on, but Greenbacker Joseph L. Smith and other moderate men prevailed and the Fusionists went home. By then Chamberlain was far away; he had gone to New York to address a Bowdoin alumni dinner.

Much of what happened in Augusta in those winter days may have been consigned to the dungeons of history, but one thing is clear. Chamberlain had preserved the peace and protected the institutions of the state without a gun being cocked or a soldier called to duty. But he received only initial credit. When the Republicans achieved victory, a writer for one of their newspapers enthusiastically announced, "Such rejoicing was never before witnessed at the Capitol. . . . What a scene in the House at the appearance of Blaine, Morrill, Davis, Hale, Chamberlain! What thunders of applause! What mighty manifestations of joy! How the rock-ribbed building shook with the clamor and excitement!"[13]

The writer then fired several verbal salutes, the first one to James G. Blaine, "whose powerful brain, great experience, untiring energy, and unflinching courage, made him the real leader in the struggle." And not far below this, "to Joshua Chamberlain, the heroic holder of the fort, the noble soul that stepped into the gap, assumed the responsibility, and saved the state from anarchy and bloodshed."

It was one of the few tributes paid to Chamberlain by the Republican press. But it accurately reflected the impression of Chamberlain's part in this affair left with the people of Maine. Decades later, well into the next century, the older generations spoke with gratitude of the man named Chamberlain who had saved the state from civil war. Persons who were children at the time of the crisis in Augusta recorded memories suggesting the deep current of fear that was flowing through Maine. Harriet Blaine Beale, James G. Blaine's daughter, wrote of an experience at the Blaine House. "I remember my Mother lifting me out of bed one night and saying 'Look! Do you see those men?"[14] She recalled looking through the window and seeing a line of men, black against the snow, standing guard around the house.

Fannie Hardy Eckstrom (1865–1946) wrote: "My own father took over fifty men, armed, and himself carried a rifle-barrel in a big umbrella and stock in his over-coast breast pocket, with a hundred rounds of ammunition, expecting to have a fight in the streets. But for General Chamberlain they would have had a bad time in the state capital that year."[15]

The case had drawn national attention. Thomas Nast, the great caricaturist of the day, was intrigued by the spectacle presented by Chamberlain, protecting the Fusionists against the Republicans one day and on the next day protecting the Republicans against the Fusionists. It reminded him of another legendary man in the middle, the early colonist, John Smith; that and the name of the Fusionist governor-elect Smith, suggested an idea to him. He drew a cartoon for *Harper's Weekly* (issue of February 7, 1880) showing Blaine and Chamberlain in Native-American dress, with Chamberlain as Pocahontas protecting a supine figure labeled "Smith's Sidewalk Legislature" against Blaine in the role of Powhatan standing over them wielding a large cudgel.

Speaking to the Bowdoin alumni at the Westminster Hotel in New York on January 29, Chamberlain turned the recent events in Maine into a credit for their alma mater. According to a newspaper report, which follows in part, he proclaimed that the college back in Brunswick was but a small part of the real Bowdoin.

By far the greater part of Bowdoin College, both as to power and influence, as well as in respect to numbers, are out in the world

A February 7, 1880, Harper's Weekly *cartoon by Thomas Nast. The caption reads: "POWHATAN BLAINE: Just let me give him one whack to show how strong I am. POCAHANTAS CHAMBERLAIN: No, don't Jim, you'll make a mess of it."*

doing manly, noble work for it. A noble instance of this kind cannot fail to rise to your minds, an illustration which stands before us today, for I need not remind you that half of the members of the Supreme Court of Maine are graduates of Bowdoin College. (great cheering.) You have a right to be proud that half the members of the Supreme Court, from the Chief Justice of fourscore to the youngest member, are brethren of ours, who received their bent toward loyalty, clearness of thought and right in the old college where all of us learned them.

Gentlemen, in that confusion of tongues which we have had there lately in our trying times in that (a voice, "fusion of tongues") (great laughter). Well, I call it "confusion," but I don't know what to call it—in that maelstrom—in the questions, the cross-questions, in that chaos of governors without a government—there was needed a clear and authoritative voice affirming the principles of constitutional law and constitutional government . . . which was heard above that chaos. . . . Gentlemen, when I say that the voice of the Supreme Court was the voice of Bowdoin College, I do not stretch the point. (Applause.)[16]

At this time Chamberlain did not realize that one of these brethren on the supreme court was to participate, either inadvertently or intentionally, in one small part of a plan by the Republican leaders to discredit Chamberlain and get him out of the way for good.

This was Chief Justice John Appleton, class of 1822, seventy-six years of age. At the height of the crisis, or one of the heights, Chamberlain had sent to Judge Appleton, on a midnight train to Bangor, a letter that was perhaps too hastily conceived.

Augusta, Jan. 12, 1880

My dear sir,

Mr. Lamson has borne himself so honorably & has aided so much in trying to bring about a peaceful solution, that I have come to entertain a high respect for him.

I earnestly hope it will be found that Lamson is entitled to be recognized. In that case I can see a way out.

Of course the court can only give us the law; but where the "letter" is less killing than the "spirit," it might be possible to temper justice with mercy.

Sincerely yours,
J. L. Chamberlain[17]

In a letter to Justice Appleton written nearly a year later on December 30, 1880, Chamberlain explained his meaning: He thought that Lamson should be recognized for the purpose of putting a set of questions to the court. This would have been plain to Justice Appleton, if he had previously received a list of questions that Lamson had prepared, but (as Chamberlain learned later) Lamson never sent the questions.

What prompted this December 30, 1880, letter to Appleton was an earlier erroneous report that on January 12, 1880, Chamberlain had written to Appleton urging that Lamson be recognized as *acting governor,* which would mean recognition of the Fusion legislature as legal. This report indicated that C. A. Boutelle, Blaine's close associate on the Republican state committee, had somehow obtained his January letter to Appleton and was going to use it to portray Chamberlain as a traitor to the party who had been ready to sell out to the Fusionists. "I can't believe," Chamberlain now wrote to Appleton, "that Capt. Boutelle has my private letter to you."[18]

What had brought all this to the surface was a rumor that Chamberlain might be a candidate for the U.S. Senate. The general himself had little to do with this. Starting and running an all-out campaign to get himself elected was not his style; he seems to have thought of himself as a Cincinnatus who would be called from his plough when the people wanted him, as they had once called him to serve as governor. The *Boston Herald* put it this way: "Gen. Chamberlain's attitude in relation to the Maine Senatorship is the true one for a man to occupy who is in every way competent for the high position, and still retains a sense of the eternal fitness of things. 'It has not been my habit,' he says, 'to make myself a candidate for any office whatever, but when called to a public trust, I have endeavored to fulfill it to the best of my ability. . . .' Maine would do herself an honor and the country a real service by sending Gen. Chamberlain to the Senate." The *Herald* repeated this endorsement a few days later but with doubt, observing that there was not much chance of "getting so far outside the old machine."[19]

Clearly, the old machine was geared to destroy Chamberlain's candidacy. On Monday, January 2, 1881, the *Portland Avertiser* ran a story that began:

> General Chamberlain was in the city Saturday, and a representative of the *Advertiser* conversed with him concerning the rumor published in the *Greenback-Labor Chronicle* a few days ago, in these words.
>
> The *Chronicle* has learned from a reliable Republican who was a member of last winter's Legislature and has been elected this year, that while Joshua L. Chamberlain was in command of the forces at the State House, he wrote the court then in session in Bangor, earnestly urging that the court recognize the Fusion Legislature, as in his opinion it was in every sense legal, and the only legal one Maine could have that year. On his experience as Governor and knowledge of the law and precedents Chamberlain made this appeal. C. A. Boutelle, of Bangor, now has that letter in his possession and is holding it menacingly over Chamberlain's head. If Chamberlain comes up as a formidable candidate for the Senate, this letter will be published.

Boutelle, a former Navy man, was owner and editor of the *Whig & Courier,* a Republican newspaper in Bangor, an aggressive member of the Republican state committee, a friend of James G. Blaine, and a soon-to-be Republican member of Congress. There was no mistaking a negative word from him as being a thumbs-down signal for Chamberlain from the party.

In the interview published in the *Advertiser* Chamberlain effectively refuted this grossly inaccurate report, but he must have realized by now that his public career was over. No party wanted him. He had angered the Democrats and Greenbackers for not yielding to their claims. He had angered the Republicans for the same reason and for not doing as he was told to do by the party leader. He might have had great popular support if he had gone to the public aggressively as a candidate for the Senate. But as he once said, he hated the idea of seeming to ask the public for something and being denied—a remark betraying sensitivity and pride that disqualified him from being an effective politician. Had he been in favor with a party, he would have—with his common sense, vision, speaking ability, and adherence to principle—served the country well as a cabinet member, diplomat, or in another nonelective office. But upward avenues were now closed. It was all over for Chamberlain in the world of government.

And worse than that. The next-to-last paragraph of *The Twelve Days* reads, "For a long time after this those who desired to secure office or contracts under the State or National Governments were obliged to represent themselves as not friendly to the General."[20]

The achievement in Augusta represented the high point in Chamberlain's postwar life. John Graham, who investigated the "count-out" affair thoroughly and with a scholar's impartiality in preparation for his 1981 master's thesis, pointed out that Chamberlain received the Medal of Honor for his heroism in leading the 20th Maine at the Battle of Gettysburg and said, "Maine would have done well to award him some sort of similar honor for the service he performed with equal gallantry in 1880. It is due to him, more than anyone else, that this was not a story about another bloody civil war."

But unlike what happened after the triumph at Little Round Top, Chamberlain's career from the Augusta victory onward went mostly downhill. In 1883 he resigned the presidency of Bowdoin, undoubtedly because of the frustrations he had experienced at the college in attempting to modernize its curriculum and because of his health, as well. His physical condition may also have been a consideration in his choosing not to engage in an active political campaign. Periods of acute illness caused by his deep pelvic wound from the Civil War seemed to come and go. In March 1883 he was examined by Dr. Joseph Huckins Warren of Boston, who urged him to stop work, have a change of surroundings in Florida, and undergo an operation. Remarkably, Warren even offered to go with him and take his instruments along in case an emergency operation was needed. This degree of solicitude is probably explained by the fact that Warren was a graduate of Bowdoin's medical school in the class of 1853 and so must have been an acquaintance and perhaps a friend of Joshua Chamberlain, class of 1852. Warren did operate on Chamberlain in Boston on April 19, 1883, and pronounced the operation a success, but it left the patient weak and unwilling to continue as president of Bowdoin. On July 11, 1883, the governing boards issued a gracious and appreciative statement summarizing his services to the college as professor and president and bidding him an affectionate farewell.

At the outset Bowdoin had seemed to promise another possible chapter of an epic life. Now his feelings were reflected in a letter he wrote in February 1884: "My dear Professor Johnson: I thought it best to resign the Presidency at the last Commencement, and I want to say, to set a caution against your young ambition, that however pleasant and useful the life of a College Professor may be, that of a President, in I may say any of our common or best New England colleges, even, is about the most thankless, wearing, and wasteful life that can be undertaken. I have had two very attractive Presidencies offered; but no more of that sort of thing for me if I can help it."[21]

The addressee was probably Henry Johnson, and if so Chamberlain's words were taken to heart, for Johnson, a shy and friendly member of the Bowdoin faculty, never became a college president. Instead he achieved a distinguished reputation by virtue of his published poems, a highly regarded translation of Dante's *Divine Comedy,* and as a valued professor at Bowdoin for forty years.

CHAPTER TEN

Family Fortunes

Visitors to Brunswick, Maine, driving into the town at night, see the high, square illuminated white tower of the First Parish Church, the town's most prominent landmark. Many who are Joshua Chamberlain enthusiasts know that this church had much to do with his family life. Few will realize that they are looking at a real oddity—a Gothic style church made of wood. This may have been a concession by the architect, Richard Upjohn, to Maine resources and Maine frugality.

When the church was designed in the mid-1840s, Upjohn—whose greatest work is represented by Trinity Church in New York—presented the parishioners with a set of plans that shocked their Puritan sensibilities. It showed a church in the form of a cross, with transepts opening out to each side just in front of the pulpit and with a vast interior somewhat like that of a cathedral, open and unobstructed except for the arches, braces, and pillars supporting the roof high overhead—the whole thing smacking too much of popery for Congregational stomachs.

Upjohn's plans might have been thrown into the Androscoggin River had it not been for the able pastor of the First Parish Church, the Rev. George Eliashib Adams, D.D. A twig on the same tree that had produced presidents John Adams and John Quincy Adams, the Rev. Dr. Adams was an intelligent man with a sense of humor who did an effective job of selling the church design to his parishioners and to his ministerial brethren in nearby towns. The new church was built and was dedicated in 1846.

In the cruciform design, the main shaft of the cross stood east and west, the arms north and south. These arms, or transepts, held galleries. The

The First Parish Church, Brunswick, Maine.
COURTESY FIRST PARISH CHURCH.

south gallery, by agreement between Bowdoin and church authorities, was occupied by the college students, whose attendance was compulsory.[1] The boys in the front row were in the habit of sitting with their feet up on the railing, so that the congregation in the main body of the church had the view of a long row of boots. Adams once remarked that he couldn't tell whether there were bodies attached to these boots or heads attached to the bodies. His first glimpse of Joshua Chamberlain, who entered Bowdoin in 1848, may well have been only of the soles of his boots.[2] If so, it was not long before Joshua emerged from this anonymity. Active in the choir, he became acquainted with Frances (Fanny) Caroline Adams, the pastor's adopted daughter. Fanny was the natural daughter of another Adams, an uncle of the pastor in Boston, and at the age of four or five had been given over to the care of Dr. and Mrs. Adams, who were childless.[3]

Fanny and Joshua fell deeply in love. She was infatuated with him, he even more so with her. There were reasons for this enchantment on both sides. Chamberlain was physically attractive, and even if he came from the back-country—as Brewer might have been regarded by citizens of coastal Maine—he was highly intelligent and appreciative of the arts, especially music. His proficiency in music has been overlooked, overshadowed perhaps by his martial glories. As a boy in Brewer he had practiced on a crude bass viol, on which he had to use a cornstalk for a bow. At Bowdoin this talent blossomed. In his senior year Chamberlain became conductor of the church choir and organist. Fanny also had musical talent; she occasionally served as church organist. Among her other attractions was that she was a Boston Adams and the daughter of the pastor, and in the mid-nineteenth century the Congregational pastor was "high-up" in the community—not very well paid, but "high-up"—and for an ambitious young man like Joshua Chamberlain coming out of the backcountry this did nothing to lessen Fanny Adams's charms.

They had a long engagement. Following his graduation from Bowdoin in 1852, they were separated for three years while Joshua attended Bangor Theological Seminary and Fanny, for the most time, taught music in a school in Milledgeville, Georgia. When they both returned to Brunswick, Joshua as an instructor at Bowdoin, they were married on December 7, 1855, in the First Parish Church by Dr. Adams.

Joshua's musical talent was one of the things that made him acceptable to the pastor. Adams had a fine voice; so did Chamberlain. The two of them sang together at several funerals—there were many of these for children—and on other and happier occasions. When the great war came along, Chamberlain's advance to the rank of major general heightened the regard Adams had for him. At the age of sixty-three he went to visit General Chamberlain when he and his troops were in camp near Washington preparing for the grand victory review of the Union armies on May 23, 1865. Adams kept a journal—a habit he continued throughout this long and difficult journey—and parts of it provide us with rare glimpses of Chamberlain's army life. The elderly clergyman visited the wounded, held services for the soldiers, lived in a tent, ate army rations, and endured army discomforts and army diseases. His diary entry for May 22 includes a description of Chamberlain, ill but as usual carrying on unflinchingly, and a mention of speeches given during the presentation to Gen. Charles Griffin of a pin made by Tiffany and Company—an image in jewelry of the Fifth Corps badge, a red Maltese cross. A part of this diary entry follows:

Everybody busy today with ordinary affairs & preparations for the review tomorrow, & the presentation tonight. Supply trains, officers & others on horseback, aides, orderlies, rushing from point to point, men coming for passes, all sorts of papers, all sorts of complaints, dissatisfactions, crooks, quirks. The Gen. pretty miserable but constantly working. Dr. De Witt never saw a man who would continue working so when really unfit to move. Am getting up a diarrhea, which troubles me much & makes me fearful about tomorrow. [Adams was planning to attend the review.] So Dr. De Witt gives me a pill of opium & camphor to take tonight. The presentation comes off at 5. Weather good. A fine time. C's speech very good. General Griffin's reply simple & appropriate.

After collation, General Hayes, Major Batchelder, etc. were called out. Also Mr. Geiger of Phila. Also *myself*. Told them I was glad to see 'm; would have 'listed myself but 1st was too great a coward & 2nd was too old. Had no sons to send unfortunately, so sent some of my boys from Bowd. Coll (I call 'm my boys.) & not content with that sent my son-in-law Gen. Chamberlain. (Applause: "Cd. not have done it better.") Wound up wishing I could be permitted to wear the badge of the Corps. I would be glad to preach in it after I get home. Whereupon 4 were immediately pinned upon my coat by 4 officers. One that had been through the whole war by a German capt.[4]

The question of whether or not Adams actually did preach a sermon back home with the Maltese cross of the Fifth Corps attached to his clerical garb is not answered by any record now at hand, but there is an undocumented understanding that this is exactly what he did.

After serving the First Parish Church for forty years and in the seventieth year of his life, Adams felt the need of a new challenge and departed for East Orange, New Jersey, where he successfully organized a new church and died on Christmas Day, 1875. He had been more than an ordinary father-in-law to Joshua Chamberlain, and his loss was felt deeply. Ideally as a man grows older, one generation passes away as another comes on to surround him with fresh warmth and capabilities. With one exception—the family produced by his daughter Grace—this did not happen to Chamberlain. His mother and father, to whom he was greatly devoted, died in the 1880s. His brothers Horace and John died of a lung disease, probably tuberculosis, in 1861 and 1867 respectively. His brother Tom, who had served with him so loyally and well in the 20th Maine, began drinking after the war, suffered from heart and lung disease, and died in 1896. His sister Sarah had two children, but they were off to the north in Brewer, Maine, and Chamberlain had little contact with them. His son, Harold Wyllys, never married and failed to be self-supporting in occupations he undertook. The removal of the Rev. George Eliashib Adams's stalwart figure from the family circle therefore meant more than the ordinary loss of comfort and support to Joshua and Fanny Chamberlain. In 1882 they gave to the church in his memory the large stained glass window that dominates the east wall of the church, the first colored window installed in the building. Chamberlain never belonged to the church; he retained his membership in the First Congregational Church in Brewer, his native town, all his life.[5] He was, however, a member of the First Parish, the corporate body supporting the church. He bought and occupied a pew. He served on committees. Referring to the stained glass window, the church history remarks, "It is a memorial to Dr. Adams, but it also is a constant reminder of the service and loyalty of General Chamberlain."[6]

The First Parish Church held other memories closely related to the Chamberlains. In one pew, number twenty-three, Harriet Beecher Stowe, wife of a Bowdoin professor, on March 2, 1851, a day when Chamberlain as a student should have been in attendance, had seen her vision of the death of Uncle Tom. In 1964 Martin Luther King preached in this church, thus bringing to full circle, a century later, the struggle for freedom, from civil war to civil rights.[7] Mrs. Stowe was, in Lincoln's words, "the little woman that wrote the book that made this great war"—the Civil War that brought Chamberlain fame.

In her relationship with Joshua the war had been Fanny's greatest rival. He had gone off to it at the age of thirty-three, leaving her with two small children, Harold Wyllys and Grace. Even worse, in the fall of 1864, after a few months at home recuperating from a severe wound that beyond all question would have excused him from further service, Chamberlain had gone back to combat duty before he could mount a horse or walk a hundred yards.

Fanny was of a disposition that ran strongly toward the arts. In addition to being a musician, she also was a painter. If any of her paintings still exist, their locations are unknown, but a letter reveals a few of the titles: *Magdalen, Madonna, Angels, Hamlet,* and *The Roman Campaign*; somehow these titles give us a glimpse of her taste and aspirations.[8]

The few existing photographs of her do not show a woman of overwhelming beauty, and yet the fault here may have lain in the failings of nineteenth-century cameras and their operators. Chamberlain's letters to Fanny leading up to their marriage testify to a powerful sexual entrancement.

Consonant with her artistic leanings, Fanny was a lover of beautiful styles and fabrics in clothing and in the early days of the marriage was a shopper and a spender. A close friend wrote letters scolding her for this, but Chamberlain seems to have made few protests. Nor did he complain much about another outstanding trait: Fanny's independence. Even when Joshua was away at war Fanny would sometimes leave their two children in the care of a relative and go off to Boston or New York. Another instance of this trait: Although her adoptive father was pastor of the First Parish Church and she was its occasional organist, Fanny did not become a member.

After the war Fanny's situation changed a great deal and for the worse. She had to live with a man who kept himself furiously busy, who was away from home a great deal, and who was continually irritated and frustrated by pain and illness arising from his war wound. There is little doubt that this wound impaired their marital relations. It does not take a urologist to conclude that a man with a recurring fistula at the base of his penis cannot have an altogether satisfactory sex life. As his courtship letters indicate, a strong sexuality was part of Chamberlain's nature, and any deprivation must have been a depressant to his spirit and an abrasion of the peculiar masculine pride that hinges upon this bodily function. Yet his love for Fanny continued unabated, and there are many evidences of his devotion. As far as the records show, there was only one time when the marriage was in serious trouble. On the night of November 19, 1868, when Chamberlain was governor of Maine and when he was about to retire in his quarters in Augusta after a hard day at the office, a staff member came into his room and said he wouldn't have bothered him but something potentially ruinous was afoot. Fanny was telling neighbors that Chamberlain was pulling her hair, striking and otherwise abusing her, and she was going to sue for divorce. It is possible that Fanny, resentful at being left alone again, created this dramatic situation as a means of getting her husband's attention. She accomplished this. After a sleepless night, the method of response that he expressed in a letter to her was well chosen.[9] He wisely ignored her specific accusations. To call them untrue would be an attack on her veracity. To admit them as true would brand him as a wife-abuser. Instead he focused on her wish for a divorce, which he would not deny her. But then he went on to point out that she should consider the negative effects on her, on the family, and on him. This rational reaction may have been just the one to cool Fanny's emotions so that reconciliation could occur. Exactly how it did occur is not recorded, but by the time Chamberlain became president of Bowdoin College three years later, a caring and affectionate relationship had resumed and would continue until her death.

In the last decades of the century, the picture of Fanny changes. She is much less independent. She seems to grow smaller—is often referred to in family correspondence as "Dear little Ma," or in other endearing diminutives. She becomes more reclusive and unwilling to travel, preferring to remain at home in Brunswick. She is more dependent on her daughter Grace, her son Wyllys, and Joshua, when he was available (much of the time he was away from home). The reason for this change—or certainly a large part of the reason—was that Fanny, who had always had trouble with her eyes, was slowly going blind.

Joshua Chamberlain's life in the last sixteen or seventeen years of the century strike one as falling into the sequence of a dream in which there is no connection between episodes, bizarre things happen, and the dreamer has an uneasy sense of being far away from his settled home or habitation. His

executive experiences as an army officer, governor, and college president
had led him to believe that he could be successful as head of a business. In
fact, early in his presidency of Bowdoin he became for a while president of
an industrial company. This information comes from Dwight B. Demeritt Jr.,
author of *Maine Made Guns & Their Makers,* who in his research noticed a
couple of stories in the *Lewiston Journal* dated July 17, 1873, and January 9,
1874. The stories dealt with the Evans Rifle Manufacturing Company of
Mechanic Falls, Maine, which Demeritt describes as Maine's only mass-
producer of firearms in the nineteenth century. The first story reported that
the directors of the newly organized company had met and elected Joshua L.
Chamberlain president. The second, written about six months later, said that
the directors had met and elected Adna C. Denison president in Chamberlain's place.

These stories raise a question: How was Chamberlain able to be president of a college (his position in 1873) and head of an industrial company
at the same time? A look at his correspondence for 1873 seems to provide
the answer. On July 8 of that year he wrote a letter to Bowdoin's governing
boards resigning from its presidency. "A spirit seems to possess the College
with which I cannot harmonize," he commented.[10] But he was persuaded to
remain at Bowdoin, and this would explain his replacement by Adna Denison as president of the rifle manufacturing company.

Brief as it was, this venture into the world of business was significant.
Undoubtedly Chamberlain was lending his name as an inducement to
investors and customers. It was one of the most famous military names in
the country, and it would be invaluable to the rifle company when it
approached army boards or other purchasers of rifles. But there was a weak
spot in the arrangement. Chamberlain was vulnerable to being kicked out
after the business was successfully under way and the directors saw no further need of his distinguished reputation and the cost of his fee or salary.
This cycle of events did not take place with the Evans Rifle Manufacturing
Company, but the episode may have set the pattern for a number of executive positions that Chamberlain assumed in the 1880s and 1890s in a business career that was generally unrewarding.

In the early 1880s, on a recreational visit to Florida, Chamberlain saw
it as a land of great opportunity. He returned to the Sunshine State and, with
other investors, became involved in a land development company with
headquarters in Ocala and land on the west coast. A railroad was needed to
open up the development, and so a company was formed to build it. These
ventures necessitated the raising of capital; as a result Chamberlain had to
spend much of his time in New York. One of his letterheads dated April 2,
1888, shows his situation at that time:

The Florida West Coast Improvement Company
constructing and operating the
Silver Springs, Ocala and Gulf Railroad
Vice-Presidents Office
56 Wall and 59 Pine Streets[11]
Joshua L. Chamberlain
Vice-President

Chamberlain also rented an apartment at 101 West Seventy-fifth Street (a strange milieu for him), where he and (sometimes) Fanny lived off and on. His son Wyllys lived in Florida for a while, practicing law and helping to supervise his father's businesses. The Florida activities of both father and son proved unsuccessful, and so they returned to the North, where in further enterprises, including presidencies and directorships for Chamberlain, fortunes still eluded them.

In addition to his business connections, Chamberlain was involved in a curious variety of undertakings. In the early 1890s he was president of a New York school, the Institute for Artists and Artisans, for which he tried to establish a summer school extension at his oceanside home named Domhegan, located on a beautiful point of land jutting out into the Atlantic near his home in Brunswick. For a while he was president of the *New England Magazine.* And he served as editor for a series of volumes entitled *Universities and Their Sons,* for which he wrote a scholarly introduction.

He belonged to or presided over more than twenty societies and associations centered upon such subjects as political science, genealogy, geographic interests, Egyptian exploration, philosophy, history, religion, blindness, military and veterans' affairs, relief work, and so on. Much in demand as a speaker, he gave dozens of lectures. It was as though he was determined to be so frantically busy that he would not leave himself a moment for life's ordinary pleasures.

In the early 1890s Wyllys evaluated his father's business career in a letter written from New York to his mother. Since this letter also conveys an unintended evaluation of his own career, it is well to precede it with some background information about Wyllys. He graduated from Bowdoin College in 1881, attended Boston University's law school, and would have been edging into his forties as the century ended.

Wyllys did not do well as a lawyer. From time to time his father had to lend him money. Probably the reason he did not do well was that he wanted to be an inventor and spent much of his time working on electromechanical devices. Chamberlain tried to divert him into other channels but finally gave up, and Wyllys kept on tinkering. He had been at Bowdoin during the final years of Chamberlain's scientific department; perhaps this had stimulated his interest in inventions or—more likely—he was inspired by the examples of Thomas Edison and others whose fertile brains at this time were revolutionizing the world and founding vast fortunes. Unfortunately none of Wyllys's inventions caught on.

Wyllys never married. He lived with his parents most of the time, in New York and Brunswick, and then after his mother died in 1905, with his father in Brunswick and Portland. Judging by city directories, he was an electrician and the proprietor for a time of the Chamberlain Electric Company in Portland. He probably lived with or near his married sister, Grace Allen, in Massachusetts until his death in 1928. Wyllys seems to have been a likeable sort and undoubtedly was a great comfort and support to his mother during her declining years when Chamberlain was so often away from home. Wyllys apparently was not in robust health. Here is a letter he wrote to his mother about himself and his father sometime in the very early 1890s.

My dear little Ma,

I owe you an apology for not answering your good letter before; but have been engaged in a sort of struggle for subsistence and trying to decide what to do. I am still in the stage of being neither sick nor well; but there are some things I can do, easier than others.

I am writing some articles for the papers, which I have not heard from yet but think they will bring something. If published, will send you a copy. I have developed a strong scientific and mechanical bent, about the only strong bent I have had since the time I was so absorbed in natural history.

Besides my "Summer plan" that I worked up so much while I was in Boston, I have gotten up a process and mechanism for an auxiliary car motor, and also for a *locomotive* for street use, both of them. More correctly, I have invented *improvements* in that line, which are so *radical* that I have come to the conclusion (from all the scientific works I have read) that they will prove *patentable,* and if so will sell within a year, or less. There is also a *starter,* different from anything I have been able to find among all the recorded inventions of this country, which I think will be valuable. It all came upon me so forcibly and suddenly that I did not hardly dare to postpone working it up till I saw my own way out; as such things often depend on records, and I have repeatedly surprised my self by the way my investigations have borne out my ideas.

My plan is to collect the various fees now due me for services here and in Fla, and what I can from my writing; and then go on my summer enterprise & vacation combined—getting strong from my outing, at any rate. And I will not come back till I have gotten more money than I started with, anyway. With the proceeds, or part, I then intend, in the Fall, to *test* my inventions, one after the other, till proven practicable, *apply for patents,* & reinvest what surplus there may be left, keeping enough to keep the pot boiling, till I can sell a patent, and meanwhile to get into a good *patent law office,* where both my scientific and mechanical insight, as well as my five years *law,* will all be not only useful, but *necessary* to success. This will involve practice in the U.S. courts, which happens to be *just the same as in Florida,* and mostly in chancery, which I like most!

I feel deliberately certain of all these points, so my courage is good, tho' I am out of health and out of money just at present. I am eating about 3 lbs. of steak (chopped) every day now, and digesting it. My blood began to improve in quality and strength months ago so it is not "if I get well but *when* I get well." That is the way I look at all these things. Just think on that way of putting it and see if it don't help over many a hard place.

It has been such a tough old time for us both now, that perhaps it is better that you were not in it, after I have good reasons for hoping that in not over a year, I will be in a position to give you and poor old Father a good *lift,* after all, and see you both able to follow up the advantages you have. So keep young, and we will have some fun, yet. I don't feel as old by a good deal as I did ten years ago when I was *stranded* on the post graduate course. Fact.

Two of Father's companies are coming to the front, three of them. I hope he will see that he gets something for himself out of them. But I am coming to realize better than ever what you have seen so long, that our man can't be best at *everything,* and Father can not ever be relied upon to look out for himself, but always for that other fellow. I think my outlet is providentially timed, so as to be a relief before things get any worse, Father has sunk so much money, and gotten his property most of it tied up besides. I don't say this to worry you, but think it best for you to know something of how things stand. Just as soon as these companies are beginning to prosper, they begin to *retreat,* and cut down Father's share. It makes me very mad.

However, Father stands it very well, on the whole, and his reputation is still very high, in every way.

By the way, it happened only a few days ago that a Boston gentleman came to Father and made him a handsome offer to go in with his people in developing a company to manufacture a new steam-storage street-car-locomotive, which will compete with all my inventions! Isn't it funny? He will try to help them. If mine beats his I will divide with him, anyway.

Want to see you and Dear Dad awfully.

With much love,

> Always yours,
> Wyllys[12]

The best-situated member of the family was Joshua and Fanny's firstborn, Grace, also called Daisy. In 1881 she married Horace Allen of Boston, a lawyer whose prosperous career gave her a life unvexed by financial worries. The Allens produced three daughters. Wyllys begat no heirs. Joshua's male line ended with him.

The decline of Chamberlain's fortunes in the last years of the century was added to the distress of painful illnesses caused mainly by the old wound from Petersburg. The operation that Chamberlain had at the hands of Dr. J. H. Warren of Boston on April 19, 1883, did not have a lasting benefit. On that day, when he was coming out of the ether, Daisy had written to "My darling little Ma" that Dr. Warren had pronounced it "as successful an operation as he had ever made."[13] But the following letter, written from New York City three years later, tells a different story about Chamberlain's physical condition. It also tells much about his relationship with Fanny and his family and, in fact, with the world.

A few words of explanation may aid in the reading of this letter. The narrative it conveys begins in Grand Central Station on Sunday, December 5, 1886. Joshua and Fanny have been living in a hotel. Now Fanny is going to the home of her daughter, Grace Allen, in Boston. After she departs Joshua leaves the hotel and goes to the home of Dr. Francis W. Upham, then sixty-nine years of age, and his wife, Elizabeth K. Upham, then fifty-one, at 44 West 35th Street, between Fifth Avenue and Broadway.

Chamberlain mentions "the elevated road"; there were several of these at the time. The train he takes to the vicinity of Dr. Upham's home is on the Sixth Avenue line. Upham is not a medical doctor but an honorary LL.D. He has been a lawyer, a college professor, and is now a writer. He graduated from Bowdoin—as did a whole flock of Uphams. This is the link with Chamberlain. A "young Mr. Upham" appears in the letter as a worker on Wall Street. He is the son of Dr. Jabez Baxter Upham, who *is* a medical doctor; he had been a surgeon in the Civil War; he is now retired but comes to Chamberlain's bedside when he is called to do so. Chamberlain's illness seems to involve a flare-up of malaria he is known to have suffered from during the Civil War, but his speaking of chills that are running "from hip to hip" suggests that his old wound is seriously aggravated. Still confined to his bed, Chamberlain has been sick a week when he begins this letter. Although with the kindest of friends, he is far from his family and home. In this sense of separation—from Maine and from the character and occupation his early career seemed to predict—the letter strikes a sad note that resonates throughout his life in the closing years of the nineteenth century.

44 West 35 St.
New York
Dec. 13, '86

My dear Gracie:

You & dear Mamma must not think I would let all these long days pass without a word from me.

But I really have not been able to write until now your dear beautiful letter makes it impossible not to do so.

I was not well for several days before our poor tired "little one" went from me to you. When she went I stood on the bridge in the gallery of the Grand Central Depot and watched the train bearing away—at first so slowly but strongly & surely—my dear one committed to its trust, till it had passed out of sight, and only the circling wreaths of steam told of its track. Then that vanished.

I turned back to the desolate hotel—only for a moment entering the deserted room—& gave orders that completed the scattering of the things which outwardly had made our little home for so many weeks & months, the big trunk to an office "downtown," & the two hand bags to Dr. Upham's, to which latter place I afterwards brought myself—depressed in body & in mind. There was a dinner party there that evening, and all remarked my *peculiarly* "poor looks."

The next day was stormy, the snow gusts whistling in the air & circling around in eddies & making the fences & posts & yards look like a field of graves. I was here at Dr. Upham's you understand.

But I had to come out & be entertained & to spend the day in a false position, & had but little rest. I went to dine with the [word illegible] & they let me sleep on the sofa an hour or two. It was peaceful & restful there—a sort of "Saint's rest."

Monday I went down town & tried to carry forward my work but with little success—still feeling very ill.

Tuesday 7th was my wedding day & I still tried more than ever to write my letter to "Mamma."

It was a cold north-east weather day. I went down to the Wall Street office & the moment I secured completion of the long pending business—the "contract," of which Mamma knows—I felt a sudden severe illness—first in my head—then in my limbs—then all over me. I rose to go, but sank into a chair.

The kind friends there—not Wall Street "sharks" I assure you nor "Bulls & Bears" to me—took me, or led me (I could walk) to the nearest station of the elevated road & young Mr. Upham, of the office (not a near relative of my host but a son of Dr. J. Baxter Upham) . . . came up with me. Half way up I had to go out on the platform to get a breath of the stormy air—the atmosphere in the cars made me deathly sick. I was none too soon; for the moment I got out there, I threw up my breakfast (which had been quite simple) & which I perceived was all in its crude state, just as I had swallowed it four hours before. When I got to the house, here, the spasmodic congestive chills through the body, seemingly from hip to hip, were intensely severe, and my feet and hands grew cold as ice. Everybody of course flew to me. I was enveloped in hot water bottles & flannels, in bed, of course. Young Mr. Upham telegraphed for his father Dr. Baxter Upham, a very skillful physician. Mrs. Upham telegraphed my own Dr. Jackson, who lives 7 miles away but on the line of the elevated road & Dr. Francis Upham ran for Dr. Fordyce Barker, perhaps the most eminent physician in the city. I was soon seized with violent fits of vomiting, which made pretty thorough work of my stomach, & they thought afterwards may have "saved my life"—but I think that puts it rather strong.

Young Upham meantime gave me a hot-water-mustard foot bath, and in an hour or more I was in a gentle perspiration & the pains greatly relieved. But I knew it was a sharp attack; and as the pains crept into the region of the heart, I did not know what was coming but thought it best to give instructions about many things, & to give your address, & that of my home friends & of many in this city who would wish to be near me in case of need.

But I told Mrs. Upham not to send any word unless it became necessary—not at any rate while I was conscious.

I was not in the least frightened, nor afraid, but I was thinking much of "Dear Mamma" & you & poor Wyllys, I knew not where.

Dr. Baxter Upham came first of the physicians. He searched for tokens of heart disturbance & of pneumonia in both of which matters he is an expert. He was soon satisfied there was no pneumonia, & the disturbed action of the heart he believed to be only effect of the shock & of the pain—which I know was true, for I have no disease of the heart.

While he was with me Dr. Jackson came. I was much easier then, & I felt that Dr. Jackson knew about me well enough to give a true diagnosis, & also to put me in the right line.

He said that all that had been done to meet my case was just right. He said the attack was the result of a long overworked and overworn nerve & vital force & that he thought the malaria in my blood had rushed out & seized me & dragged me down. He did what was right—gave me a little acetate of ammonia & a little quinine, & left me much better. In the evening Dr. Barker came & added a slight treatment.

Dear, kind Mrs. Upham, as Mamma will readily know, was ready to lay the universe at my feet, & in truth did really overwhelm, & perhaps overload, me with attentions & suggestions & questions I could not answer for multitude, minuteness & persistency, & this she still does.

So I pulled through three or four days—the three doctors coming in, out of kindness, every few hours, to keep hold of me, and after that I had only the weakness & the wretchedness of the reaction to endure. I have not yet left my bed as a home, but I am sitting up now—for my second essay at sending you a letter. (It is now Tuesday 2 p.m.)

Mrs. Upham wanted to write to you, but I wanted to do that myself, and so it is only now that I have thought it best to let you know all about it. Had I needed you, or had things grown worse with me, I would have had you informed at once. But as it was no good could come of making you anxious & agonized.

Mrs. Upham was sure I could come down to a dinner she was to give last Saturday, & to which she had invited several distinguished people to meet me, & I at the time thought I might be able just to go down for an hour & let her telegraph Horace to send my package of fine clothes from Boston. I thought at any rate you would believe I was not having a very bad time as I was sending for my best clothes.

They came & I thank Horace for his kind & prompt attention.

Now, dears, I am "all right," & hope by tomorrow to go down town a while in the middle of the day. I have everything done for me that "money," & perhaps "love," could command. So I suffer for nothing except for the sight of my dear "ones."

I am thankful for all the love & mercy God has shown us, & I think of it much.

How kind it was in Horace to cheer me that lonely Sunday with the telegram! I insisted on keeping it right beside my face, until your letter came. Now, I substitute that for it. Our dear one, I know, is happy, sheltered & cherished in her precious daughter's home. Wyllys is well. My brother & sister are well. So, as Cicero would say, "I am well."

Do not fear or worry for me. I shall go on now, with care & caution & will keep you informed of my condition. With a heartfull of love to you, my dearest ones, I am always yours,

J. L. Chamberlain[14]

CHAPTER ELEVEN

Echoes of Martial Glory

W hile it might be said that Chamberlain did not have a wholly successful career in politics, education, and business following the Civil War, there was one sphere in which his reputation was firmly enshrined—the world of active and veteran military men. The officers and enlisted men who had watched this scholar-teacher rise from an inexperienced lieutenant colonel to a brevet major general in fewer than three years continued after the war to hold him in high regard, and for at least four decades the opinions of this group had considerable weight. For example, one almost had to have been in the war and done well in it to get anywhere in politics, as evidenced by the fact that, after Andrew Johnson, for the rest of the century every elected president of the United States except one had a good war record, four of them having risen to the rank of general by brevet or otherwise. The exception, Grover Cleveland, had a good excuse. When the war broke he and his two brothers drew lots to determine which one of them would stay home and take care of their widowed mother. Grover lost (or won, depending on how you look at it) and hired a substitute when he was drafted.

Chamberlain did not have the political talents or disposition to parlay this asset beyond his election to four terms as governor of Maine. But the esteem and admiration awarded him by Civil War veterans, including some of the top general officers still in service, was made evident by their election of Chamberlain to high offices in veterans' organizations and his prominence in the affairs of those organizations.

The Grand Army of the Republic, of course, was one of the groups in which Chamberlain was eminent; he served for a time as commander of the GAR's Maine department. Of more lasting importance was his membership in the Military Order of the Loyal Legion of the United States, a verbal mouthful commonly condensed to MOLLUS. One had to be or to have been an officer to belong to the Loyal Legion, but the rules, unlike those of the GAR, allowed descendants of officers to be members, so the organization, founded in 1865, has continued to this day, and claims to be the nation's oldest chartered Civil War institution. Its associated but separate Civil War Library and Museum at 1805 Pine Street, Philadelphia, is a Civil War researcher's paradise—three floors of books, relics, and manuscripts. One can look up from his or her studying to see uniforms and accoutrements worn by Generals Grant and Meade, the saddle on which General Reynolds was riding when he was killed at Gettysburg, and other things of interest to the Civil War student.

Chamberlain was an early member of the order, as indicated by his insignia number (62), and was a commander of the MOLLUS Maine branch, or commandery as these branches were called. (At this writing the Maine commandery is nonexistent, but there are hopes that it may be revived.) Chamberlain may well have become national commander in chief, but in the early days of the Loyal Legion it was the practice to select for this position some eminent officer of the army or navy regular service; for example, the great Army of the Potomac corps commander, Gen. Winfield Scott Hancock, served as acting or actual commander in chief from 1879 to 1886, and he was followed by Lt. Gen. Philip H. Sheridan from 1886 until his death in 1888. One exception to this practice was engineered with the aid of Chamberlain himself. It took place at the Loyal Legion's national headquarters, then at 723 Walnut Street, Philadelphia, in mid-October 1888. The state commanders and other high officers had gathered there to elect a new national commander in chief, to succeed Sheridan, and one of the possible candidates was Rutherford B. Hayes, who had come out of the war as a brevet major general but had not been a regular army officer.[1]

In a way Rutherford B. Hayes was another Joshua L. Chamberlain. As an officer of volunteer troops in the Civil War he had been a great success. He looked back on the war as a glorious experience, more important in his life than even the presidency. It was only natural that he and the war hero of Maine would take to one another immediately. He was also favored by Chamberlain because he was the president often credited with ending Reconstruction.

In 1876 Hayes won the Republican nomination from James G. Blaine and then ran against Democrat Samuel J. Tilden. The election was disputed, two sets of returns having been sent in by each of four states, three of them Southern. Congress appointed an electorial commission to settle the matter. The commissioners awarded disputed votes to Hayes, allowing him to win by one electoral vote. Keeping a promise to the Southerners, Hayes then withdrew all remaining troops from the South. Chamberlain wrote him a three-page letter a few days after his inauguration expressing his satisfaction with "the opening acts of your administration." He continued: "No small part of that satisfaction is in the evidence that the views set forth in your letter of acceptance have suffered no shock, and that you stand as the champion of honest peace and constitutional liberty. The hopes of the country hang on the realization of these ideas."[2]

The ideas Chamberlain referred to, put forth in the previous autumn by Hayes while accepting the nomination, encouraged the Southern states to believe that their rights would be recognized and their prosperity promoted.[3]

Some Democrats, smarting from defeat, complained that Hayes's victory in the election was an act of larceny—that there had been a quid pro quo in the promise of troop withdrawals. In the disputed state election in Maine of 1879–80 a few Democrats went so far as to say that they were "counting out" Republicans to get even with the Republicans for their theft of the presidential election of 1876.[4] However he came to be president, Rutherford B. Hayes turned out to be a good one, in Joshua Chamberlain's eyes. Their meeting at the Loyal Legion gathering in Philadelphia is partially described in a diary entry by the former president dated October 18, 1888.

> General Chamberlain told me after our meeting at the Library that if I was modest, I would have to leave the chair, for he was agoing to nominate me for Commander-in-Chief on the unanimous request of all present—about thirty members. The election was fixed for the afternoon. . . . In the afternoon meeting when General Chamberlain rose and spoke of his embarrassment in speaking in the presence of etc., I immediately left the chair to General Gregg, commander of the Pennsylvania commandery, and left the hall. I met in the office of the library Dr. William H. Engle of the State Library of Pennsylvania. . . . We soon heard applause in the room adjoining.[5]

The applause followed a typically graceful speech by Chamberlain in which he commended Hayes's previous services to the order. When he came to discussion of the custom of having only officers of the regular service as commander in chief—the prime obstacle in the way of choosing Hayes—he demolished it very effectively. "However fitly we might recognize the merits of some one of the distinguished officers of the Regular Service whom we have now, I am sure, in our minds and hearts, we present here a man who has been Commander-in-Chief of both the Army and Navy."[6] Hayes's diary continues: "In a few moments Governor Chamberlain came to me in the office where I was talking with Dr. Engle and announced to me that I was chosen unanimously Commander in Chief."

Hayes's mention of the library is a reminder of the Loyal Legion's contribution to Civil War literature. It was the custom of various commanderies to have papers read before them and to publish these papers. Known today as the MOLLUS War Papers, they are important historically because they were written in most cases by people who had witnessed or experienced the events they described. The Maine and Pennsylvania commanderies published papers read by Chamberlain, some of which were incorporated in his book *The Passing of the Armies,* published by G. P. Putnam's Sons in 1915.

Important as was his recognition by the GAR and MOLLUS, perhaps the most significant honor Chamberlain received from veterans was being elected president of the Society of the Army of the Potomac at Gettysburg in 1888. In a letter to his daughter, Grace Allen, he wrote, "The reunion at Gettysburg was remarkably interesting—25,000 pilgrims returned to their old fields—many distinguished officers. It was a remarkable honor, on such a field & such an occasion, for one who was only a colonel on that field to be chosen President of the Society of the Potomac. . . . I was not a candidate, & it was a surprise to me for there were candidates who 'ranked' me out of sight."[7]

As Chamberlain suggested, many of the leading generals and other officers who had served in this army were still around, some of them prominent in public life. Yet the veterans who voted must have sensed that no one could personify more than Chamberlain the Army of the Potomac. He was a civilian turned soldier. This was a citizen army. It was an army of initially untrained men who had learned the arts of war at the price of great suffering. Chamberlain could never speak or write about it without emotion. And he thought of how in future wars the suffering might be minimized. Could a professional standing army large enough to fight a major war be maintained? Financially and politically he knew that would be impossible in the United States. A sensible alternative would be a program of peacetime military training of civilians, using a professional army as a training cadre around which an expanded organization could be built. To some extent the Fifth Corps of the Army of the Potomac, in which Chamberlain had served, was an ideal realization of that concept; it was a civilian body with a professional military skeleton. Its Second Division, initially at least, was made up of regular army troops, and most of its commanding officers in the superior positions were West Pointers.

Chamberlain thought well of the regular army people and they of him. But in one respect, he believed, the volunteer troops were superior to their professional brethren. As he put it, "They represented the homes and ideals of the country, and not only knew what they were fighting for but also held it dear."[8]

Chamberlain elaborated this point in 1889 when, as president of the society, he spoke at a meeting in Orange, New Jersey. The following bit of information serves as a background: In the presidential election on November 8, 1864, the soldiers of the Army of the Potomac voted in the field and their votes were tabulated in the field—a circumstance that never since has occurred in time of war. The agonizing choice was between Lincoln, who advocated the war's continuance, and McClellan, whose Democratic Party had adopted a platform declaring that the war was a failure and should be ended by a negotiated peace. This imposed a test of resolution unique in the history of armies. To some extent the soldiers were voting on whether they would fight on or go home. The Army of the Potomac voted decisively for Lincoln; it was an army enduring brutal punishment that voted to send its lines charging again upon parapets where thousands of voters would meet certain death.

At the Society of the Army of the Potomac meeting in Orange, Chamberlain responded to a greeting from the governor of New Jersey, in part as follows:

> And now pardon me a word in behalf of those for whom I am to return your greeting. I desire that the friends with us today, especially the younger portion, who may not be so familiar with the history of the country in its details, may be reminded of what manner of men these are before you. When his Excellency the Governor mentioned that space of twenty-five years ago I could not help thinking, comrades and gentlemen, of that dark and bitter year, 1864, when the hearts of almost all men, and I don't know but of some women, were filled with fear at the aspect of things for our country's honor and the hopes of all seemed trailing in the dust; when all the newspapers here were filled with foreboding and (the gentlemen of the press will forgive me) almost upbraiding us of the

army at times that we were not in Richmond; while in Washington even prominent members of Congress were beginning to forsake the great President and form plans other than his and when the issue of our cause seemed to have settled down as in a cloud upon almost every heart in the country; and I desire to say here today that in this Army of the Potomac whose suffering and losses were such in that same year of 1864 that we were not called upon or permitted to report our casualties during that whole campaign from the Rapidan and Rappahannock to the James and Appomattox, for fear the country could not stand the disclosure, in this army there was no faltering nor thought of despair. These men before you and their comrades of all men I ever heard of, kept up their heart and hope and loyalty to the President and the great cause, holding up their bleeding and shattered forms, and protesting that never, while one man of them could hold the field, should that flag be sullied in the dust or the honor of the country go down in shame. I want these honorable gentlemen to bear in mind, and these beautiful and sympathetic ladies, and these youths, that it was the word character, as well as the physical force of these men of the Army of the Potomac that made them patriots and saviors of their country. These are the men for whom it falls to my honorable and happy lot to speak today, and to respond for to your welcome, and say that they are deserving of it.[9]

As notable as the esteem of veterans' organizations was the recognition awarded Chamberlain by officers of the regular and active army, such as took place during a funeral service for General Grant in 1885. Grant died on July 23 of that year at Mt. McGregor near Saratoga. In planning for the funeral, his family recalled that the general sometime prior to his death had written a memorandum naming three places from which he wanted a burial place to be selected—West Point; Galena, Illinois; and New York City. Why New York? one might wonder. Grant's answer is reported to have been, "Because the people of that city befriended me in my need."[10] This is the city where he bought a home in 1881, where he became a partner and invested all his money in a banking house that went broke and left him penniless, and where, afflicted by cancer, he had heroically begun the task of writing his *Personal Memoirs,* which earned half a million dollars and saved his family from destitution. During this period many helpful and dependable friends had come to his support. The family chose New York as his burial place, with Central Park as the selected spot.

U. S. Grant's temporary tomb in Riverside Park, New York.

A brief flurry of protest appeared in the public prints. Some people thought that Grant's tomb ought to be in the Washington area—at Arlington or the Soldier's Home—but the *New York Times* asserted that New York City was "the nation's real capital." The paper also explained that more people would see the tomb here because "everybody who visits Washington, it may be assumed, visits New York, but everybody who visits New York does not visit Washington."[11]

There was one important change, however. It was the suggestion of New York's mayor to erect the tomb in Riverside Park, not in Central Park. As reported by the *Times,* "He thought that the greatness of the man should call for a structure unique and magnificent, to which the surroundings should be fitted, and that a place should be selected in which the monument could stand, not as the chief among many statues or structures, but as the only structure, in isolated grandeur."[12]

The Grant family quickly came around to the mayor's view and made Riverside Park its final choice. With that, frenzied preparations began. While a committee formed to raise funds for a permanent tomb was launching a nationwide campaign, a temporary structure was designed in twenty minutes and built in about a week. Railroads and ferries were readied to bring hordes of people into New York. Everyone who was anybody from President Grover Cleveland to P. T. Barnum planned to attend the services. Papers reported that the pallbearers would include Sherman, Sheridan, Adm. David Porter, and former Confederate general Joseph E. Johnston. When invited, Johnston, who was in Portland, Oregon, at the time, traveled night and day without stopping in order to reach New York in time. Fitzhugh Lee and other former foes were also there.

Elaborate floral displays were prepared—one described as a cannon having a body made of yellow roses, with wheels constructed of dark purple immortelles. In charge of the funeral ceremonies in New York by order of the War Department was Gen. Winfield Scott Hancock, who was now in command of the Division of the Atlantic and Department of the East with headquarters on Governors Island.

Grant's body arrived by train in New York on August 5 and was conveyed amid the sounds of tolling church bells, mournful band music, and the cadenced tramp of military escorts to City Hall, where it lay in state until the morning of Saturday, August 8. Then began what was undoubtedly the longest funeral procession ever to take place in New York City, watched by what was reported to be the largest crowd ever assembled in the city up to that time. It was made up of military, municipal, fraternal, and other marching groups of every description and included a long line of carriages in which important people rode. The route went from City Hall up Broadway to Fourteenth Street, over Fourteenth to Fifth Avenue, up Fifth to West Fifty-seventh Street, thence by various ways to Riverside Drive and up to Riverside Park—about seven and a half miles. Organizations that wanted to could fall out at Fifty-seventh Street, but a large part of the parade, including the carriages of dignitaries, went on to the park. One attendee, former president Rutherford B. Hayes, wrote in his diary that the drive took five hours, that there were perhaps fifty thousand people in the procession, and that the watchers (presumably in midcity) stood five deep on each side of the street.

The carriage segment of the parade was organized in the following order of precedence: immediate family with relatives and close associates, such as Grant's former cabinet members and military staff officers; President Cleveland; the vice president; Supreme Court and cabinet members; Senate and House delegations; former presidents; foreign ministers; state governors; and so on down the line of officialdom. A few minutes before ten o'clock the family and other immediate mourners entered carriages from the Twenty-fourth Street side of the Fifth Avenue Hotel. Joshua Chamberlain, who happened to be staying nearby at the Victoria Hotel at Fifth Avenue and Broadway, was placed in a carriage not far behind the president, according to a letter he wrote to Fanny that evening. How this happened is not fully explained, but the letter indicates that General Hancock, his old compatriot from the Army of the Potomac, was responsible.

Victoria Hotel
New York 8 Aug. '85

My dear Fanny
The great scene is over. Grant is laid in his tomb. You may imagine—few others can—how strange that seems to me.

That emblem of strength & stubborn resolution yielding to human weakness & passing helplessly away to dust. I wish you could have seen the faces of Sherman & Sheridan & Hancock as they stood over that bier before the body was laid away.

What thoughts—what memories—what [word illegible]—passed through those minds! The pageant and the tribute of honor were grand—worthy of a great nation. I wish now very much that I had brought Wyllys with me.

This is the last of the great scenes, at least for this generation. I will tell you more about it when I get rested a little, or after I come home. By Genl. Hancock's kind attentions I was treated with marked distinction—too much in fact.

I had a carriage directly in the group of cabinet ministers & the most distinguished men of the country. It chanced that I was far ahead of the governors of states & the officers of the army! I would not have chosen that position because it was too much. But Genl. Hancock's staff officer did not seem to understand that I was only a private citizen.

I was also in the same line with the senators chosen as chief mourners. It strangely happened that *Governor Connor* of Maine was left out without notice & without provision by carriage for a place in the procession.

I stopped my carriage when I saw him & took him & the commander in chief of the Grand Army into my carriage & my place—far ahead of that to which they would have fallen if they had had a carriage.

By this means they had a chance to see the whole ceremony & at the burial service they were with me not ten feet from the central scene, the casket before the tomb door, while the last services were paid—the last prayer offered—and the bugler stepped to the front & sounded with trembling lips *the tattoo!* the evening roll call—you remember—the end of day—the signal of silence & darkness. They who stood about—most of them—could not feel all that said to me. I looked in vain for a face that seemed to express what I was feeling. But not till I saw the faces of Sherman & Sheridan & Hancock did I meet that resemblance, & that deepened my own feeling.

The great men of the nation were there. But nothing seemed great to me—but what was gone; except the multitudes that crowded miles on miles, & the tokens of mourning that overshadowed the city.

Grant himself seemed greater now than ever. And he is.

I am glad I saw it all, & I was admitted to a near place.

Do not think me foolishly egotistic. It is not that spirit that prompts me to speak of myself; but you know that I have had great & deep experiences—& some of my life has gone into the history of the days that are past.

I will probably go to Phila. & West Virginia next. Address care of M.C.C. Church, Parkersburg, West Va.

> Good night & all blessings
> Yours   J. L. C.[13]

Among the thoughts that passed through Chamberlain's mind on that long carriage ride must have been the memories of Grant's visit at his invitation to Brunswick on August 2, 1865, to attend the commencement exercises at Bowdoin College. In one of the ceremonies Chamberlain had presented Grant with a honorary degree. At the commencement dinner there had been a pleasant little interchange between the two of them. Addressing the diners, Chamberlain had said, "I have tried to get General Grant to speak, but he says 'No,' and when he says that word he means it. Lee knows it means something." Here Grant had broken in and said, "I continue to fight it out on that line."[14]

Grant's *Memoirs* was issued in December 1885, and Chamberlain must have been moved when he found himself mentioned in it. In his book *U. S. Grant and the American Military Tradition,* Bruce Catton described the completion of the *Memoirs* while Grant was dying of cancer. According to Catton, after Grant finished the manuscript he had a few afterthoughts. He wrote a few pages of paragraphs that he wished to be inserted at certain places in the manuscript, and on the very last page was an "insert" about the way Col. Joshua Chamberlain was wounded at Petersburg and how for his bravery Grant made him a brigadier general. This, apparently, is one of the last things Grant wrote; forty-eight hours later he was dead.

This is the way it appeared in the published memoirs.

Colonel J. L. Chamberlain of the 20th Maine was wounded on the 18th. He was gallantly leading his brigade at the time, as he had been in the habit of doing in all the engagements in which he had previously been engaged. He had several times been recommended for a brigadier-generalcy for gallant and meritorious conduct. On this occasion, however, I promoted him on the spot, and forwarded a copy of my order to the War Department, asking that my act might be confirmed and Chamberlain's name sent to the Senate for confirmation without any delay. This was done, and at last a gallant and meritorious officer received partial justice at the hands of his government, which he had served so faithfully and so well.[15]

"Meritorious"—that was a key word in Chamberlain's life in that it differentiated his military and civilian careers. In the bloody business of war, although it may take a while, incompetent people must eventually be thrown off and meritorious ones raised up—otherwise goals will not be reached and destruction may ensue. In civilian pursuits courage, intelligence, and character do not necessarily bring success. That Chamberlain, simply on his merits, had achieved a remarkably high status in the army is verified by several records—one of them, strangely, in the archives of the First Parish Church in Brunswick, Maine. As previously mentioned, the First Parish's pastor and Chamberlain's father-in-law, Dr. George E. Adams, in the spring of 1865 visited Chamberlain in his camp near Washington, where troops had gathered for the triumphal Grand Review, which began on the morning of May 23. Here is part of Adams's diary entry for May 20.

All around from time to time the Bugle-call for this or that Brigade, then soon the drum & fife, summons to the evening roll call—i.e., Tattoo. C. has been to the city tonight to see Sheridan, in behalf of Griffin, to whom Meade is hostile (on acct. of his habit of severe criticism). G. fears that he should be displaced from command of the Corps. Sheridan says no, he shall not be disturbed. Sheridan seemed delighted to see a 5th Corps man. C. also saw Grant. C. would rather have a Brevet than a full Maj. Gen. The brevet is a permanent honor, a rank that cannot be resigned.

There are two rather striking disclosures here: first, that Chamberlain stood high enough so that he could successfully intervene at higher headquarters on behalf of his own immediate superior, the able but somewhat abrasive Gen. Charles Griffin commanding the Fifth Corps; and second, that his goal was "permanent honor." This honor was certified when in August 1893 Chamberlain received in the mail a small package from the War Department's Records and Pensions Office, with a return receipt requested. When opened, it was found to contain the Medal of Honor, more popularly known as the Congressional Medal of Honor, the nation's highest military decoration, awarded for gallantry in action. Today such an award would provide the occasion for an elaborate ceremony, but in the late nineteenth century the postman was often the only representative of the federal government to make an appearance. The citation was for "daring heroism and great tenacity in holding his position on Little Round Top against repeated assaults and carrying the advance position on The Great Round Top."[16]

Chamberlain was highly pleased by this award. But he probably never in his most extreme fantasies imagined that his name would echo even further down the corridors of military history.

CHAPTER TWELVE

A Battle Remembered

And Gentlemen in England, now a-bed
Shall think themselves accurst they were not here;
And hold their manhoods cheap whiles any speaks
That fought with us upon Saint Crispin's day.

—Henry V, Act IV, scene iii

Having been a key participant in the Civil War, Chamberlain had to endure the refighting of its battles, which began to intensify in the last decade of the nineteenth century. Some of the refighters were afflicted by the trouble Mark Twain once reported. "When I was younger, I could remember anything, whether it happened or not, but I am getting old, and soon I shall remember only the latter."[1] That was part of the difficulty—certainly some of the veterans remembered things that had not happened—but many more had simply enlarged what of necessity had been only a narrow view of an event into a version of the whole. And many had been misled by rumors. Chamberlain was often plagued by correspondence and at times confrontations arising from this miasma.

A typical canard was quashed in a statement by Chamberlain that appeared in the *Southern Historical Society Papers*:

> And right here I wish to correct again that statement so often attributed to me, to the effect that I have said I received from the hands of General Lee on that day his sword. . . . I never did make that claim even, as I never did receive that sword.

As I have said, no Confederate officer was required or even asked to surrender his side arms if they were his personal property. As a matter of fact, General Lee never gave up his sword, although, if I am not mistaken, there was some conference between General Grant and some of the members of his staff upon that very subject just before the final surrender. I was not present at that conference, however, and only know of it by heresay.[2]

Although both of Chamberlain's promotions beyond colonel and most of his honors had been won in service other than that with the 20th Maine, a regiment he commanded for only a few months, the focus of his fame remained disproportionately on Little Round Top, where he and his men, on the edge of annihilation, had routed the Confederates with a desperate charge. After the war extended discussions of what really happened in that fight began to take shape. *The Attack and Defense of Little Round Top* by Oliver W. Norton, published in 1913, has been thought of as the most accurate account of the action on Little Round Top, dealing with all the regiments involved. Norton's method was to collect after-action reports by commanders involved, plus the accounts of a dozen or so historians, and analyze all this material—a task he was well fitted to do because he had been there as the bugler accompanying Col. Strong Vincent, the brigade commander. Even so, in the introduction to his book Norton wrote, "There is no part of the battle of Gettysburg . . . the facts in regard to which have been less understood, because more misrepresented, than the struggle for the possession of Little Round Top." One of the reasons, he thought, was that both brigade commanders of the dominant Union brigade were killed—Colonel Vincent at Gettysburg and his successor, Col. James C. Rise, ten months later—so they never had the opportunity to write their reminiscences after the war. As for the historians whose accounts Norton examined, he wrote that "no two of them agree in their descriptions of what took place on Little Round Top."[3]

Concerning the action of the 20th Maine, probably the most thorough and penetrating study ever made was that by Dr. Thomas A. Desjardin in the early 1990s. He collected more than seventy recollections written by some twenty Union and Confederate survivors of the engagement, took his own measurements and compass bearings for the preparation of new maps, explored dozens of record and manuscript depositories, talked to many authorities, and wrote the fascinating book *Stand Firm Ye Boys from Maine* (1995). In his research he found that even Norton may have made mistakes; for example, Norton emphatically denied that one regiment was in a position which it seems in fact to have occupied for a time.[4]

The disagreements among the 20th Maine veterans originated in a common phenomenon often demonstrated in psychology classes. An instructor arranges to have something bizarre suddenly happen, then asks the class members to write brief accounts of what they may have seen. A great variety of stories results. In the fighting at Little Round Top this variety was amplified by the stress of battle, the narrow fields of vision afforded to soldiers who were taking all possible cover behind rocks and trees, and the thick clouds of smoke that Civil War weaponry produced. Add to this the failings of memory over the years, and it was not strange that veterans had different impressions of what had happened. Among these impressions, the one likely to draw the most attention and controversy was the idea that Chamberlain had not been as important as people thought in initiating the famous charge. Disagreements about this and other matters took place, naturally enough, at reunions, most notably one at Gettysburg in the late 1880s.

In 1886 the survivors of the 20th Maine erected on Little Round Top a simple rectangular-faced monument made of Maine granite on a spot where, it was judged by a committee, the colors had been placed in the battle. On October 3, 1889, the monument was dedicated, with members of the Twentieth Maine Regiment Association, their families, and others gathered around it to hear the dedicatory speeches. By this time published accounts by a few veterans had appeared.

One of these was *Army Life: Reminiscences of the War,* by the Rev. Theodore Gerrish, a book that covers the entire service of the 20th Maine regiment. This is a fairly good book, long in the public domain, that has been often borrowed from by modern Civil War writers and filmmakers. In fact, Desjardin took the title for his book *Stand Firm Ye Boys from Maine* from one of its pages, even though his research for the book had led him to conclude that Gerrish was not even present at Gettysburg. The various items of conflicting evidence regarding this are presented here because they illustrate the difficulty of getting at the truth after decades have passed, even though many records and documents exist.

Desjardin discovered, from regimental and hospital records available from the National Archives, that Gerrish was absent sick in hospital during the period when the battle was fought. This was a time of great stress and long marches, when regimental record keeping was not at its best, so that part of the evidence might have been suspect. But the hospital records are more difficult to question. They show Gerrish was in hospital not only at the time of Gettysburg but for other periods (illness struck more frequently than bullets in the Civil War). They also show a long absence caused by a wound; he was shot through the ankle in the battle of the Wilderness. Obviously, for the periods of absence he depended on the eyewitness accounts of his comrades in gathering material for his book.

Now for a conflicting record. By the 1890s it had become such a distinction to be known as having participated in the battle of Gettysburg, that the state of Maine established a commission, on which Chamberlain served, which undertook to prepare a book that would report on each of the fifteen regiments, battalions, batteries, or other Maine units that fought in the battle; it would also include lists of participants—a task of devilish difficulty, with absolute accuracy a highly questionable goal. On March 4, 1897, Albert E. Fernald of Winterport, who had been a sergeant in the 20th Maine at Gettysburg and who later as a lieutenant earned the Medal of Honor, wrote to Chamberlain, probably in response to an inquiry about Gerrish. He told Chamberlain that Gerrish was not at Gettysburg. Either the letter reached Chamberlain too late—after the book had gone to the printer—or there was still doubt in Chamberlain's mind, for when the commission's book *Maine at Gettysburg* was published in 1898, Gerrish was listed as being present with Company H.

An added perplexity: As previously mentioned, in 1886 the survivors of the 20th Maine placed a monument on Little Round Top on a spot where a committee, meeting there in 1882, had judged that the colors had stood; Gerrish was a member of that committee. Why had he been chosen for that responsibility if he had not been there when the battle took place? He was a Methodist minister, gave the required prayers at 20th Maine reunions, and seems to have been well regarded by his fellow veterans.

Still another oddity: Gerrish wrote another book published in 1887, entitled *Life in the World's Wonderland.* It was a travel book about a trip Gerrish made through the Northwest and up the inland passage to Alaska. In Spokane he meets with a man with a GAR badge on his breast. They exchange memories of Gettysburg. "Were you there?" the man asks him. Gerrish replies, "Yes, I was in the Twentieth Maine. We fought on Little Round Top that day."[5] But there is another undated edition of this book in which this incident does not appear and nothing is said about Gerrish's being at Gettysburg. Which book is to be believed? The whole affair illustrates the difficulty of determining precisely, after a passage of years, what happened at any tumultuous event.

Historian William B. Jordan Jr. has characterized descriptions of what happened at Little Round Top, including those of the participants, as like the story of the blind men and the elephant; one of the men getting hold of a leg describes an elephant as being "very much like a tree," another getting hold of a trunk describes it as something else, and so on. On that basis history has been improved if Gerrish was not present on Little Round Top. If he was there he would have had his head behind a rock or tree and taken the battle to be very like something it was not. If he was not there, he would have gained from his comrades a cross section of impressions and a much wider view of what happened. Oliver Norton, after examining the accounts of many historians concerning the battle of Little Round Top, said that one of the best was written by the man who was farthest away—the Comte de Paris, across the Atlantic. This may have been the case with Theodore Gerrish. At any rate this is what he wrote about the battle's climax:

> A critical moment has arrived and we can remain as we are no longer; we must advance or retreat. It must not be the latter, but how can it be the former? Colonel Chamberlain understands how it can be done. The order is given "Fix Bayonets!" and the steel shanks of the bayonets rattle upon the rifle barrels. "Charge bayonets, charge!" Every man understood in a moment that the movement was our only salvation, but there is a limit to human endurance, and I do not dishonor those brave men when I write that for a brief moment the order was not obeyed, and the little line seemed to quail under the fearful fire that was being poured upon it. O for some man reckless of life, and all else save his country's honor and safety, who would rush far out to the front, lead the way, and inspire the hearts of his exhausted comrades! In that moment of supreme need the want was supplied. Lieut. H. S. Melcher, an officer who had worked his way up from the ranks, and was then in command of Co. F, at the time the color company, saw the situation, and did not hesitate, and for his gallant act deserves as much as any other man the honor of the victory on Round Top. With a cheer, and a flash of his sword, that sent an inspiration along the line, full ten paces to the front he sprang— ten paces—more than half the distance between the hostile lines. "Come on! Come on! Come on, boys!" he shouts. The color sergeant and the brave color guard follow, and with one wild yell of anguish wrung from its tortured heart, the regiment charged.
>
> The rebels were confounded at the movement. We struck them with a fearful shock. They recoil, stagger, break and run, and like avenging demons our men pursue.[6]

The part about the hesitation immediately drew sharp denials from some of the 20th Maine veterans. Nobody hesitated! Nobody quailed! The part about Holman Melcher aroused an extended controversy—in fact, it is still going on and may never end. Melcher was an admirable solder whose story is well told in the book *With a Flash of His Sword,* edited by William B. Styple (1994). After distinguished service and honorable wounds in the war, he had a successful career in business politics. His brief account of the battle published in 1885 modestly makes no mention of his own part in the fight; he describes Chamberlain as giving the order to fix bayonets and the charge as beginning almost before the colonel could say anything more.[7]

This is close to what Chamberlain wrote in his official report: "It was imperative to strike before we were struck by this overwhelming force in a hand-to-hand fight, which we could not probably have withstood or survived. At that crisis I *ordered the bayonet.* The word was enough. It ran like fire along the line from man to man, and rose into a shout, with which they sprang forward upon the enemy. . . ."[8] The order to fix bayonets was, of course, equivalent to an order to charge, bayonets being a weapon that cannot be used at a distance; and it is quite evident that the men understood it as such. Joshua Chamberlain wrote at least three reports of the battle; in only one of these did he say that he ordered a *charge.* For his presumably final report, the one that appeared in the *Official Records,* the word "charge" does not appear, and he wrote "I ordered the bayonet."[9]

When veterans of the 20th Maine and their families gathered on Little Round Top in early October 1889 for the dedication of the regiment's monuments on Little and Big Round Tops, they listened to a program that concentrated on memories of the battle—and compared these memories with their own. The head of the regimental association, Holman Melcher, now mayor of Portland, was presiding. The Rev. Theodore Gerrish was present to take care of the opening prayer and the benediction; so was Albert Fernald, and one wonders what conversation he and Gerrish may have had. President Melcher announced he would introduce the regimental historian, Howard L. Prince, who would be followed by General Chamberlain.

Prince, who had been quartermaster sergeant of the 20th Maine at the time of the battle, began his talk by frankly admitting that he had not been present at the fight on Little Round Top. He had been within the sound of the guns but was conducting a load of shoes toward Gettysburg for the footsore regiment. His talk was a long one; on the whole it seemed remarkably accurate, and he explained a number of things. For example, he said that "the front surged backward and forward like a wave. At times our dead and

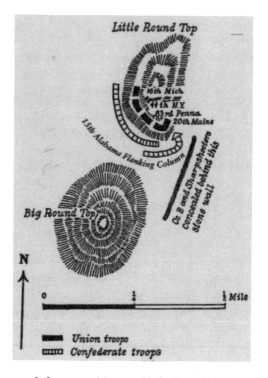

Infantry positions at Little Round Top.

wounded were in front of our line, and then by a superhuman effort our gallant lads would carry the combat forward beyond their prostrate forms."[10] When Melcher, in command of Company F, suggested an advance of his company, he was doing so, Prince said, in order to cover the wounded. Yet just at that moment Chamberlain had decided to take the offensive with his whole regiment and "the one word 'bayonet' rings from Chamberlain's lips like a bugle note, and down that worn and weary line the word and the action go, like a flash of lightning through the powder-smoke."[11]

One great fear of a Civil War infantry commander was that of being flanked, when the enemy could fire lengthwise down his line of soldiers and failing to hit one would be almost sure to hit another, so that the fire was doubly effective. This, as Chamberlain explained later, was one reason why he did not want Melcher to break the line and take his company to a forward and separate position where he might get into that predicament.

In his address following that of Prince, Chamberlain agreed with his version of the Melcher incident and added a bit of conversation. Melcher had come up to him and said:

> I think we could press forward with my company, if you will per-mit me, and cover the ground where our dead and wounded are."
> "You shall have the chance," was my answer. "I am about to order a charge. We are to make a great right wheel." What he did, you who know him know. What you did, the world knows.
> I am sorry to have heard it intimated that any hesitated when that order was given. That was not so. No man hesitated. . . . Nobody hesitated to obey that order. In fact, to tell the truth, the order was never given, or but imperfectly. The enemy were already pressing up the slope. There was only time or need for the words, "Bayonet! Forward to the right!"[12]

Chamberlain's honest admission that the order to charge was never given opened the way to new interpretations of that critical moment—one that Melcher not only led the charge, but that he suggested it, and further that neither Melcher nor Chamberlain was responsible; it was an impulsive for-ward movement of the whole regiment. This, if it happened, was a some-what unlikely thing for a well-trained Civil War regiment to do, but it was a wild affair, and this story remains as one of the hypotheses that were set afloat. Maj. Ellis Spear remembered that although he was in command of the left wing he never received an order to charge; he couldn't see the right of the regiment but he heard shouting from the center and saw an advance beginning there and continuing to the left.[13]

Quite contrary to anything like this is the version set forth by Michael Shaara's Pulitzer Prize–winning 1974 novel and the deservedly popular film *Gettysburg*, that grew out of it; these have Chamberlain shouting "Charge!" waving his sword, and leading a rush down the slope in the way we think of Teddy Roosevelt charging up San Juan Hill. This novelized and filmed version has been set upon by some historians, who seem to forget that they are quarreling with a fiction and who also forget that no matter what the truth is or what they write in its elucidation, this is the way the event will be remembered by 98 percent of the general public who are aware of it. This is the way mythology proceeds—carrying forward essen-tial truths unencumbered by factual details.

Another point of disagreement that came up at the 1889 reunion had to do with the "refusal" of the regiment's left wing, that is, its being bent back at nearly a right angle with the rest of the line to keep the 20th Maine from being flanked by the large Confederate force seen to be moving in that direction. This is a maneuver for which Chamberlain has often been commended in military classrooms. Whose idea was the "refusal?" And who alerted Chamberlain to the danger it was designed to avert?

Historian Howard Prince said that "we must conclude that as there is substantial agreement on the main features of the action, these disputed details were seen from different points, or were viewed at different stages as parts of the whole. Now it is well known that our gallant Lieut. Nichols always maintained that he first made known the extent of the Confederate line to Col. Chamberlain, and the Colonel in his official report says that his attention was called to it by an officer from the center, which was about Nichol's position, and that then mounting upon a rock he was able to discern it for himself, and took the action already described. Major Spear is equally sure that he called Col. Chamberlain's attention to it before the regiment was fairly under fire, and that the new disposition was then made."[14]

In his remarks following those of Prince, Chamberlain said, "I take note . . . of the surprise of several officers to hear that it was some other than a single one of them who came to me in the course of the fight with information of the enemy's extended movements to envelop our left. Now, as might well be believed of such gentlemen and soldiers, they are all right; no one of them is wrong."[15]

Another portion of Chamberlain's address reflected his annoyance at some of the after-action analyses that were going on. "You see there may be stories apparently not consistent with each other, yet all of them true in their time and place, and so far as each actor is concerned. And while everyone here, officer and soldier, did more than his duty, and acted with the utmost intelligence and spirit, you must permit me to add the remark that I commanded my regiment that day."[16]

Chamberlain was much more critical in a letter to Ellis Spear written on November 27, 1896, in which he said:

> The Melcher incident is also magnified. He is now presented to the public as having suggested the charge. There is no truth in this. I had communicated with you before he came and asked me if he could not advance his company and gather in some prisoners in his front. I told him to take his place with his company; that I was about to order a general charge. He went on the run, and did, I have no doubt, gallant service; but he did no more than many others did. . . . There is a tendency nowadays to make "history" subserve other

purposes than legitimate ones. "Incidental" history, even if true in detail, can be made to produce what used to be called in our logic, "*suggestio falsi.*"[17]

There is evidence here that the cogs of Chamberlain's memory, like those of his old comrades, were beginning to slip. He writes "gather in some prisoners in his front." They were not prisoners; they were wounded soldiers. In this same letter he mentioned a story being put forth on behalf of Walter G. Morrill, commander of Company B at Little Round Top. Just prior to the Confederate attack Chamberlain had sent Morrill and his company out at some distance to his left to guard his exposed flank. There they had been cut off from the regiment by the Confederate advance and had taken cover behind a stone wall. Then, when the 20th Maine charged, they rose up and fired into the Alabamians from their rear, contributing greatly to their alarm and desire to be gone. In his letter to Spear, Chamberlain wrote:

> Now, it seems, it was Morrill who won the battle. He did good and praiseworthy work. But one might ask why he did not make some demonstration while Oates was advancing on us, and not wait until we had fought him as long as we could stand and then turned on him and got him running.
>
> The "whole truth" is sometimes quite different in its bearings from what is called truth. But to make a part-truth displace the whole is not in accordance with old-fashioned ethics.[18]

There is reason to believe that Chamberlain himself did not fully understand all that happened after he gave the order to fix bayonets. In his official reports and later recollections he pictures his left wing coming up into line and then the whole line, with its right anchored on the 83rd Pennsylvania, swinging around in a great 'right wheel" as he called it, with the regiment describing nearly a half circle, the left passing over the space of half a mile. There is some confirmation by Amos M. Judson of the adjacent 83rd Pennsylvania, whose book published in 1865 was one of the first if not the first of the regimental histories—written early enough to be uncontaminated by the author's reading of other accounts. Judson described what happened as seen from the 83rd's position—whether by him or someone else he does not say. "The Twentieth Maine continued their pursuit, their line swinging around a moving pivot, like a great gate upon a post until its left had swept down through the valley and up the sides of Big Round Top."[19]

In Casey's *Infantry Tactics,* the manual used by the 20th Maine, there is no command "Battalion right wheel" for a regiment in line of battle, and Chamberlain certainly knew this. In his official report he placed the two words, right wheel, within quotation marks. But the idea has persisted that there was a military maneuver by this name and it was executed by the 20th Maine. It is likely that this was a formation forced into being by the topography, with the valley and the sides of the Round Top defining it, and that it was preceded by some rather chaotic action on the left. Researches by Dr. Thomas Desjardin indicate that the initial charge by at least part of the left wing went in an entirely different direction and resulted in the capture of a number of Confederates to the east of Little Round Top, where they would have been hidden from Chamberlain and any observers in the 83rd Pennsylvania.

In 1902 William Oates, who had commanded the 15th Alabama attacking the 20th Maine, contributed to the general confusion. He and the survivors of his regiment wanted to place a monument on Little Round Top marking the farthest advance, or high-water mark, of their July 2, 1863, attack. There followed a wrangle lasting two or three years involving Oates, Chamberlain, the Gettysburg Battlefield Commission, the secretary of war, and others. Oates wanted the monument placed at a position that would indicate that his attack had penetrated so far as to be in rear of the 20th Maine's brigade. Chamberlain objected. He wrote to Oates, "It is really my desire to have your monument set up, only let us make sure of our ground for the sake of historical fact."[20]

Chamberlain even criticized the position of the 20th Maine's monument. In his address at its dedicatory exercises he had told his old comrades that if they had wanted to put the monument where the colors had stood, they had put it in the wrong place. But the 20th Maine monument was never moved. And the 15th Alabama monument was never erected.

Whatever happened in the murky uproar about Little Round Top, Chamberlain came out of it with a reputation among fellow officers in the Fifth Corps and among his men as an effective commander. And if there was any question about his leadership it was proven at many other places, including Big Round Top, which has been overshadowed by the action on the smaller hill. In one of the far-inland regions of Maine the son of a man who fought with the 20th Maine on Little Round Top remembered his father saying, "Hell, we wasn't no heroes. We just got caught up there and had to fight our way out."[21] It was a good definition of a common variety of heroism—trapped people having to fight their way out. Little Round Top was essentially a defensive battle, won out of desperation.

Big Round Top was something else. The top of this larger hill, about a quarter of a mile south or a little southwest of Little Round Top, offered an artillery position that would command not only the smaller hill but the whole battlefield. That, Oates had recognized, when he had been forced to lead the 15th Alabama up the big hill to clear it of sharpshooters he did not want to leave in his rear. With the fight on Little Round Top over and night coming on, Chamberlain's corps commander looked at the rocky, wooded mass looming ominously over the field and recognized the danger it presented. He asked Col. James C. Rice, now commanding Chamberlain's brigade, to take that big hill. Rice turned to a fresh brigade of Pennsylvanians that had just come up and asked their commander, Col. Joseph W. Fisher, to do so. Fisher, as Chamberlain remembered it, "emphatically declined,"[22] even though he was supposed to be defending the sacred soil of his own state. He had reasons for declining: It was getting dark; the ground was difficult and unknown to his men; it would be uphill against Confederates who were lying behind good cover, resting their rifles on protective boulders, waiting for the noise of climbing attackers stumbling in darkness among the rocks and bushes. There would be flashes of fire, a hail of lead, the screaming of wounded, and the brigade could leave half its men lying on the hillside after this ill-considered advance. So Colonel Fisher must have thought.

Rice then turned to Chamberlain and said, "Colonel, will you do it?" and Chamberlain might have responded, "Are you joking, sir?" He had only about half his force left, and they were in bad shape. In the words of Lt. Samuel L. Miller, "The casualties of battle, together with the details to bury the dead and bring up ammunition, had reduced the ranks of the Twentieth to 200 muskets. The men had just passed through such an ordeal as only those who have experienced the horrors of war can comprehend; one man in every three had been shot down; they were exhausted, hungry and thirsty."[23] Yet when Chamberlain accepted the assignment to take Big Round Top, they willingly followed him up its rocky slopes in an extended line of battle with fixed bayonets and orders not to fire, so that their small number and positions would not be revealed. And so—taking some fire but not returning it—they secured the heights and captured more prisoners.

The assault was not as difficult as it promised to be, but that does not alter the fact that it was one of the most frightening experiences in the history of the regiment—and an outstanding example of leadership. The men trusted Chamberlain's judgment; they followed him; they did what he told them to do; and everything turned out right.

In summary, of all that has been said or written about the events on the Round Tops on July 2, 1863, the most convincing statement is the one made by Chamberlain on October 3, 1889, "You must permit me to add the remark that I commanded my regiment that day."

In refighting the war Chamberlain more than held his ground, but it took hours, days, and weeks of time, particularly in trying to determine for the public record who was at Gettysburg and what they did there. As he, and the nation, grew older and as memories of the battle came to have an almost sacred meaning, this work seemed very important to him. If there was any evidence at all that a man was on that hallowed field, Chamberlain wanted him to have credit for it, even if by this policy absentees got mixed into the lists of those present.

Some of the correspondence he had with survivors of the 16th Maine Regiment illustrates his efforts and concern. The veterans of the 16th Maine, it should be explained, were people with whom Chamberlain had an emotional attachment second only to that he had with men of the 20th Maine. This was probably because the situations of the two regiments at Gettysburg had been so much alike and their fates so different. Like the 20th on the second day of the battle, the 16th on the first day was ordered to hold an area of ground "at all costs"—in the case of the 16th so that its division could withdraw and escape the overwhelming Confederate advance that swept the Union forces from the field on that day. The 16th fulfilled its mission, but it was practically destroyed. Only thirty-eight men and four officers stood at day's end. All other members of the regiment had been killed, wounded, or captured. The chaotic condition of the 16th made meaningful record keeping difficult. And this was why, nearly thirty-five years afterward, the survivors of the 16th Maine needed help in making up their list of men present at Gettysburg—help that Chamberlain provided. The people he wrote to in the correspondence that follows (in order of their appearance or mention) were Charles Hamlin, chairman of the executive committee of the Maine Gettysburg Commission, which was preparing the book *Maine at Gettysburg*; Abner R. Small, adjutant of the 16th Maine at Gettysburg; and Charles W. Tilden, who had commanded the 16th Maine at Gettysburg.

Chamberlain's letters are reproduced at some length because they provide another good example of the fog that time casts over memory.

Brunswick, Jan. 20th 1897

Dear General Hamlin:—

I have just returned from a week's absence, during a part of which I went over very carefully with Captain Verrill the matters he has so ably undertaken to look after. I now find your valuable letter enclosing a list of men of the 16th Regiment present for duty at the battle of Gettysburg. This you say was made out by Lieut. Wiggin. Not knowing of the existence of such a list I had persuaded Major Small, busy as he is, to aid me in making up such a list, which after much labor is just now complete as he could make it.

But it is a remarkable fact, and one which illustrates the difficulty of arriving at the exact truth even in plain matter of fact in preparing "war histories," that the two lists so carefully made up differ so much as to be almost unrecognizable as intended for the same.

Major Small and I have labored very hard, and long, to get the truth; and in some respects Lieutenant Wiggin's list seems to be most accurate, from the specifications he makes as to detached service on the part of some men of whom we had not discovered this. Still, the list of names is greatly at variance in the two cases. I have returned both to Major Small, and he and I may have to have another sitting over the matter. . . .[24]

>─┼─◆>──O─<◆─┼─<

Brunswick, Jan. 20th 1897

Dear Major Small:—

After my long afternoon with Captain Verrill I went to New York, where I received your list of names of men at Gettysburg, and General Tilden's comments on the rule of leaving off men not then actually in the line of battle. I fully agree with him that the names of men present at the battle even if not "in it," as teamsters, clerks, musicians, etc. should be recognized and assigned to their true place in the list. I would not put on the list the names of men sick in Washington, no matter how deserving they may be of mention and remembrance, for character, or for duty elsewhere. But all who were at Gettysburg should, I think, be on your list, with remarks in case of those not expected to be in the line of battle. They were in their places, doing their duty.

But now, on arriving home this morning I find from General Hamlin a list made up, he says by Lieut. Wiggin; which differs as to the names of the men in the several companies from the list we have so widely as to be almost unrecognizable as intended for the same. In some of Lieut. Wiggin's companies, there is a tremendous preponderance of sergeants and corporals, and men we were sure were either off, or on, appear in his lists in quite the contrary categories. What can I do but send both lists to you for your final judgment and decision? I do not know enough to undertake to determine such matters. Kindly revise, and return.

How about your map? Captain Verrill was expecting it when I left him.

Joshua L. Chamberlain[25]

>—+◆>—O—<◆+—<

Brunswick, Jan. 24, 1897

General C. W. Tilden:—

Hallowell

My dear General:

I have got the list of men at Gettysburg into the best state possible under existing conditions. I now submit it to you for your careful eye before we put it into the hands of the printers.

Major Small has got his final revision of the names entitled to go in. I agree with you that those on detached service not known to be elsewhere should be treated as in their proper place of duty. You will find them on the list. Also the sick, after July 3rd, even if we do not feel sure they were in or at the battle, and possibly some who did not wish to exert themselves to get there; but there were few such in your regiment, or in any Maine regiment; and I would rather take the chance of putting in some men who were not in the battle than the chance of leaving off a single man who was there. You could hardly believe how much pains and solid labor Major Small and I have put into this list business. I combined all that Major Small had done with what Lieut. Wiggin had prepared, and then went over the whole work of both, and over all other possible sources of information, as I wished the list accurate as possible.[26]

>—+◆>—O—<◆+—<

Brunswick, April 16th, 1897

Dear Major Small:

You will rejoice with me when I inform you that after truly incredible labor I have succeeded in consolidating the paper made up from your History and that presented by Lieut. Wiggin, so as to get them both within the limit required by the Executive Committee of the Gettysburg Commission, and have forwarded them all complete to Gen. Hamlin at Bangor. I had to take this work with me on the road to Washington and set the type-writers at it by dictation wherever I could catch the time, place and them.

The proofs will, I suppose, come to you, and to General Tilden, and you can criticize and correct as you may feel inclined.

I have done my last best, and am only ashamed of my own high-wrought, but entirely true remarks before your brave and loved survivors, where my affection may have betrayed itself.

Well, God made me so; I can't help it.

With no little of it to you and yours,

> I am ever, faithfully yours,
> Joshua L. Chamberlain[27]

The "remarks" referred to near the close of the letter are found in *Maine at Gettysburg* in the section devoted to the 16th Maine, as Address of General Chamberlain, and were his response to the toast "Gettysburg" at a banquet in honor of the 16th Maine and the 5th Maine Battery at the city of Gardiner. When he mentioned the flag, which the men of the 16th carried from the field torn up in bits and secreted in their clothing, it is reported that "the long repressed feelings of the hearers broke into wildest demonstration, in the midst of which a member of the regiment arose and took from his breast pocket a star of the old flag, at which the assembly lost all control of itself."[28]

CHAPTER THIRTEEN

"You've Done Enough at Gettysburg"

The war with Spain in 1898 and our nation's acquisitions overseas as an aftermath excited great controversy in America. Thomas Brackett Reed resigned from Congress in protest against what he considered to be unconstitutional and rampant imperialism. Theodore Roosevelt thought it was a bully little war, just the thing to toughen up the military muscles of a nation that was going soft, and that the territorial expansion would mean new markets, increased employment, the advance of civilization into haunts of barbarism, and other benefits.

Joshua Chamberlain, for all his scholarly background and quiet demeanor, was a Theodore Roosevelt kind of man. If Chamberlain had had his way, he would have been in Cuba for the war. On April 22, 1898, he wrote to the secretary of war offering his military service.[1] On the same day he wrote to one of Maine's senators in Washington outlining a plan for using New England troops.[2] The recommended force would consist of one regiment each from Maine, New Hampshire, and Vermont; two regiments from Connecticut; and three from Massachusetts, and he would be glad to assume command of it. His wound, he said, was better than it had been for years, and he could not but think that his day was not over for service to his country. Joshua Chamberlain was then nearly seventy years of age. On April 30 the secretary of war wrote thanking him for his patriotic letter and promising that he would keep it on file in case an opportunity arose.

Chamberlain was, no doubt, highly chagrined by this reply—also by the fact that his onetime opponent, William C. Oates, who commanded the 15th Alabama at Little Round Top and who was now a prominent politician in the South—was accepted for service as a brigadier general at the age of sixty-four. So was the considerably younger Adelbert Ames, who had been Chamberlain's commander in the 20th Maine.

By then Ames, who had married well, was a wealthy and influential man and a chum of John D. Rockefeller. Considering his own financial condition, Chamberlain would have chafed even more at Ames's being in the war if he had read the *New York Herald* of July 22, 1898, which reported that Blanche Butler Ames was to charter the ninety-six-foot yacht *America* and sail it to Cuba well provisioned with a crew of twelve and anchor it where her husband would have it for rest and recreation between battles. In August of that year General Ames wrote a letter to a veteran of the 20th Maine expressing his regret that he could not attend that year's reunion of the regiment and asking to be remembered to his old friend Joshua Chamberlain.[3] Ames told the veteran that although thirty-five years separated his two commissions—one from Lincoln and the other from McKinley—he felt like a youth again when he reached San Juan Hill and heard the bullets and shells whizzing past. It is to be hoped that Chamberlain never saw that letter.

As for overseas dominions, Chamberlain's attitude toward these can be determined from his seeking, in 1898, an appointment to become governor of the Philippines. A merciful Providence denied him this appointment. The Filipinos had been fighting the Spanish for their independence and they went right on fighting the Americans. This bloody guerrilla war in the jungles and hamlets of the Philippines, rife with atrocities, a foretaste of the Vietnam War, lasted well into 1902, and before it was over more Americans had lost their lives than were killed in the war with Spain. It was not the sort of war that Chamberlain would have known anything about. He was spared a nasty experience.

In late 1899 Joshua Chamberlain and his friends conducted an intensive campaign aimed at getting him appointed collector of customs in the port of Portland. At the time this was one of the busiest ports in the country, and the collectorship, in terms of prestige and salary, was one of the biggest plums on the federal fruit tree. Backing Chamberlain in this effort was a strong group; typical of its members were a wealthy industrialist, a justice of the Maine Supreme Court, the chairman of the Republican county committee, a judge of probate, and the customs collector at another Maine port. Prominent attorneys and politicians brought influence to bear. Hundreds of Maine citizens signed petitions. A snowfall of letters descended upon President McKinley and Maine's senators and representatives in Washington— all urging the appointment of the honored old general.

Chamberlain's advocates soon learned that one of the chief objectors to his appointment was Sen. William P. Frye, with whom he had exchanged verbal shots over the hanging of Clifton Harris when Chamberlain was governor of Maine and Frye was the state's attorney general. In an attempt to soften the senator, the supreme court justice wrote to Frye referring to the Harris case and asking him to forget former differences because Chamberlain was old, ill, and poor—and his wife was totally blind. Ellis Spear wrote to Congressman Amos Allen calling attention to Chamberlain's distinguished service in the war, the severity of his wound, and the distress that poverty would bring to a man of his pride and sensitivity. Chamberlain's financial picture was not quite as dark as his friends painted it. He owned a considerable amount of real estate, a ten-ton schooner, and some good investments; but his business failures undoubtedly had left him "cash poor," and without added income he would soon have to start selling off these properties.[4]

But in spite of such letters and support, reports from Washington continued to indicate that Chamberlain had no chance to become collector. Amos Allen, the representative in Congress from the district of Maine that included Portland—thus a key actor in the drama—was favorably disposed toward Chamberlain (he was a Bowdoin man, class of 1860, which may have helped), but he was caught up in a predicament. He knew Chamberlain could not be appointed collector. There was a secondary position in the Customs House—a good job—that of surveyor, and he would have liked Chamberlain to have that. But the powers to whom he was beholden had promised the surveyorship to Charles M. Moses, who was then the appraiser in the Customs House. It occurred to Allen, or to somebody, that if Chamberlain could be persuaded to accept the surveyor's slot and throw his support to Moses for the collectorship, the whole problem would be solved. "This matter," Allen wrote," has been an awful trial to me."[5]

Chamberlain's supporters, including his physician, Dr. Abner O. Shaw, urged him to go along with this little chess play. Shaw was not only one of Portland's most eminent physicians, he was also a shrewd and active player in southern Maine politics. When he died in 1934 at the age of ninety-six, one of the life accomplishments noted in his obituaries was that he had been a prime mover in getting his friend Thomas Brackett Reed into Congress. But his advice to take the surveyor's job may have been more medical than political, considering Chamberlain's shaky health. He pointed out that the duties were easier than those of the collector, the salary ($4,500) was good, and he would not have to do the political work expected of the collector. Chamberlain wrote to Allen on Christmas Day, 1899, approving

the deal and saying that his friends were well pleased with it. (He avoided saying that *he* was pleased.) In February 1900 Allen wrote to Chamberlain telling him that he was recommending him for surveyor and that he would enjoy the job—it would give him leisure time and a comfortable income.[6] In March Chamberlain was officially notified of his appointment.

The position of surveyor was not quite as cushioned with comfort and leisure as Congressman Allen and others had said it was in coaxing Chamberlain to accept it. The first ten words of the customs regulations job description told the story: "The Surveyor is the outdoor executive officer of the port. . . ." The surveyor had to be out in the weather much of the time, and the waterfront on a windy winter day was not the ideal place for a man in his seventies. The regulations went on to describe his duties. He "supervises the force of inspectors, weighers, measurers, gaugers, and laborers. He takes charge of all vessels arriving from foreign ports and reports their names and character to the collector. He supervises the discharge of their cargoes and the lading of merchandise exported or transported in bond, or exported for the benefit of drawback. He ascertains and reports the quantity and proof of all imported spirits and of all spirits exported in bond. He has charge of the admeasurement of vessels for registry and for the adjustment of the tonnage tax."[7]

When the old surveyor was indoors in his office he found the Portland Customs House a comfortable, dignified, and pleasant place to work. The gray stone building (still the Customs House in 1998) is of Italianate style with a granite exterior and marble halls within. The central chamber, with its very high ceiling, its multicolored marble-faced walls and counters, gold leaf decorations, floors of alternating squares of red slate and white marble, and a high-standing mahogany clock in the center, resembles the interior of an old London bank.

In many ways it was an ideal position for his declining years—a safe harbor after a hard voyage. But pride was involved. The collectorship had previously been a job awarded to former governors, senators, and the like. That Joshua Chamberlain had not been awarded this post could be taken as an indication of how far his political worth had fallen. To his close friends he expressed a great deal of bitterness. The collectorship would have been a position of power and prominence representing an active governmental role. The surveyorship, he wrote to Gen. John T. Richards, "has nothing of this character or history about it. It is essentially an obscure office, tending to keep one out of notice, as well as out of responsibility."[8] A good job, yes, he was saying—but not if you have been a major general, a state governor, a college president; then it was demeaning.

After he had been on duty a few months he took a leave of absence and went on a trip to Italy. Although he almost died overseas when his wound became infected, it was one of the great experiences of his life—a happy highlight among the dark vicissitudes of his later years. Upon his return he was interviewed by reporters from a couple of Portland newspapers who were diligent in reporting his impressions of the journey.[9] He left New York in early November on the steamship *Columbia* of the Hamburg-American line. The first stop was Gibraltar. "The soldiers there," Chamberlain said, "made a fine appearance. In fact, I watched for some time a battalion of English soldiers and must say it was the finest I ever saw." The ship arrived at Naples one morning before dawn and anchored in the bay. "A heavy storm sprang up and the lightning was terrific. To complete the awful grandeur of the scene Vesuvius began to throw up its fires lighting up the scenery. . . ." The ship went on to Genoa where, after a few days' visit, Chamberlain and a group arranged a trip back to Naples by land. Then to Rome and a nearly disastrous spell of illness, caused, he wrote, by "a state of weather which had been unknown in Rome for 100 years—bitterly cold and rainy. The insufficient means of warming the houses made the cold and dampness almost intolerable. The result was I took a severe cold which caused inflammation of my wound and I became very ill."

Chamberlain wrote to Collector of Customs Moses on December 1, "The case was critical . . . and my friends thought it necessary to remove me as soon as possible to the better conditions of Egypt. Of course I am absolutely prostrated, but everything is being done for me." The friends included Dana Estes, Maine native and a prominent Boston publisher. Estes and his sister accompanied and cared for Chamberlain on a trying journey to Egypt, by a Dutch–East African liner through the Suez canal to Ismailia, then by train to Cairo.

Once in Egypt Chamberlain recovered very rapidly and was up and off again. He told one of the Portland reporters, "Early in January I made the trip up the Nile by steamer to the first cataracts, landing at and visiting all the pyramids, monuments, tombs and temples on both sides of the river." He made one eight-hour side trip riding on a donkey. "I saw the famous quarry from which the granite for all the obelisks, even the one in Portland and the one in Central Park, New York, was taken. On the Nile hundreds of men were working on the most marvelous piece of engineering I ever saw. It was the dam across the river, one mile and a half wide. . . . This dam will double the agricultural area of Egypt."

Chamberlain saw improvements blossoming everywhere—in industry, agriculture, education, living standards. His deep and lifelong interest in education found much to admire; "almost a revolution," he thought, in methods and instruction. "I visited all of the institutions, from the great university at Cairo, where there are thousands and thousands of students from all over the Mohammedan world, and which is the oldest institution in the world, through government schools and the very remarkable schools of the American mission, down to the primary schools. Their methods of instruction really give us something to learn as to making knowledge available and greater."

These advances in Egypt, Chamberlain concluded, were all due to English management and influence. This represented a distinct turnabout from his attitude toward England immediately following the Civil War, which was decidedly anti-British. Some of this animosity, no doubt, stemmed from the fact that in the War of 1812 the British had sailed up the Penobscot River and burned his grandfather's shipyard. When he was governor of Maine, in 1867, he had warned against the consolidation of the provinces to the north into modern Canada, seeing it as a threat to United States security. Speaking to the Maine legislature, he had likened it to the French empire in Mexico and condemned it as part of a conspiracy to "environ us with Monarchies." By now fear of all such dangers would be anachronistic; British colonialism looked fine to him.

Chamberlain left Egypt on February 7, 1901, arrived in New York on February 26, and left there at once for Portland on the steamer *Horatio Hall*. "Since my return," he told a reporter in a March interview, "my health has been fairly good. The trip abroad was of great benefit to me not only physically but also mentally. The new scenes and ideas one gets across the Atlantic freshen him up wonderfully and he returns to his post of duty with renewed zest and vigor."

Originally commissioned as surveyor of the port by the administration of President McKinley, Chamberlain was later appointed by those of Roosevelt and Taft. He grew fond of his associates in the Customs House, and they of him. He did not treat the job as a sinecure, and he worked at it long past the time when most men were able to retire. Even in his unimposing position a hero's mantle clung to him. The *Portland Daily Press* had this to say of him on July 2, 1912, the forty-ninth anniversary of the battle at Little Round Top:

> Gen. Chamberlain is now serving his 4th term. For all of his 84 years there is hardly a day when he is not in his office as surveyor. Regularly he makes his examination of the men in his care. He attends to his duty at all times and takes the greatest pleasure in doing so.
>
> Of all the men at the custom house there is none more beloved than Gen. Chamberlain. When he leaves his office for the big main room, he is generally surrounded by the clerks who always have a word of greeting for him.
>
> On the coldest days last winter the surveyor was to be seen around the Grand Trunk docks when the ocean steamships came in. Closely muffled up, attended by his friends, he was always a conspicuous and interesting figure. It was not unusual for officers on the ship to inquire as to the distinguished man's identity and when they learned who Gen. Chamberlain was, they touched their hats to the famous veteran.

Chamberlain was always in demand as a speaker, and he was still accepting some of these invitations. He found himself in distinguished company when the town of York, Maine, was observing its 250th anniversary. On August 5, 1902, he spoke on York common from a platform that was loaded with celebrities, including Maine's great writer, Sarah Orne Jewett, editor and novelist William Dean Howells, humorist Mark Twain, and Thomas Brackett Reed, who had successfully combined humor with politics. Mark Twain was spending part of that summer in a rented cottage near the summer home of his friend William Dean Howells, and someone had roped him into the celebration—probably Reed, who was also a close friend of Twain.

Chamberlain was the leadoff speaker, and he gave a graceful, pleasing talk on the value of traditions, the bright virtues of Yorkian ancestors, worthy to be emulated, and so on. When Thomas Reed spoke, he noted his ancestors came from York, but he had had hard work to discover that they ever existed, and they certainly held no positions of great emolument, judging from his own financial condition when *he* arrived. Mark Twain gave one his typical rambles, full of absurdities and personal clowning. Speaking of the content of the talks that had preceded him, he said that he was a little deaf but not so much as to miss hearing the many compliments, all of which, he was sure, had referred to him. For example, when Chamberlain had mentioned, "the intellectually brilliant,"[10] Twain had noticed that the former governor had been looking straight at him.

In contrast, Chamberlain's talk had been fairly serious. Did he have a sense of humor? Most of his writing that remains to us is gracious, engaging, interesting but usually quite serious. He thinks up nothing absurd, nothing conforming to what Immanuel Kant once defined as the cause of laughter: "The sudden transformation of a tense expectation into nothing." Yet there are light and playful touches in some of his correspondence with Fanny in their days of courtship. And sometimes his expressions had a sardonic twist, such as that having to do with his wounding at Petersburg, where his blood soaked the ground. "I am not of Virginia blood; she is of mine."[11] Or when he said, in his dissection of Attorney General Frye's argument for Harris, that a plea based on "previous bad conduct" was "a novelty in jurisprudence."

And certainly if not a great originator of humor, Chamberlain could use it, as when, in speaking to the Chamberlain Association of America in Boston on September 8, 1898, he spoke thus of the theory of evolution. "I would say of this introduction of new relations [he was speaking of the apes], as Lincoln said to the book agent, 'For people who like that kind of book, that is just the kind of book they would like.'" Among the users of this great line have been not only Abraham Lincoln, but also Artemus Ward, Max Beerbohm, and possibly an unidentified ancient Greek. A British writer, Hilary Corke, called it "The world's best book review." Joshua Chamberlain's use of the line entitles him, at least, to consideration as an appreciator, if not an originator, of good humor.

Three weeks after speaking at the anniversary in York, Chamberlain met Theodore Roosevelt, who was then the nation's president. Roosevelt made a speech in Portland, and Chamberlain, with other dignitaries, sat with him on the platform. At one point in the speech Roosevelt turned to him on the platform and said, "I was greeted here not only by your Mayor, not only by other men standing high, but by you, General, to whom it was given at the supreme moment of the war to win the supreme reward of a soldier . . . and may we keep ourselves from envying him because to him fell the supreme good fortune of winning the medal of honor for mighty deeds done in the mightiest battle that the nineteenth century saw, Gettysburg"—a verbal salute that was followed by loud applause.[12]

It was a great day in Portland, with flags, bunting, and other displays all along the streets that Roosevelt toured. Over the portico of the West End Hotel a lifesize dummy of a horse, borrowed from a local harness shop, was placed with a hotel porter dressed in a khaki uniform sitting astride it. When the presidential party passed, this "roof rider" and Rough Rider Roosevelt waved to each other vigorously. Afterward the citizens of Portland, if they had thought of it, could have congratulated themselves on seeing another unique spectacle; the conductors of two of the most famous charges in American history—Roosevelt's up San Juan Hill, Chamberlain's down Little Round Top—sitting together on the same speaker's platform. If George E. Pickett had been there, the roster would have been complete.

After he became surveyor of the port, Chamberlain established a residence in the New Falmouth, one of Portland's finest hotels, while retaining his home in Brunswick. Legislator and historian Herbert Adams has studied Portland city directories and other records bearing upon Chamberlain. His notes indicate that this hotel was located on Middle Street, a convenient walk from Commercial Street, where the Customs House is situated, near the waterfront. The New Falmouth was host to many famous public figures including Ulysses S. Grant, Theodore Roosevelt, and in 1960 Richard Nixon, being demolished for "urban renewal" shortly after Nixon's stay. The site, Adams says for the benefit of Chamberlain pilgrims, is now a bank plaza on Middle Street across the street from the bronze statue, *The Maine Lobsterman.*

As her blindness progressed, Fanny had become increasingly depressed and reclusive. She did not accompany Chamberlain on his trip to Italy and Egypt. Chamberlain wrote from his office or hotel offering "a pleasant change by bringing you to Portland."[13] But she did not join him in his quarters there. In the summer of 1905 she fell and broke her hip. Fanny died on October 18 of that year and was buried in Brunswick's Pine Grove Cemetery. On the back of her gravestone the world "Unveiled" is incised.

During this period Chamberlain continued to suffer from intermittent illnesses. Col. Kenneth McAllister, M.D., of the Brooke Army Medical Center and consultant in infectious diseases to the U.S. Army surgeon general has studied Chamberlain's medical history and believes that these illnesses were caused by infections of the wound-damaged pelvic bones, urinary tract infections, and quite possibly, tuberculosis, the family disease (Joshua's brothers Horace, John, and Tom all died of it.)

In the autumn of 1909, although retaining the home in Brunswick, Chamberlain sought to make life a little easier for himself by purchasing a home in Portland at 211 Ocean Avenue, soon afterward redesignated 499, the street number it bears today. Ocean Avenue lies generally north of downtown Portland, separated from it by Back Cove. In 1909 it ran through a pleasant suburban area. Chamberlain could look from his upper windows at the city across green fields and the sparkling water of the cove. The house was near a trolley line that offered convenient transportation to either Brunswick or downtown Portland.

Wyllys lived with him in the house on Ocean Avenue, and they probably rode the trolley together to work: Chamberlain to the Customs House, Wyllys—according to the research reports of Herbert Adams—to a building not far away at 123 Commercial Street, where he operated the Chamberlain Electric Company, which apparently lasted only two or three years. City directories list him as an electrician. He was undoubtedly still working on inventions; Chamberlain had written several years previously that he refused to do anything else.

It may have been from the house on Ocean Avenue that Chamberlain sent a note to Robert Peary on October 5, 1909, because he said he was disabled by old war wounds and could not greet Peary on his visit to Portland Harbor following his triumphant return from the North Pole. He wrote: "I regret much not to be able to avail myself of the opportunity given by the visit of our Boarding Officer's launch this morning to pay my respects to you in person but have to send my deputy instead who appreciates the privilege."[14] Peary—Bowdoin class of 1877—was one of the products of the short-lived engineering course that Chamberlain had introduced at the college.

Old boys from his past of another variety—Civil War veterans—represented a constant burden for Chamberlain all through his postwar years. They wrote to him seeking his help with pension claims, medical treatment, missing records—every sort of personal problem. He became a veterans' father figure, at the cost of thousands of hours of his time.

The heaviest of these burdens in service of the veterans fell upon Chamberlain when he was eighty-four and in very poor health, still nursing damages of his severe wound from Petersburg and still being cared for by Dr. Abner O. Shaw.

The occasion was the fiftieth anniversary of the battle of Gettysburg and a reunion celebrating that event initiated by the commonwealth of Pennsylvania and the federal government. These two offered to provide quarters, subsistence, and medical care for all honorably discharged veterans of the Civil War who could get to Gettysburg, and this included former rebel soldiers of the southern states. The state governments made corresponding offers. Maine's offer was a bit more restrictive; the state would provide free transportation to and from Gettysburg, and free subsistence and medical attention during the journey, for *only* those veterans who had actually been on the field at the time of the battle, July 1, 2, and 3, 1863.

All well and good. But making the arrangements in Maine was a bigger job than anyone had anticipated. There was the planning of transportation for five or six hundred veterans and for their living quarters in a section of a great tent city that would be set up at Gettysburg.[15] Then there was the problem of reaching the veterans. Where were they? How were they to be notified? Also, how would the sheep be separated from the goats? There surely would be some applicants for the free trip who had never been within a hundred miles of Gettysburg, and a few who had not even been in the war.

To handle details on a national basis, a Battle of Gettysburg Commission was set up with offices in Gettysburg and Harrisburg, Pennsylvania. And the state of Maine, for its representative on this commission, appointed its foremost veteran, Gen. Joshua L. Chamberlain. In many ways the appointment was ill considered. Chamberlain did not have sufficient secretarial help to handle such a big job. In partial awareness of this situation, Elliott T. Dill, the adjutant general of Maine, wrote to him:

December 16, 1912

Dear General Chamberlain:

I am in receipt of a letter from Governor-elect Haines enclosing copy of his letter to you relative to detail work in connection with the Gettysburg celebration.

I beg to assure you that anything which this office can do to relieve your Commission of detail work in connection with the Gettysburg Semi-Centennial will be most cheerfully performed. You will understand that the office will not venture to offer suggestions but will be ready at all times to co-operate to the greatest possible extent.

I most heartily concur in the Governor's suggestion that "You have done quite enough at Gettysburg already" and it will be a pleasant recollection to me as a younger man to know that I have assisted you in any way.

Sincerely yours,
Elliott T. Dill
The Adjutant General[16]

Chamberlain replied in a letter that he typed himself, with only a few errors.

> United States Customs Service
> Port of Portland, Maine
> December 17th, 1912

General Elliott T. Dill:—

Dear General:

I thank you for your kindly letter. I have no doubt of your willingness and ability to do everything possible to make things and people go right in the matter of the Gettysburg Fifty Year celebration. But it will be impossible to prevent hundreds of old soldiers writing to me to give them some special attention. The mere answering of these letters would be beyond my power. And I need my time and strength for other imperative duties. Even without this Gettysburg business, my old-soldier applications for assistance in some way or another gave me more than I could carry alone in the way of correspondence. Think of what must be done in the way of keeping account of each and all the men who are finally warranted as entitled and able to go to Gettysburg! And the thousand details connected with tickets, and journeying that must be attended to in some office here at home!

I will not weary you with more of this; but will enclose a letter just received from the Massachusetts Commission.

I have only this old typewriter to work with, and my own unpracticed hands, this morning. Please excuse informalities.

> Yours as ever,
> Joshua L. Chamberlain[17]

During the winter of 1912–13 the adjutant general's office relieved Chamberlain of most of the detail work, but since his name remained on the official list, papers from the national commission kept coming to him and it seemed impossible for him to disengage completely. In April he suggested that he resign and that the governor appoint the adjutant general as the Maine commissioner. The governor would not hear of it. Instead, he appointed a friend of Chamberlain, Col. Frederic E. Boothby of Portland, to work with him as a sort of co-commissioner and to relieve him further of administrative duties.

Still Chamberlain could not let go. He considered the position more than honorary; it was a responsibility, he thought, and he participated actively. In one area—that of who was eligible for the free transportation to Gettysburg and who was not—he intervened quite significantly. By April, after placing notices in the newspapers and corresponding with GAR posts and regimental associations, the adjutant general's office had received more than five hundred applications from men who claimed to have been in the battle. Were the claims correct? The people in the Maine adjutant general's office, all of them considerably younger and less experienced than Chamberlain, thought they had taken care of this matter. All they had to do, they thought, was to look in the book entitled *Maine at Gettysburg* published by a state commission in 1898 and listing, supposedly, all the Maine men who had participated in the battle according to the records. Chamberlain, of course, had been through all the pitfalls of preparing that book, and he made some amendments. For example, a Joseph Tyler had been listed in the book as being "on special duty or service" at the time of the battle, which left in doubt the question of whether he was on the field or not. Joe Tyler was the regimental bugler; at 20th Maine reunions he brought tears to the eyes of the veterans by blowing the old calls. Chamberlain wrote the adjutant general in his behalf: "He was the Principal Musician of my old regiment, the 20th Maine, and was a most competent and faithful man in every line of duty. He was prominent in the engagement on Round Top at Gettysburg."[18]

He also intervened in a matter of more general importance. The principal record attesting to a man's presence or absence at Gettysburg was the monthly return of the regiment for June 30, 1863, the day before the battle began. Chamberlain wrote a letter explaining the inadequacies of this record.

499 Ocean Avenue, Portland, April 25th, 1913

General Elliott [Dill]

The Adjutant General

Augusta, Maine

Dear General:—

I have made diligent search among my books and papers for evidence in regard to the presence in the battle of Gettysburg, of Hosea B. Small, of Newport, and W. C. Keegan, of Lewiston. I am entirely unable to certify as to the fact in either case. I will, however, make a statement of fact possibly bearing on the matter concerning participation in that battle by members of the 20th Regiment, Maine Volunteers.

We had very hard marching two or three days before that battle, and during this time quite a number of men became exhausted
or disabled. To such I gave permission to "fall out" of the column
of march, with instructions to overtake us as soon as they were
able, by following the wagon trains by night, or in any other way
they could. Several of these men, I should say, most of them—did
come up on the morning of July 2nd, at Gettysburg, and took their
places in the ranks, and did their best, although by no means in perfect condition for duty. These men deserve special consideration,
and I hold them in such, whoever and wherever they may now be.

This gives a good general ground for the state of the case in
these instances. It would account for their being reported "absent
with leave" or not appearing for roll-call, on June 30th. They are
supposed to be truthful men, and I should give weight to their
statements—especially if these tallied with my notes and clear
recollections as to general conditions. If they were in the battle
under such circumstances, it would be a great wrong to them to
bar them out of the privileges now offered to veterans of Gettysburg. While I cannot vouch for the truth of their claim, I should
vote for it in a court of inquiry.

Very truly yours,
Joshua L. Chamberlain[19]

Probably as a result of this letter, the adjutant general's office did make an
effort to evaluate veterans' claims going beyond the official records.

On May 15 and 16, 1913, an important meeting of the national commission at Gettysburg was scheduled, and Chamberlain decided that he
should go. On April 29 he wrote the adjutant general, "I have promised to
be present at the meeting May 15th, although I am suffering something of a
pull-down just now. I shall take my old regimental surgeon, Dr. A. O.
Shaw, of Portland with me for attendant and guardian. He was not with the
regiment at Gettysburg; but I shall take him as my guest, and at my own
private charge. I really do not dare to go without him."[20]

He returned from Gettysburg on May 20, worn-out, and was immediately sent to bed by Dr. Shaw, who had had to attend him almost constantly
during the trip. But he was up the next day, pecking away at his typewriter
and turning out a three-page, single-spaced report on his activities on the
old battlefield. One thing Chamberlain had been concerned about was the
effect of the long journey on aged veterans. As planned, the Maine delega-

tion would leave Portland on a special train at 7 P.M. on Saturday, June 28. There would be Pullman accommodations, with two men in each lower berth, one in each upper. The train would go to Grand Central Station in New York. They would then board omnibuses and ride down to Pennsylvania Station. The train from there would take them to Gettysburg, arriving on the evening of Sunday, June 29. They would have only box lunches for food on the way—and it would be very hot at this time of year. In part of his report Chamberlain wrote:

> Hospital tents will be erected in various convenient portions of the field These are part of the general provision. But considering the years that have passed since the youthful services of our veterans, and the consequent diminution of physical energies, the hard journey from Maine to Gettysburg, and the privations of camp life in the extreme heat of early July, I regard it as highly probable that a considerable number of our veterans will require medical and perhaps hospital treatment in the course of their visit; and I have asked permission to make use of two of our tents for hospital uses if needed. I have no doubt this will be granted, and that the surgeons accompanying our State veterans will find favorable conditions in camp for exercising their care.[21]

Other accomplishments: When he found that all the hotel rooms in town were reserved, Chamberlain obtained quarters for Maine's governor and his staff at Pennsylvania College (today Gettysburg College); he recommended routing procedures that would prevent a traffic jam with trains being held for miles and hours away from the camp; and he arranged for a location of the Maine section that would place its veterans close to the areas where most of them fought and close to the Great Tent. This tent, he reported, would seat more than ten thousand people and was arranged so it could be divided into numerous separate compartments where regimental and other unit reunions could be held—and those people in Maine who wanted to hold reunions had better send their requests right away to a person and address he gave. The Great Tent was also where the main exercises would be held, including a talk by President Wilson.

So Chamberlain was able to make these and several other contributions to the reunion, but when the great days came, he was not there. Dr. Shaw absolutely vetoed the idea of another trip to Gettysburg—the strain and fatigue would be too much. On July 21 Chamberlain wrote to Colonel Boothby expressing his pleasure at hearing that the affair had been such a success. His comment: "The State of Maine made as worthy an appearance *this* July as it did fifty years ago. We are all proud to belong to her."[22]

There is little doubt that the effects of Chamberlain's May trip to Gettysburg hastened the onset of his final illness, which began in November 1913 and ended with his death on February 24, 1914, at his home in Portland. Quickly thereafter the name of Joshua Chamberlain slipped into shadow. Overwhelmed by World War I, the Great Depression, and World War II, Americans completely forgot him.

One of the last persons to see Chamberlain alive was Francis M. O'Brien, then a small boy whose family lived in the neighborhood. He and some other children were playing in the snow in front of the O'Brien home when a man came along—evidently in a hurry—a man who asked Francis to deliver an envelope to General Chamberlain. Francis took the envelope and went to the Chamberlain house, where, he remembered, a lady came to the door and invited him in. He explained that he had a letter for General Chamberlain. She suggested that Francis deliver it himself and conducted him into a room where he saw—lying in bed and propped up by pillows—an old man with white hair and a sweeping white mustache. Francis approached the bed and handed over the envelope. Chamberlain glanced at it, looked at him and said to the woman, "Now there's a good boy. Give him a nickel."[23]

Francis O'Brien went on through life to endear himself among thousands of book lovers as Maine's preeminent antiquarian bookdealer and bibliophile. Four years before his death on May 23, 1994, Bowdoin College gave him an honorary doctor of letters degree. The citation said in part that he had "rubbed shoulders with both Joshua Chamberlain and James Joyce." In the previous three decades the general had risen from the ashes of oblivion to be ranked with the famous names of literature and history.

CHAPTER FOURTEEN

Fame Returns

In the early 1920s the Maine commissioner of schools thought it would be a good idea if the state had a book that acquainted children with the famous people Maine had produced. Selected by the Maine Writers Research Club, the authors of this book included Percival P. Baxter, a governor of Maine and the donor of Baxter State Park; Laura E. Richards, popular author of the day; Kate Douglas Wiggin, another well-known Maine writer; and other persons of intelligence and talent. The book they produced was entitled *Just Maine Folks*. Published in 1924, it told the stories of about fifty women and men who had been prominent in the life of Maine and the nation. It will hardly be believed today that Chamberlain was not among them.

Within ten years of his death the name of Joshua Chamberlain had dropped completely out of sight. It was as though the events of those years, principally World War I, had blotted him out. Few people came to visit his grave in Brunswick's Pine Grove Cemetery. The site was disturbed only by the sound of traffic passing on the Bath Road and the sighing of wind in the overhanging branches of the pines. This shroud of silence and forgetfulness hung over him for another two decades.

Then, slowly at first but with increasing momentum, a remarkable restoration of his name and fame took place. Involved in the Chamberlain resurrection was a series of events, one building upon another, often in a way so serendipitous as to create wonder whether or not some supernatural influence might be at work.

The Chamberlain renaissance was, one might almost think, planned by Chamberlain himself. He did many things that ensured his survival on the pages of history and literature, the most important of which was his employment of the written word, that foremost agent of survival. It is perhaps not too much to assert that if a person or an event is not written about, after the passing of a generation or two, that person never lived; that event never happened. A familiar example is seen in the old photographs nearly everyone has around the house showing people whose identities have completely vanished because no one ever wrote names on the backs of the pictures. The tide that sweeps us toward oblivion is very powerful. In the words of Ecclesiastes, "There is no remembrance of former things, nor will there be any remembrance of later things yet to happen among those who come after."[1]

Yet Joshua Chamberlain was a man who would not be swept away. The written word preserved him. Some of these words originated in speeches and were lost because they were not written down. But many speeches and interviews were recorded by reporters and many were preserved by Chamberlain in manuscripts that he saved. Chamberlain also wrote many articles, and his best writing appeared in an outstanding book, *The Passing of the Armies,* published in 1915, after his death, by G. P. Putnam's Sons. It is an account of the twelve days of war preceding Appomattox and is unique in its genre; there is no other book by a combat participant who had the cultural background and literary skill to describe what he experienced so movingly and so well (if the reader can overlook a few passages of overcolored prose). There is a curious ethereal quality in this work—a sense of otherworldliness combined with realistic descriptions of this last campaign. It was destined to endure—with some fortuitous assistance provided by copyright law. Until the Copyright Act of 1976 became effective on January 1, 1978, the first term of copyright protection lasted twenty-eight years and in the twenty-eighth year, no sooner and no later, the copyright could be renewed for another twenty-eight-year term. If it was not renewed, protection of the work ceased.

Copyright on *The Passing of the Armies* should have been renewed in 1943, but by then the original holders of the right, Chamberlain's daughter and son, Grace and Wyllys, had died; and the grandchildren either forgot about it or saw no possibility of reviving a book so long out of print by a forgotten author. This failure to renew cast the book into the public domain, so that without charge or obligation any writer could use excerpts from it and any publisher could reprint it. This happened. Several writers have reproduced passages from the book; it has become known as a classic; and at least two publishers have issued reprint editions.

In this and other writings and recorded speaking, Chamberlain had built up a tremendous reservoir of information about himself, and this information had flowed on through time like a mountain stream that cannot be contained. If one historian failed to come across the stream and dip into it, another certainly would.

One instance of the volume of this information can be seen in the Maine *Adjutant General's Report,* volume I, 1864–65. After the war the adjutant general asked certain Maine officers to send him narratives of their service for use in preparing a series of individual military histories for this report. Chamberlain's letter in reply ran to about thirty-six hundred words and filled the equivalent of seven pages in the volume. This was by far the longest narrative except for that of Bvt. Maj. Gen. Charles H. Smith of Eastport; his covered nine pages. The history of Bvt. Maj. Gen. Adelbert Ames filled about a page.[2] The self-declared military achievements of many officers were such that they filled only half a page. There are now (1998) dozens of books and other publications dealing with Joshua Chamberlain. When they are read with careful attention to notes identifying sources—if these are given—it will be seen that most of the information originated with Chamberlain himself.

The first nationally read writer after 1915 to dip into the Chamberlain legend was Kenneth Roberts, the author of *Arundel* and other popular historical novels. In June 1938 his nonfiction book *Trending into Maine* appeared, and in it was a chapter entitled "Maine Stories I'd Like to Write." Among these stories were those of several Maine regiments, including the 20th Maine, and a few pages about that regiment were almost entirely about Joshua Chamberlain.[3]

Ten years later English historian Arnold J. Toynbee, in his *A Study of History,* called Maine "a relic of seventeenth century New England inhabited by woodmen and watermen and hunters."[4] The enraged Roberts wrote an article for *The Saturday Evening Post* entitled, "Don't Say That About Maine," which castigated Toynbee and called attention to Maine's contributions to civilization, including Joshua Chamberlain.

The next step in the Chamberlain revival, although it has been little recognized as such, was the publication of Bruce Catton's books. These included *A Stillness at Appomattox,* for which he received the Pulitzer prize in 1954. Obviously the title of his book was suggested by Chamberlain's description of the Confederate troops as they marched past his own to surrender—"an awed stillness rather and breath-holding, as if it were the passing of the dead!"[5] In Catton's works only minimum attention was paid to Joshua Chamberlain but they had an important effect in popularizing Civil War literature, and so prepared the way for Chamberlain's entrance upon the stage.

The Twentieth Maine: A Volunteer Regiment in the Civil War (1957) by John J. Pullen opened the next channel of information. In this book about the war as seen through the eyes of one regiment, Chamberlain was the leading character, and it is credited with bringing him to the general public's attention. As often occurred in the Chamberlain renaissance, supernatural aid seemed to attend its progress. It began in the early 1950s as a short story that was rejected by several magazines—fortunately—because had it been accepted there probably would have been no book. An outline was sent to J. B. Lippincott, where it "went in over the transom," meaning receipt of a manuscript that has not been solicited or presented by a literary agent. Such manuscripts landed in a "slush pile," which in a large publishing house could amount to hundreds or even thousands of manuscripts a year. The "slush pile" is typically trash; looking for a publishable manuscript in it is like looking for one in a dumpster. By some miracle *The Twentieth Maine* was picked out and published.

The book had good reviews and was one of the nonfiction nominees for the 1958 National Book Award, but it was far from being a best-seller; this edition alone would not have spread popular awareness of Joshua Chamberlain. The chance to do that came from *Reader's Digest Condensed Books,* which then had a subscription of more than two million and an even wider distribution, since these books were seen for years after publication selling for fifteen or twenty-five cents in yard and used-book sales. Proofs of *The Twentieth Maine* were sent to *Reader's Digest,* but the editor assigned to it for a trial condensation reported that the task was impossible, and that seemed to be the end of the line. But then another editor of great literary talent, who had read the proofs, Lucia Alzamora Reiss, asked if she might try her hand at it.[6] Her name must be listed among those who have furthered the fame of Joshua Chamberlain, for her try succeeded and *The Twentieth Maine* appeared in the condensed books in the winter of 1958.

In 1960 the first full-length biography of Chamberlain appeared, *Soul of the Lion* by Willard M. Wallace. It has already been mentioned that most of the information for Chamberlain literature came from Chamberlain himself. The history of this title provides an example. In the battle of Quaker Road on March 29, 1865, Chamberlain happened upon Gen. Horatio B. Sickel lying on the ground with a shattered limb. He sat down by the wounded officer and tried to provide what comfort he could. Sickel looked up at him and whispered, "General, you have the soul of the lion and the heart of the woman."[7] Unrestrained by modesty, Chamberlain passed the compliment on to posterity. It appears in his book *The Passing of the Armies,* and part of it went on from there to become the title for Wallace's biography.

In 1974 Chamberlain appeared as one of the principal characters in the Pulitzer prize–winning novel *The Killer Angels* by Michael Shaara. The novel served as the basis for the film *Gettysburg,* opening in theaters in 1993 and first appearing on television in 1994. In writing his novel, Shaara borrowed information liberally from *The Twentieth Maine* in scenes involving Chamberlain and this regiment.

Again the copyright law favored the advancement of the Chamberlain legend. Although *The Twentieth Maine* remains under copyright protection, this protection does not extend to the facts and figures in a work of nonfiction—not even if the nonfiction information has been revealed for the first time after long research. If it were otherwise, learning in many fields of knowledge wold be greatly retarded. (An opposite system prevails in the world of fiction. Borrowing material from a novel, which is purely a product of the author's imagination, can result in a lawsuit for copyright infringement.)

In 1992 Alice Trulock's book *In the Hands of Providence* added a great deal to the public's knowledge of Chamberlain. The research behind this book was extensive. Other books and articles about Chamberlain and collections of his writings have appeared, but the most powerful agents of his popularization, coming in the 1990s, have been the movie and television screens, augmented by videocassettes. And the theater has not neglected Joshua Chamberlain. In 1996 the musical *Chamberlain* played to packed houses in the Maine State Music Theatre in Brunswick.[8]

A lesson has been learned. While the printed word is necessary in the perpetuation of a historical figure, in immediate effectiveness it cannot compare with the dramatic or theatrical presentation. Following the film *Gettysburg,* based on the novel *The Killer Angels,* what can only be described as a nationwide explosion of interest in Joshua Chamberlain took place. And at Gettysburg itself, according to Supervisory Park Historian D. Scott Hartwig, except for Robert E. Lee, today the participant in the battle best known to visitors coming to the park is Joshua Chamberlain. Hartwig believes there are reasons for this. He comments:

> The Chamberlain of the novel and film was the citizen soldier that Americans can identify with—a man of noble virtues, highly educated yet modest, brave, honest, and sensitive. Chamberlain was also a winner, triumphing over seemingly great odds on the blood-soaked slopes of Little Round Top. As Gen. George S. Patton once said, "Americans love a winner." Americans flock to where Chamberlain stood at Gettysburg for all these reasons, and because they

know what he did. There are many heroes of Gettysburg who remain in obscurity, their great deeds undiscovered except by a handful of students and buffs, who know that in a battle of 165,000 people, there are many who perform above the call of duty. Chamberlain is also famous and popular with Americans because when we peer beneath the veneer of the man portrayed in historical fiction, we discover that the real Chamberlain was every inch as stalwart a fellow as we believed and hoped he would be.

When any figure is subjected to continuing fictional and theatrical treatment, which encourages and indeed requires a certain license, that figure begins to take on mythical qualities. Certainly that has been the case with Joshua Chamberlain. With his portrayal moving from nonfiction to fiction and to dramatic visual presentation, it was only natural that Chamberlain would become more and more a mythic figure. He invites an inverse comparison with John Wayne.

Wayne arose from being a figure of one dimension, in fact less than one dimension—an ephemeral image on a screen with no more substance than a shadow—to become, in effect, a real person, a hero to militant national leaders, and a recipient of a medal from Congress hailing him as a great American. Chamberlain, who actually performed heroic acts of the sort that Wayne accomplished only in an imaginary world, was to some extent transformed from a real person into a myth. In some respects he followed the Greek pattern of a hero—a person of exceptional gifts, struggling against powerful forces, suffering injury, descending into the underworld, rising again. To society this kind of figure has its value. Joseph Campbell, in his book *The Hero With a Thousand Faces,* writes, "It has always been the prime function of mythology and rite to supply the symbols that carry the human spirit forward, in counteraction to those other constant human fantasies that tend to tie it back."[9]

One evidence of the mythic charm that has attached itself to Chamberlain is seen from the fact that places important in his life have come to be regarded as shrines. At Gettysburg people place around the 20th Maine monument that stands on Little Round Top flowers, money, garlands, poems, and other tributes to his memory—as they do on his grave in Brunswick, Maine. Thousands visit his former home in the same town, now a museum. Here the register shows names and addresses from all over the country and the world. Chamberlain has sometimes been referred to as a cult hero, but this is a misnomer. The visitors are men, women, and children of all ages and cultural levels. They range from scholars busy preparing their footnotes to camera-packing tourists wearing T-shirts on which Chamberlain is pictured and his name is emblazoned. Chamberlain postcards, portrait-bearing clocks and wristwatches, pins, pens, night-lights, busts, banners, statuettes, and mementos of all kinds may be purchased. In 1997 a credit card bearing on its face a picture of Joshua Chamberlain leading the charge at Little Round Top was introduced; wags have remarked that this is a most appropriate illustration for a credit card. An excellent brew named Chamberlain Pale Ale was introduced in the early 1990s. Chamberlain might be described as the founder of an industry dedicated to the celebration of his fame—also as an inspiration of the arts. There is a profusion of paintings showing him in battle scenes, and limited editions of these paintings are being sold, some of them at very high prices. Among collectors, any piece of paper bearing Chamberlain's signature is a much-wanted item. A canceled check may go for $300 to $400, a letter for $1,000 to $2,000.

On February 24, 1996, an item seen in the *New London Day* aroused considerable interest. It was on the page on which memorial notices appear—the sort of notice that typically begins "in loving memory of. . . ." It read

In Memoriam

in Memory of

Joshua Lawrence Chamberlain

who died February 24, 1914

Major General V Corps

"The soul of a lion and

heart of a woman"

The idea of paying a newspaper to run such a notice eighty-two years after the death of its subject did not seem strange to David Rathbun, the retired shipyard executive who placed it.

CHAPTER FIFTEEN

Recall to Service

In 1982 at the U.S. Army Command and General Staff College at Fort
Leavenworth, Kansas, a lieutenant colonel of infantry, Boyd M. Harris,
was assigned to write a field manual on leadership. In studying past
leaders and battles Colonel Harris was impressed by the record of Joshua
Chamberlain, who—in his words—was "a major example of what a leader
must be, know and do."[1] After passing through the army review circuit
with approval and favorable comments the manual was officially published
in October, 1983, entitled *Field Manual (FM) 22-100: Military Leadership.*
The first chapter recounts the story of Chamberlain and the 20th Maine at
Little Round Top and incidents of Chamberlain's service throughout the
rest of the war follow. In several sections he is referred to as illustrating
actions and characteristics of an ideal military leader.

Sad to relate, Colonel Harris died of cancer eighteen days before his
field manual was published; therefore it has not been possible to question
him about his selection of this premier military model or to express surprise
at his elevation of Chamberlain to this status more than a century after his
brief military career had ended. Why had he not chosen Stonewall Jackson
or Robert E. Lee? Colonel Harris might have answered that they played in
the wrong league. But what about George S. Patton Jr., who, some would
say, was the greatest combat commander who ever lived?

It is a revealing exercise to compare Patton and Chamberlain using the
principles set forth in *FM 22-100* as standards. They were alike in many
respects, although different in appearance. For example, both understood the
importance of bearing, or physical behavior. According to Colonel Harris:

Illustration from the U.S. Army field manual Military Leadership.

"Bearing is shown by posture, overall appearance and manner of physical movement. Your bearing is an outward display to others of the state of your feelings, fears and overall inner confidence. Your bearing can either hurt the confidence of your soldiers or help inspire them."[2]

By all accounts, Chamberlain had this quality. Gen. Charles Griffin once said, "It is a magnificent sight to see Chamberlain in battle." He also said that Chamberlain seemed to be absolutely fearless and that amid the uproar of the fight his mind functioned as clearly and deliberately as it would have if he had been home in his study.[3] At the battle of Quaker Road (another bit of information passed on by Chamberlain himself) he was even cheered by the Confederates as he rode dashingly around, covered with blood from his and his horse's wounds, rallying his troops to resume an attack.

In his book *Stand Firm Ye Boys From Maine* Thomas Desjardin observed that Chamberlain's physical behavior or bearing had much to do with the 20th Maine's victory at Little Round Top. Even though Chamberlain had been ill for several days on the hot long march northward to Gettysburg, suffering from sunstroke and other maladies, he still managed to walk calmly among his men—demonstrating personal bravery and coolness in a way that strengthened their confidence.[4]

As for Patton, he was superb in projecting an inspiring presence. His obvious method was to be, himself, the very image of combativeness, enthusiasm, and courage and to enthrall the men under his command so that each of them, in some degree, would become the embodiment of these same martial virtues. One exercise of this technique was demonstrated through a remarkable speech. It is seen in the opening of the movie *Patton,* with the general, played by George C. Scott, standing in front of a giant American flag, apparently in an auditorium, speaking to troops who are about to enter combat for the first time. A veteran who heard Patton deliver this speech in person—a more robust version of it—gives us this description: "There was no flag in the background. The talk was delivered in the muddy square of a French town, on a gray winter day, with Patton standing on a platform made of two or three packing cases. He made a wonderfully impressive sight—a *big* man, tall, erect, wearing his polished helmet, his ivory-handled revolver and so on. He spoke in a high-pitched, very penetrating voice. His appearance and his words could never be forgotten."[5]

The same veteran remembered being present at a ceremony that took place when the Third Army met the Russians in Austria. A Russian general grabbed Patton and—much to his obvious disgust—kissed him on both cheeks. In so doing he knocked Patton's helmet off, exposing the general's snow-white hair. The image of manly vigor and warlike power that Patton projected (at the age of nearly sixty) was to some degree simply great showmanship, which was apparently one of the leadership tools that both he and Chamberlain made good use of.

Without stretching the imagination too far, it is possible to see Chamberlain standing on the same packing box platform. Of course his talk would have a different tone. According to the people who knew him best, if you met Patton over a dinner table, you would find him to be an erudite, cultured, perfect gentleman. But when he gave a talk to troops it was laced with profanity, obscenity, sacrilege, blasphemy—anything to make his words memorable to soldiers. Chamberlain, with his powers of rhetoric and oratory, would have achieved the same result; but he certainly would not have said, as Patton did—according to the veteran who heard his speech— that a rifle or a machine gun that is not being fired "is of about as much use as a pecker to the Pope."

As for the content of Patton's speech, Chamberlain probably would have said the same things, one way or another. The veteran who heard Patton remembered:

> His talk had mostly to do with his own practical principles of warfare—one of which was that a determined, aggressive attack, even though it seems risky, will usually cut down on casualties. For

example, he made the point that infantry soldiers advancing and fired upon should not "hit the dirt" as the saying goes. He said the Germans were using an old trick. They would have mortar or artillery pieces registered to hit a certain area. When our solders reached that area the Germans would put on a sudden and violent burst of machine gun fire—they could fire straight up into the air, it didn't matter; upon hearing it the inexperienced soldiers would throw themselves on the ground and while they were thus immobilized down would come the shells, causing immense casualties. Keep moving, Patton advised, and forget about fox holes. "You must shoot at the German," he said, "and keep on shooting. If you don't know where he is, shoot at where you think he is. But if you go out there holding your gun in one hand, and getting up and lying down and wandering around, then I will have to write letters to mothers and wives and sweethearts saying that Willie Jones got his ass shot off because he didn't do as he was told."[6]

This emphasis on the attack was, of course, Chamberlain's philosophy, as demonstrated in several battles, particularly the one at Little Round Top, in which his regiment probably would have been destroyed had it not fixed bayonets, charged, and routed the Confederate opponents.

But according to the Army's field manual, there is more to leadership than being aggressive and putting on a show. The manual points out that the good military leader must be tactically and technically proficient—must study and acquire substantial knowledge.[7] Chamberlain certainly fulfilled that requirement, as evidenced in a significant letter from Chamberlain to his wife written from an army camp in October 1862. He wrote, "I study, I tell you—every military work I can find," and he asked her to send him his copy of a book called *The Art of War*,[8] a work by Gen. Baron Antoine-Henri de Jomini, a participant in the Napoleonic wars and one of the nineteenth century's greatest military writers. Early in 1862 J. B. Lippincott had published an English translation. Chamberlain's possession of it indicated that his study went far beyond standard texts such as Casey's *Infantry Tactics.*

As for Patton, he was probably the greatest student of military history the U.S. Army ever saw. He had a huge library of books about campaigns that went all the way from modern wars back to those of remotest history, and he studied them avidly. Further, he sometimes startled people by claiming that he had participated in some battle that took place centuries ago. Chamberlain had this same mystical streak in him. Once when he was asked about the rumor that George Washington had been seen riding over the hills just before the battle of Gettysburg, he would not deny that it could have happened.[9] When visiting Gettysburg after the war, he felt a strong sense of spiritual presence.

The Army field manual designates creativity as another element of good leadership, and it cites Chamberlain's tactics on Little Round Top as an illustration: "Colonel Chamberlain's decision to extend his line and to charge showed creativity and imagination. Previous training had not addressed those types of situation, but his mind created the correct answers under the great stress of battle."[10] Here the influence of Jomini's *The Art of War* may possibly have been at work. The book was not really written for regimental commanders; it mostly has to do with the logistics, strategy, and grand tactics involved in the management of armies; but it did introduce an important thought—that though there may be three or four immutable principles of warfare, war is not an exact science; it is an art, and Jomini even identified the art as a *drama,* replete with human passions and complications.

There is no doubt that Patton also read Jomini. He, too, was a creator of "dramas," and an innovator—particularly in the use of armored vehicles. The army had come out of World War I with the idea that tanks should be part of the infantry—should be used in crushing down barbed wire, demolishing machine gun nests, and so on. Patton, who had been a cavalryman, promoted the idea that tanks should be formed into separate units that would make wide flanking moves and deep penetrations into enemy territory. Although he never got full credit for it, in the period between the two world wars Patton did much to develop not only the machines, but also the tactics for their use—resulting in the armored divisions that were so successful in World War II.

A number of comparisons have now been considered wherein Chamberlain and Patton are seen to have shared essential qualities for good leadership. Both could inspire their men through bearing and presence. Both were aggressive in the attack. Both studied hard and were technically proficient. Both were creative. Extending the comparison a bit beyond the manual, both were extremely determined men. For example, both had to overcome a physical disability early in life. Chamberlain had a speech impediment; he stammered badly when he came to words beginning with certain consonants. Patton had dyslexia, which made his schooling a struggle. They overcame these handicaps through sheer determination, a lifelong quality that sustained them under many difficult circumstances. Another similarity: Both men loved war; to Patton it was life itself, and he didn't mind saying so. Chamberlain was less direct: When he wrote to his wife describing the hardships and dangers of war he also told her that none of them could make him want to go back to teaching again.[11] Clearly he was enjoying a soldier's life. In his book *The Passing of the Armies* he disagreed somewhat with Sherman's statement that "War is hell," remarking that while war is terrible, it does bring out some of men's higher qualities.[12] On the part of both Patton and Chamberlain this inclination existed despite their painful battlefield wounds. A further likeness: Both officers were examples of that rather peculiar but not uncommon combination (one thinks of Stonewall Jackson)—a man who is both warlike and religious. Chamberlain graduated from a theological seminary and was a practicing Christian, active in his hometown church. Patton read the Bible faithfully—the Old Testament rather than the New, one would imagine, and he was famous for some of his wartime prayers (composed by his chaplain but delivered or circulated by the general with great dramatic effect).

So far the comparisons generally depict the two men in equally favorable light. But here is a point where Patton drops behind—a sad part of his story. *FM 22-100: Military Leadership* declares that a good leader must not only know human nature and know his soldiers, he must also know and be in control of himself.[13] In a notorious incident Patton failed to meet this requirement. He was led astray by the great empathy he had for his front-line troops. He often told those men that they were the ones who were winning the war. He was deeply moved by their sacrifices and often visited the wounded in hospitals. The other side of the coin was that he was enraged by anyone who seemed to be shirking his duty.

In the summer of 1943, while visiting a hospital in Sicily, Patton encountered a young soldier who had nothing visibly wrong with him. When asked why he was in the hospital, the man replied that it was his nerves—he couldn't stand the shelling—whereupon Patton lost his temper, slapped the man, yelled at him, called him a coward, and made a terrible scene. This and another slapping incident very nearly prompted Eisenhower to fire Patton and send him home in disgrace. He was able to save the situation by ordering Patton to apologize personally to the men he had slapped and to every unit of the Seventh Army. If—as nearly happened—Patton had been removed, the United States forces would have lost a great combat commander and the invasion of Europe in the following year might have gone very differently. This is a powerful illustration of how the actions of a leader, even in a small matter, may have far-reaching consequences.

Standing in contrast is Chamberlain's handling of a group of transferred soldiers from the 2nd Maine who came to the 20th Maine as replacements in May 1863, a large part of them in a state of mutiny as the regiment moved toward Gettysburg. The army leadership manual devotes several paragraphs to this. Here is the way Chamberlain described it.

> One hundred and twenty of these men from the Second Maine were recruits, whom some recruiting officer had led into the belief that they should be discharged with their regiment at the end of its term of service. In their enthusiasm they had not noticed that they were signing enlistment papers for "three years of the war"; and when they had been held in the field after the discharge of the regiment they had refused to do military duty, and had been sequestered in a prisoner's camp as mutineers, waiting court-martial. The exigency of our movement the last of May had not permitted this semi-civil treatment; and orders from the Secretary of War had directed me to take these men up on my rolls and put them to duty. This made it still harder for them to accept, as they had never enlisted in this regiment. However, they had been soon brought over to me under the guard of the 118th Pennsylvania, with fixed bayonets; with orders to take them into my regiment and "make them do duty, or shoot them down the moment they refused"; these had been the very words of the Corps Commander in person. The responsibility, I had thought, gave me some discretionary power. So I had placed their names on our rolls, distributed them by groups, to equalize companies, and particularly to break up the "esprit de corps" of banded mutineers. Then I called them together and pointed out to them the situation: that they could not be entertained as civilian guests by me; that they were by authority of the United States on my rolls as soldiers, and I should treat them as soldiers should be treated; that they should lose no rights by obeying my orders, and I would see what could be done for their claim."[14]

Chamberlain omitted a couple of things from his account. He did not say that while the 2nd Maine men were in the prison camp their rations were cut off; they hadn't eaten for three days, and he fed them immediately. Nor did he mention that he promptly wrote to the governor of Maine on their behalf. His talk to the mutineers dealt with the situation honestly. It made no promises that could not be kept. But his plain speaking, humane treatment, and understanding of their problem won the men over. Nearly all of them returned to duty and fought with the 20th Maine at Little Round Top, where almost certainly the added force of these combat-hardened veterans made the difference that led to victory. If it is assumed that the 20th Maine saved the Union that day, it must also be assumed that these mutineers, recovered by Chamberlain, saved the 20th Maine, some of them suffering wounds and death in the process. Another example of how leadership in a small matter can have far-reaching consequences.

Among the eulogies following Chamberlain's death in 1914 was one written by Edwin S. Witherell, who said he had served in Company D of the 2nd Maine Regiment and Company E of the 20th Maine—a combination indicating that he had been one of the group that included the mutineers. It follows, in part:

> I was transferred to his regiment from the 2nd Maine the last day of May, 1863, under the circumstances which made it hard for those who were put in a strange regiment, and it was there that those men transferred came to know the sterling qualities of this man. He seemed to feel with us the unpleasant features that were ours as we were placed in different companies, among new faces, and he—from what I have since learned—urged upon the officers and men of his command to show us that we were to be received with all consideration and shown all due courtesy, which soon won from us the devotion and love which increased with the months and years that we were with him.
>
> The afternoon of the 2nd of July, 1863, on Little Round Top at Gettysburg, amid the awful carnage, gave us to see what was in the calm, quiet man who watched every portion of his line with the care of a father . . . and in every way striving to encourage the officers and men in that hour of death struggle. . . .
>
> . . . in all the walks of life, his life was a constant uplift to those who came in contact with him. . . . At the regimental reunion in Lewiston, Me. in August, 1912, the men who gathered there were so wrought up on his entry to the hall that they wept and laughed and cheered until it seemed that the town itself could hear us.[15]

Again turning to *FM 22-100,* this leadership manual places great emphasis on ethical behavior. One sentence: "If you compromise your personal integrity, you break the bonds of trust between you, your soldiers, and your leaders."[16] There are many violations of ethical behavior that can be fatal to effective leadership. One occurs when an officer, instead of sending friends or favorites into danger, sends others instead, or favors a personal relationship in some other way. Author Carlo d'Este in his book *Patton, A Genius for War* relates a questionable incident that took place shortly after the Third Army crossed the Rhine. D'Este writes that Patton learned that his son-in-law was in a German POW camp at Hammelburg more than forty miles inside the enemy lines—that at the general's insistence a raid aimed at his rescue was conducted by a task force of 294 officers and men equipped with tanks, half-tracks, and self-propelled howitzers—and that the raid turned into a bloody disaster. The son-in-law, who was wounded in the affair, was rescued a couple of weeks later by the advance of an armored division. D'Este writes that "a pall was cast over Patton's reputation that was eclipsed only by the slapping incidents."[17]

Here again there is a comparison with Chamberlain. At one critical point in the fight at Little Round Top a small area in the center of his line, around the colors, had been almost shot away. He wrote: "I sent first to the regiment on our right for a dozen men to help us here, but they could not spare a man. I then called my young brother, Tom, the adjutant, and sent him forward to close that gap."[18]

Patton and Chamberlain. The two were much alike in many ways: in courage, conspicuous gallantry, aggressive action, knowledge, creativity, religious beliefs, ability to inspire—and yet the lack of two or three qualities denied Patton the place that he craved in the pantheon of heroic military leaders. As for Chamberlain, it is a strange and haunting circumstance that he, a civilian soldier of brief experience, attained seventy years after his death the professional military reputation he secretly longed for in life.

This is one of the more remarkable aspects of the Chamberlain "resurrection." In spirit and by example he marches on in the minds of young soldiers of the active army, the army reserves, and the National Guard as they read the pages of *FM 22-100.** At Gettysburg he helped save the nation. In some future crisis his influence may help save it again.

---

*A new and more comprehensive edition of *FM 22-100* entitled *Army Leadership* was issued in August 1999. In it many examples of outstanding leadership have been added. The manual has also been expanded to deal with three levels of leadership—direct, organizational, and strategic—and to address all Army leaders including Department of the Army civilians.

CHAPTER SIXTEEN

Something Abides

There is a phrase that has great currency among Chamberlain admirers—"something abides." General Chamberlain spoke it on the Gettysburg battlefield in 1889 at a dedication of the Maine monuments. "In great deeds something abides. On great fields something stays. Forms change and pass; bodies disappear; but spirits linger to consecrate the ground for the vision-place of souls."[1] He was obviously referring to the spiritual heritage that nearly everyone senses when visiting this famous battlefield—not talking about himself.

Yet to people familiar with the phrase it means a legacy left by Joshua Chamberlain; it is something they cannot quite express in words. It can, however, be defined as a summary of his life and accomplishments. The perceptions of Chamberlain and their effect on people are remarkable—and whether they are based on something wholly real or something partly mythical doesn't really matter anymore. Something, indeed, abides.

Of course the most important bequest symbolically was the nickel the old general asked to be given to little Francis O'Brien while lying on his deathbed. On its face it said "United States of America," and there is no telling what it might have said in 1914 had it not been for the victory on Little Round Top half a century previously. The importance of this victory is recognized by respectable opinion. For example, in a *New York Times* book review Frederick Allen, managing editor of *American Heritage* magazine, has written, "This astounding, almost intimate hand-to-hand combat, far more than the hopeless Pickett's charge the next day, was the pivotal moment of the Civil War and the nearest the Confederacy came to an outright tide-turning victory."[2]

Of conspicuous importance is Chamberlain's service as a practical role model for the nation's military leaders. He has now assumed a corresponding role for some of the nation's business managers. *The Washington Post,* in an April 4, 1998, article, describes a current method of executive training in which business executives are taken to historic battlefields, where they study the actions of military commanders who won—and those of some who lost—and draw from these studies lessons in leadership that could apply in making business decisions.[3] The executives get a fresh look at the importance of clear communication, ways of motivating people, how to succeed in spite of limited resources, and other techniques that seem to stick in their minds and stay with them when they return to their daily decision-making. The *Post* reported that Gettysburg is one of the favorite fields for this and Joshua Chamberlain's defense of Little Round Top one of the most popular "classes." His handling of the mutineers from the 2nd Maine, in particular, is a rich source of leadership ideas.

As for Chamberlain's legacy from his years as governor, his vision for the State of Maine is as valid today as it was when he introduced it in his addresses to the legislature and in his 1876 Centennial speech in Philadelphia, "Maine, Her Place in History." The vision contains a warning: A state that depends too much on selling the raw products of its natural resources courts trouble. As Chamberlain put it, "When they are gone, she is gone." A prosperous future, he insisted, depends on adding value to these products and creating new products through the brainpower, skill, and ingenuity of Maine's citizens.

Closely allied with this concept is the emphasis on education passed on by Chamberlain. The University of Maine is to some degree part of his legacy. He promoted its founding and development even though it would compete with his own beloved Bowdoin. The emphasis also applied to education at lower levels. For example, he urged better training for teachers of elementary schools. "Begin at the bottom and build upward," he said. As U.S. commissioner of education to the Paris Universal Exposition in 1878 he closely studied the systems in Germany and France; he reported that people there were educated from the cradle to the grave, that there was an effort to make higher education available to all classes, and some of their methods should be adopted in America. More education for more people was an idea he always promoted.

At Chamberlain's death Prof. Henry Johnson of the Bowdoin faculty, who had begun teaching there when Chamberlain was president of the college, said: "General Chamberlain was a life-long student and knew the joys of a scholar of unusually wide interests. . . . His theories of life and action were marked by a boldness which would have been recklessness in another less thoughtful and imaginative than he. The disappointments which such a generously self-giving nature as his was destined to encounter were many but they were often worth more to the causes which he espoused than the sober successes of the cautious."[4]

In October 1997 Bowdoin dedicated the cornerstone of a new $20.5 million science complex. Those attending the ceremony who had any knowledge of Bowdoin's history could not fail to remember the ill-fated science department that Chamberlain had tried to introduce in the 1870s, representing an idea that died but soon came to life again and grew to its present importance.

Not the least of Chamberlain's contributions has been a definite and discernible inspirational effect upon many people who are impressed by his character. Reading about such a man, or seeing him portrayed in film, produces an effect that may seem to be as insubstantial as that of sunlight or the wind, and yet we know how powerful it can be in shaping an individual's life. In one of his numerous speeches Joshua Chamberlain said: "Do we not see that character is largely the result of almost infinite imperceptible vibrations from all worlds with which we are in relations, traversing our spirit and leaving their impress?"[5]

Some of the visitors at the Joshua Chamberlain Museum in Brunswick have been asked to think about this man and then write down what it is about him that has attracted and inspired them. There is a variety in their replies.

A young Californian wrote: "What I admire about Joshua Lawrence Chamberlain is his idealism and willingness to put his life on the line in pursuit of his beliefs. He was a man who had a beautiful family, respectable profession and a relatively comfortable lifestyle. Yet, when his country needed him, he unhesitatingly sacrificed everything in answering the call. While history will rightly remember his gallant victories in battle, for me, his true heroism lies in his personal sacrifice to preserve the union and to set other men free."[6]

Another young man wrote, ". . . he was the righteous, selfless non-military professional who set aside his life to fight for the freedom of others. His care and concern for his men, the nobility in his attitude (and actions) toward the enemy and the war itself make him my personal hero—a man in uniform who was so much more."[7]

Both of these admirers had the impression that Chamberlain fought to "set other men free" or "for the freedom of others." They come by this idea honestly, in fact, unavoidably. The dominant projector of Chamberlain images has been the film *Gettysburg* based on the novel *The Killer Angels,* both of which present Chamberlain speaking to a group of mutinous replacements from the 2nd Maine. Part of the talk is a moving speech on the theme of fighting for the freedom of mankind. Yet, Chamberlain's account of what he actually said had nothing to do with freedom—of the slaves or of anyone else. He wrote a great deal about fighting to save the Union, or as he once put it, "to settle the question whether we were a nation or only a bag of chips."[8] Chamberlain recognized slavery's role in causing the conflict and its sweeping away as one of the great and, he thought, divinely ordained accomplishments of the Northern victory. But that was not what he thought he was fighting for, once the fight began. Most of the soldiers as well as their commander in chief had the same declared motivation: a desire and determination to save the Union.

Yet in reality Chamberlain *was* a freedom fighter and to see this impression enhancing his image in the eyes of young men is to understand how admirable qualities are added to the hero through the workings of mythology.

Chamberlain's effect on women is sometimes expressed in more direct and personal ways. One of them wrote this: "My feeling about Joshua was that he sought me out; he spoke to me. I am still learning about him and the more I learn the more I am inspired. I look upon him as a guardian spirit and have given him the title of my honorary great-grandfather." She also wrote, "To sum up, I will say he is an attractive man. Physically, of course. (No woman could miss that!)"[9]

Another woman wrote, "I have an attraction—as well as a bond, a connection so to speak, to Joshua L. Chamberlain, and try as I might, I can't explain why (not in a short space anyway)." She entrusted the explanation to a quotation she ascribed to Ralph Waldo Emerson: "There are persons, who in my heart I daily thank for existing—persons whose faces are unknown to me, but whose fame and spirit have penetrated my solitude— and for whose sake I wish to exist."[10]

One person commented that when we think of the need for role models we usually are thinking of young people, but old people need them as well, and who better than Joshua Chamberlain stands as an exemplar in the struggle against old age, the battle that nearly everyone fights and no one wins. She wrote, "He traveled all over giving speeches, helping veterans, helping his state, doing it all while in incredible pain. Nothing I have read regarding him makes mention of any complaints on his part about the suffering. Instead of sitting down and feeling sorry for himself, he went out and lived life."[11] She is right—the worry and pain of illness, the loss of loved ones, failing physical and mental powers, declining income, the humiliation of being forgotten or no longer important—these and other penalties of being "stricken in years," as the Bible so aptly puts it, did not diminish his courage nor quench his love of life.

In addition to these comments written by visitors to the Joshua Chamberlain Museum, letters from two members of police departments seem significant—this being a line of work in which there are frequent choices between difficult or dangerous courses of action and courses that are easier but of less benefit to the community. One who found inspiration in Chamberlain is Kenneth Discorfano, who in 1994 retired from a police captaincy after twenty-five years of service in northern New Jersey. Captain Discorfano used Chamberlain as a role model in training his recruits, and in the process he became a Chamberlain scholar. In 1991, while doing research on the scene of the Quaker Road battle he noticed that there was no historical marker for the field, whereupon he raised the money for one, mostly out of his own pocket, and with the approval of the proper authorities had it installed. Discorfano has characterized Chamberlain as one who "always exhibited high ideals and uncompromising behavior," was "a symbol of steadfastness," and "the ultimate hero."[12] He also has made this unusual comment: "His awareness level was always high. I can sense this in his writing and writing that I have read about him. This is a key to me. Under stress some people develop what is commonly called tunnel vision—that is, they focus on a small portion of matter or information relative to the event; such as the barrel of a gun during a hold-up. Others, conversely, are able to analyze the whole scene before them and in fact the intense concentration allows them a wider view of persons, the event, and the details of the event. This I know first hand from my own personal experience."[13]

Next comes an extract from a letter that appeared in the June 1998 issue of *The Civil War News.* It was from Linda L. Belfiore, a police sergeant in Florida. She was writing about Chamberlain as seen in the movie *Gettysburg:* "This film not only put me on a new road of knowledge which I now study extensively, but helped me redefine myself and through continued studies gave me the courage and determination to face some very strong obstacles in my career as a law enforcement officer. After seeing the film Gettysburg I now had a hero and something to believe in. It was called 'Doing the right thing—no matter what the cost.'"[14]

One who does the right thing no matter what the cost is probably as good a definition of a hero as any that can be written, and it seems to be the impression of Joshua Chamberlain that abides. The people who knew him, heard his voice, and saw him in action have long since passed from the scene. Yet the ideas and ideals he personified have not ceased to echo in the hearts of thousands. That is the Chamberlain legacy.

Notes

Most of the notes are keyed to first words in the bibliography listings. For authors with only one entry in the bibliography only last names are used in the notes. Otherwise, further identification is given. Certain sources to which only passing reference is made are cited in full in the notes and are not in the bibliography. The following abbreviations are used for frequently mentioned sources.

BS	Bowdoin College, Brunswick, Maine.
BCSC	Bowdoin College Special Collections, Hawthorne-Longfellow Library.
LC	Library of Congress, Washington, D.C.
JLC	Joshua Lawrence Chamberlain.
MeAG	Maine Adjutant General.
MHS	Maine Historical Society, Portland, Maine.
PHS	Pejepscot Historical Society, Brunswick, Maine.
RBHPC	Rutherford B. Hayes Presidential Center, Fremont, Ohio.

PROLOGUE

1. Information for the prologue is drawn from the *Daily Eastern Argus*, 28 February 1914; *Portland Evening Express*, 27 February 1914; and *Lewiston Journal*, 28 February 1914.

2. *Historical and Pictorial Review, National Guard of the State of Maine*, xxx, 37.

3. PHS photograph of the 10th Company taken in 1915. Springfield rifles in the picture were identified by Dwight B. Demeritt Jr.

4. Edward H. Snow (1890–1977) became a respected and fondly regarded schoolmaster. He was principal of the Ardmore Junior High School, Lower Merion Township, Pennsylvania, for thirty-three years, retiring in 1956. The author met him in the late 1950s and heard from him the story of his being on the firing squad.

CHAPTER 1: A VERY PERFECT KNIGHT

1. Oates, 220.
2. Jorgensen, 60–67.
3. Maine, *Maine at Gettysburg*, 46–48.
4. *New York Times Book Review*, 12 November 1995, 28.
5. JLC, *The Passing of the Armies*, 260.
6. "That would have been too much,"—*Not a Sound of Trumpet* (booklet), Chamberlain Papers, BCSC. "I instructed my subordinate commanders"—*Portland Sunday Telegram*, 14 April 1901.
7. JLC, *The Passing of the Armies*, 261.
8. Gordon, "Last Days of the Confederacy," 190.
9. VC, *Bowdoin* 64 (spring and summer 1991):3.
10. Chamberlain, Welton, 2, 35–39.
11. JLC to his parents 14 June 1878, Chamberlain Papers, BCSC.
12. MOLLUS, *In Memoriam*, 12.
13. Smith, 5.
14. JLC to his wife, Fanny, 19 June 1864, Chamberlain Papers, BCSC.
15. Maj. Gen. Gouverneur K. Warren to Maj. Gen. George G. Meade, 19 June 1864, Chamberlain Papers, LC.
16. JLC to his wife, Fanny, 10 October 1862, Chamberlain Papers, LC.
17. JLC, *The Passing of the Armies*, 391.
18. Ibid., 385–86.
19. "Last Campaign of the War," *Brunswick Record*, 5 February 1904.

CHAPTER 2: THE RELUCTANT REPUBLICAN

1. Maj. Gen. G. K. Warren to JLC 28 August 1866, Chamberlain Papers, LC. Warren has been asked to recommend six officers from the volunteers to General Grant for positions of field officers in new regiments and JLC should inform Grant if he does not want one of these commissions.
2. *Whig & Courier*, 24 April 1866. The letter was addressed to Bvt. Maj. Gen. Charles H. Smith of Eastport and had appeared prior to its *Whig & Courier* publication in the *Eastport Sentinel*.
3. JLC, *The Passing of the Armies*, 289, 292.
4. Ibid., 288.
5. *Kennebec Journal*, 29 June 1866.
6. Ibid., 6 July 1866.
7. Blaine, *Political Discussions*, 71.
8. Ibid., 66.
9. JLC, *The Passing of the Armies*, 260.
10. *Daily Eastern Argus*, 5 January 1867.

11. Ibid.

12. Maine, *Public Documents*, address of Governor Chamberlain, January 1867, 9.

13. Ibid., 10.

14. Blaine, *Twenty Years of Congress*, 353.

15. JLC, *The Passing of the Armies*, 260.

16. Interview with Campbell B. Niven in summer of 1994.

17. Fessenden, Francis, 137.

18. BCSC, Fessenden Papers.

19. Maine, *Journal of the House of Representatives, 1868*, 25 February, 322–23. In February 1868, it may not have been known that Fessenden was going to vote for acquittal. Otherwise Thomas B. Reed may not have voted for this resolution. Reed had been the Bowdoin College roommate of Fessenden's son Samuel, who was later killed in the Civil War. At Bowdoin, Reed's money ran out in his senior year. Samuel informed his father of this, and a timely loan from William Pitt Fessenden enabled Reed to graduate. Reed never forgot this. After the impeachment trial was over Reed defended Fessenden at some risk to himself, since he was only then entering upon a political career. See McCall, 22.

20. *Whig & Courier*, 19 May 1868.

21. Kennedy, 146.

22. *Portland Daily Press*, 16 May 1868; *Kennebec Journal*, 20 May 1868.

23. *Portland Evening Express*, 27 February 1914.

24. Francis Fressenden to JLC, 7 March 1899, Chamberlain Papers, LC.

25. JLC to Francis Fessenden, 9 March 1899, Chamberlain Papers, LC.

CHAPTER 3: DEALING WITH DEMON RUM

1. JLC, *The Passing of the Armies*, 49.

2. Hendricks.

3. Achorn.

4. Sherman, 16 August 1996.

5. Dow, 160.

6. Dow, 98–99.

7. Bunker, 9–10.

8. Maine, *Laws of Maine: Acts and Resolves of the 46th Legislature*, 86–88.

9. Ibid., 85–86.

10. Maine, *Laws of Maine: Acts and Resolves of the 37th Legislature*, 35.

11. Hatch, 535.

12. Maine, *Public Documents*, address of Governor Chamberlain, January 1870, 24–25.

CHAPTER 4: THE HANGING OF CLIFTON HARRIS

1. Maine, *Maine Reports*, vol. 54, 586.
2. Quoted in *Daily Eastern Argus*, 22 January 1867.
3. Ibid., 8 February 1867.
4. Ibid., 31 July 1867.
5. Maine, *Maine Reports*, vol. 54, 588.
6. Ibid., 586.
7. Ibid., 588. The judge was Jonathan G. Dickerson, one of the justices of the Maine Supreme Judicial Court.
8. Ibid., 591–92.
9. Maine, *Public Documents*, 1868–69, report of the attorney general, 7.
10. Ibid., address of Governor Chamberlain, January 1869, 8–10.
11. Maine, *Documents, Legislative*, 1868, House n. 126; Maine, *Journal of the House*, 353.
12. McCall, 248.
13. Maine, *Public Documents*, 1868–69, address of Governor Chamberlain, January 1869, 12.
14. Ibid.
15. BCSC, Thomas B. Reed to George Gifford, 27 January 1869, Thomas B. Reed Papers.
16. Ibid.
17. Maine, *Journal of the House*, 1869, 302.
18. *Daily Eastern Argus*, 13 March 1869.
19. Ibid.
20. JLC to his mother, Sarah Chamberlain, 27 June 1869, Chamberlain Papers, BCSC.
21. JLC to the king of Prussia, 20 July 1870, Chamberlain Papers, PHS.

CHAPTER 5: MAINE AS MAINE SHOULD BE

1. Maine, *Public Documents*, address of Governor Chamberlain, January 1867, 33.
2. *Celebration of the Decennial Anniversary of the Founding of New Sweden*, 52.
3. "Two Maines," *Down East*, 44 (August 1997): 9–14.
4. Maine Development Foundation and Maine Economic Growth Council newsletter *Measuring Maine's Economic Performance*, no. 1 (20

November 1997) and no. 57 (19 December 1997) report gross state product in 1994 as roughly 26 billion dollars and tourist spending in 1996 as more than 3 billion.

5. Maine, *Public Documents*, address of Governor Chamberlain, January 1867, 37.

6. JLC, "Maine, Her Place in History," 96.

7. Ibid., 100.

8. Wells, *The Water-Power of Maine*, 8.

9. "No More Electricity," *Down East*, 44 (September 1997): 22, a reprint of an *Ellsworth American* editorial criticizing legislation passed by the 118th Legislature tending to change the role of Maine utilities from generators to retailers of electricity when so much of the state's hydro resource is still underdeveloped.

10. Maine, *Public Documents*, address of Governor Chamberlain, January 1867, 22.

11. Maine Economic Growth Council, *Measures of Growth, 1998*, 8, 9.

12. Maine, *Public Documents*, address of Governor Chamberlain, January 1867, 40.

CHAPTER 6: REVEILLE FOR BOWDOIN

1. BCSC, *Bowdoin Orient*, 26 (10 February 1873): 201.

2. According to figures compiled by Robert M. Cross, secretary emeritus of Bowdoin College, while the four classes of 1835 through 1838 had a total of 198 students (graduates and nongraduates), the four classes of 1871 through 1874 had a total of 156.

3. JLC, "The New Education," 2, BCSC.

4. Calhoun, 189.

5. JLC, "The New Education," 4, BCSC.

6. BCSC, BC Overseers Records, 1860–89, 215 (17 July 1871); 240 (9 July 1872); 244 (10 July 1872).

7. Machiavelli, 55.

8. BCSC, BC Overseers Records, 1860–89, 263 (9 July 1873).

9. George L. Vose to the Trustees and Overseers of Bowdoin College in Overseers Records, 1860–89, 281 (13 November 1873), BCSC.

10. BCSC, BC Trustees Records 1854–1906, 242 (7 July 1874); 267 (6 July 1875); 352 (19 October 1880); 381 (1882).

11. Ibid., 314 (9 July 1874); 320 (8 July 1879).

Letters Among the Following Are in the Chamberlain Papers at the Depositories Mentioned:

12. Adelbert Ames to JLC, 22 January 1875, LC.

13. JLC to Abner Coburn, 20 January 1873, PHS.

14. Abner Coburn to JLC, 1 July 1872, PHS.

15. Marriner, 174, 397, 431–32, 528.

16. JLC to Nehemiah Cleaveland, 14 October 1859, LC.

17. JLC to a Miss Low, 9 October 1872, BCSC.

18. *Portland Evening Express*, 27 February 1914.

CHAPTER 7: MUTINY OF THE BOWDOIN CADETS

1. BCSC, BC Overseers Records, 1860–89, 240 (9 July 1872).

2. BCSC, *Bowdoin Orient*, 3 (28 January 1874): 146.

3. Ibid., 4 (3 June 1874): 26.

4. This was a printed manual (Brunswick, ME: J. Griffin, 1872). A copy is in the Chamberlain Papers, BCSC.

5. BCSC, *Bowdoin Orient*, 3 (9 July 1873): 64.

6. BCSC, J. P. Sanger, Bvt. Maj. U.S. Army, to the trustees and overseers of Bowdoin College, 6 January 1874, Chamberlain Papers. One of the twenty-eight-dollar uniforms mounted on a form can be seen in Chamberlain's former home in Brunswick, Maine, now the Joshua Chamberlain Museum.

7. Anderson, 33–37. Today Memorial Hall houses the Pickard Theater.

8. This petition, dated 12 November 1873, was a printed document; see Chamberlain Papers, BCSC, *Bowdoin Orient* 3 (11 February 1874): 159.

9. Pullen, 79–81, 97.

10. JLC to parents of Bowdoin students, in printed form, 29 May 1874, Chamberlain Papers, BCSC.

11. BCSC, BC Trustees Records 1854–1906, 305 (9 July 1878); *Bowdoin Orient*, 8 (8 May 1878): 17; *Bowdoin College, A Military History*, 4.

CHAPTER 8: MAINE ON THE BRINK OF CIVIL WAR

1. Quoted in *Daily Eastern Argus*, 30 October 1879.

2. Ibid.

3. Maine, *Annual Register* for the year 1880–81, 99.

4. *Whig & Courier*, 17 November 1879. In some accounts the number of votes for House Republicans is 89 because one Republican died following his election. The *Whig & Courier* evidently assumed that he would be replaced by a Republican.

5. Quoted in *Kennebec Journal*, 8 October 1879, 2.

6. *Whig & Courier*, 19 November 1879, 2.

7. Maine, *Report of the Joint Select Committee*, 657.

8. *Whig & Courier*, 17 November 1879.

9. Quoted in *Whig & Courier*, 29 November 1879.

10. Maine, *Report of the Joint Select Committee*, 551.

11. *Whig & Courier*, 22 December 1879.

12. Ibid.

13. Ibid.

14. Ibid.

15. Ibid., 20 December 1879.

16. JLC to James G. Blaine, 29 December 1879, PHS.

17. *Whig & Courier*, 27 December 1879.

18. Maine, *Report of the Joint Select Committee*, 665.

19. Ibid., 634.

CHAPTER 9: ANOTHER ROUND TOP

1. *Lewiston Journal*, 31 December 1879.

2. Bunker, 31.

3. A statement by Alice M. Farrington, niece of General Chamberlain, made in the early 1950s. It is remembered by the author's sister Ruth Pullen, who had accompanied him to Miss Farrington's home in Brewer, Maine, on a research trip pertaining to his book *The Twentieth Maine*.

4. Dingley, 166.

5. Ibid., 169.

6. Chamberlain Association of America, *Joshua Lawrence Chamberlain Supplement: The Twelve Days at Augusta 1880*, 10.

7. Ibid., 24.

8. Ibid.

9. Ibid., 19.

10. Ibid., 24–25.

11. JLC to his wife, Fanny, 15 January 1880, Chamberlain Papers, BCSC.

12. Depository for this letter and Blaine's letters of 14 and 16 January 1880, PHS.

13. *Kennebec Journal*, 21 January 1880.

14. Maine Writers Research Club, 30.

15. Ring, 61.

16. *Kennebec Journal*, 4 February 1880.

17. Chamberlain Papers, MHS.

18. JLC to John Appleton, 30 December 1880, Chamberlain Papers, MHS.

19. Quoted in the *Portland Daily Advertiser*, 22 December 1880.

20. *Twelve Days*, 26.

21. JLC to Professor Johnson, 6 February 1884, Chamberlain Papers, BCSC.

CHAPTER 10: FAMILY FORTUNES

1. For information about the First Parish Church and the Rev. George E. Adams, see Ashby, 180, 186–89, 206, 266–68.

2. Helmreich, 114.

3. Trulock, 43, 407 n. 45.

4. Adams, George E., diary entry for 22 May 1865.

5. Rachel Clark, secretary First Congregational Church, Brewer, Maine, to the author 3 July 1997.

6. Ashby, 367–68.

7. Ibid., 229; Adams, Herbert, "King's Voice Still Rings."

8. Helen R. Adams to JLC 25 December 1905, Chamberlain Papers, BCSC.

9. JLC to his wife, Fanny, 20 November 1868, Frost Family Papers, Yale University Library.

10. JLC to Bowdoin trustees, 8 July 1873, Chamberlain Papers, MHS.

11. In the Rutherford B. Hayes Papers, RBHPC.

12. Wyllys Chamberlain to his mother, Fanny, date not certain, may be 1891 or 1893, Chamberlain Papers, MHS.

13. Grace Allen to her mother, Fanny, 19 April 1883, Chamberlain Papers, BCSC.

14. JLC to his daughter, Grace Allen, 13 December 1886, Chamberlain Papers, BCSC.

CHAPTER 11: ECHOES OF MARTIAL GLORY

1. Most of the information concerning the Military Order of the Loyal Legion of the United States came from conversations and correspondence with Robert G. Carron, commander in chief of the order, and with John J. Craft and Steven J. Wright, director and curator respectively of the Civil War Library and Museum in Philadelphia, which is associated with the order.

2. JLC to Rutherford B. Hayes, 8 March 1877, Rutherford B. Hayes Papers, RBHPC.

3. Williams, *The Life of Rutherford Birchard Hayes*, 462.

4. Bunker, 44.

5. Williams, *Diary and Letters of Rutherford Birchard Hayes*, 4: 410–12.

6. JLC, report of a speech 17 October 1888 nominating the former president Rutherford B. Hayes, RBHPC.

7. JLC to his daughter, Grace Allen, 13 July 1888, BCSC.

8. JLC, *The Passing of the Armies*, 15.

9. MOLLUS, 11.

10. *New York Times*, 24 July 1885.

11. Ibid., 25 July 1885.

12. Ibid., 29 July 1885.

13. Depository of this letter, Maine State Museum, Augusta, Maine.

14. Simon, 271 n.

15. Grant, 517.

16. *Medal of Honor Recipients*, 401.

CHAPTER 12: A BATTLE REMEMBERED

1. *Mark Twain's Autobiography* 2 vol. New York: Harper & Brothers Publishers, 1924. 1:xii.

2. JLC, "Last Salute of the Army of Northern Virginia," 363.

3. Norton 12–13. Colonel Rice did not live to write a reminiscence but he did write an after-action report dated 31 July 1863; see Norton, 205–10.

4. Desjardin, 129; Norton, 243; the regiment was the 16th Michigan.

5. Gerrish, *Life in the World's Wonderland*, 177 (1887 edition).

6. Gerrish, *Army Life*, 109–11.

7. Styple, 133.

8. Nesbitt, 91.

9. Ibid., 80–94.

10. *Dedication of the Twentieth Maine Monuments*, 20.

11. Ibid., 23.

12. Ibid., 28–29.

13. Spear, 36.

14. *Dedication of the Twentieth Maine Monuments*, 18.

15. Ibid., 27.

16. Ibid., 29.

17. This letter is from the collection of Marjorie Spear of Warren, Maine, and her late husband Abbott.

18. Ibid.

19. Judson, 130.

20. JLC to William C. Oates, 18 May 1905, Gettysburg National Military Park Library. In this depository there is extensive 1903–5 correspondence concerning the 15th Alabama monument.

21. Son of a man who fought with the 20th Maine, his name now forgotten. His words are remembered by the author from an interview while gathering material for his book *The Twentieth Maine* in the early 1950s.

22. Ladd and Ladd, 992–93.

23. *Dedication of the Twentieth Maine Monuments*, 32.

24. Abner R. Small Collection (no. 135) MHS.

25. Ibid.

26. Ibid.

27. Ibid.

28. Maine, *Maine at Gettysburg*, 63–66.

CHAPTER 13: "YOU'VE DONE ENOUGH AT GETTYSBURG"

1. Depository, National Archives, Chamberlain File.

2. Ibid; this letter was written to William P. Frye.

3. Ames, 651–52.

4. Justice William P. Whitehouse to Sen. William P. Frye, 25 November 1899, Chamberlain Papers, MHS; Ellis Spear to Hon. Amos Allen, 4 December 1899, Chamberlain Papers, BCSC. An inventory of Chamberlain's estate following his death showed a total value of $33,018, and a dollar was worth something in 1914. For example, the total for his real estate was only $10,340, but it included a tract of thirty-five acres in Brunswick between Maine and Harpswell Streets just south of Bowdoin College; his oceanside place, Domhegan, consisting of five or six acres on Simpson's Point, Casco Bay, with a building described as a summer hotel and other structures; a house and lot at 499 Ocean Avenue, Portland, and three lots in South Portland; and a house and eight acres in Brewer. His home on Maine Street in Brunswick was not included. (PHS photocopies of probate records.)

5. Hon. Amos L. Allen to G. M. Elliott, M.D., 12 December 1899, Chamberlain Papers, MHS.

6. Hon. Amos L. Allen to JLC, 2 February 1900, RBHPC.

7. U.S. Treasury Department, *Customs Regulations of the United States*, 422; Farnsworth, 297.

8. JLC to Gen. John T. Richards, 26 December 1899, Chamberlain Papers, MHS.

9. The quoted passages that follow, describing JLC's trip, are from the *Portland Daily Press*, 28 February 1901, and the *Portland Sunday Telegram*, 17 March 1901; JLC's 21 December 1900 letter to Collector Moses appeared in the *Portland Daily Press*, 10 January 1901.

10. Old York Historical and Imprint Society, 102–20; McCall, 1.

11. JLC, *The Passing of the Armies*, 27.

12. *Daily Eastern Argus*, 27 August 1902.

13. JLC to his wife, Fanny, 11 February 1903, Chamberlain Papers, BCSC.

14. JLC to Robert Peary, 5 October 1909, Chamberlain Papers, BCSC. Depository for the letters referred to in the next eight notes is the Maine State Archives Collection: Adjutant General's correspondence and records

pertaining to the 50th Reunion at Gettysburg.

15. MeAG to JLC, 6 May 1913, reporting that 533 veterans who participated in the battle had signed up to go, along with 56 veterans who wanted to go at their own expense.

16. MeAG to JLC, 16 December 1912.

17. JLC to MeAG, 17 December 1912.

18. Ibid., 31 March 1913.

19. Ibid., 25 April 1913.

20. Ibid., 29 April 1913.

21. JLC to Col. Frederic E. Boothby, 21 May 1913.

22. Ibid., 21 July 1913.

23. Author's conversation with Francis O'Brien, 11 March 1994, shortly before his death.

CHAPTER 14: FAME RETURNS

1. Eccles: 1:11, RSV.

2. Chamberlain's history is found on 330–37 of this report, General Smith's on 457–67, and Col. Ellis Spear's on 468–69.

3. Pages about Chamberlain, 43–50.

4. Quoted in Roberts, "Don't Say That About Maine," 7.

5. JLC, *The Passing of the Armies*, 261.

6. Lynn Carrick, J. B. Lippincott editor, to the author 5 November 1957, in author's possession.

7. JLC, *The Passing of the Armies*, 57.

8. *Chamberlain*, with book and lyrics by Sarah Knapp and music by Stephen M. Alper, ran from August 14 through August 24, 1996, in the Pickard Theater on the Bowdoin College campus, Brunswick, Maine (The Maine State Music Theatre).

9. Campbell, 11.

CHAPTER 15: RECALL TO SERVICE

1. Lt. Col. Boyd M. Harris to the author, 27 October 1982, in author's possession.

2. U.S. Army, *FM 22-100: Military Leadership*, 31 October 1983, 125.

3. Trulock, 208, 235.

4. Desjardin, 155.

5. Talk by Gen. George S. Patton Jr. to officers and noncommissioned officers of the 65th Infantry Division at Ennery, France, 5 March 1945, transcription by the author, in author's possession.

6. Ibid.

7. U.S. Army, *FM 22-100: Military Leadership*, 31 July 1990, 6, 41–42.

8. JLC to his wife, Fanny, 26 October 1862, Chamberlain Papers, LC.

9. *Bangor Daily News*, 1 July 1913.

10. U.S. Army, *FM 22-100: Military Leadership*, 31 October 1983, 124.

11. JLC to his wife, Fanny, 10 October 1862, Chamberlain Papers, LC.

12. JLC, *The Passing of the Armies*, 385–86.

13. U.S. Army, *FM 22-100: Military Leadership*, 31 July 1990, 4, 6.

14. JLC, "Through Blood and Fire at Gettysburg," 899–900.

15. *Daily Eastern Argus*, 27 February 1914, reprinted from the *Springfield Republican*.

16. U.S. Army, *FM 22-100: Military Leadership*, 31 July 1990, 30.

17. D'Este, 714–16.

18. JLC, "Through Blood and Fire at Gettysburg," 904.

CHAPTER 16: SOMETHING ABIDES

1. JLC, *Address at the Dedication of the Maine Monuments*, 15.

2. *New York Times Book Review*, 8 March 1998, 17.

3. Berselli, A1, A10.

4. *Portland Evening Express* and *Daily Advertiser*, 24 February 1914.

5. JLC, remarks made at the dinner of the Chamberlain Association of America, Boston, 8 September 1898.

6. Dan Revetto, Tujunga, California.

7. Mark Smith, Columbus, Ohio.

8. Untitled fragment in Chamberlain Papers, BCSC.

9. Phyllis Marshall Watson, Brunswick, Maine.

10. Una C. Dietlin, Brunswick, Maine.

11. Cheryl A. Pula, New York Mills, New York.

12. Kenneth Discorfano, Tucson, Arizona; letters to the author, in author's possession.

13. Ibid.

14. Linda L. Belfiore, *The Civil War News*, June 1998, first section, 6.

Bibliography

Abrahamson, James L. *American Arms for a New Century.* New York: Free Press, 1981.

Achorn, Edgar Oakes. "General Chamberlain." Chamberlain Papers. Bowdoin College Special Collections. Hawthorne-Longfellow Library.

Adams, George E. Diary, 1839–70. Archives of the First Parish Church, Brunswick, ME.

Adams, Herbert. "Summer in York Harbor Was Start of Twain's Fall." *Maine Sunday Telegram,* 4 August 1985.

———. "King's Voice Still Rings in Maine." *Maine Sunday Telegram* 17 January 1988.

Ames, Blanche Butler, comp. *Chronicles from the Nineteenth Century: Family Letters of Blanche Butler and Adelbert Ames, 1874–1899.* Vol. 2. Clinton, MA: Colonial Press, 1957. Privately issued.

Anderson, Patricia M. *The Architecture of Bowdoin College.* Brunswick, ME: Bowdoin College Museum of Art, 1988.

Ashby, Thompson E. *A History of the First Parish Church in Brunswick, Maine.* Brunswick, ME: J. H. French and Son, 1969.

Beale, Howard K. *The Critical Year: A Study of Andrew Johnson and Reconstruction.* New York: Harcourt, Brace & Co., 1930.

Berselli, Beth. "Cannons of Management: Executives Flock to the Battlefields for Training," *Washington Post,* 4 April 1988.

Blaine, James G. *Political Discussions, Legislative, Diplomatic and Popular.* Norwich, CT: Henry Bill Publishing Co., 1887.

———. *Twenty Years of Congress.* Vol. 2. Norwich, CT: Henry Bill Publishing Co., 1886.

Bowdoin College. *Bowdoin.* 64 (Spring and Summer 1991).

———. *General Catalogue of 1784–1950.* Portland, ME: Anthoensen Press, 1950.

Bowdoin College, Special Collections (BCSC), Hawthorne-Longfellow Library. *Bowdoin College: A Military History.*

———. *Bowdoin Orient.* Selected issues 1873–78.

———. Chamberlain Papers.

———. Fessenden Papers.

———. *Not a Sound of Trumpet.* Booklet in Chamberlain Papers.

———. Overseers Records, Bowdoin College, 1860–89.

———. *Regulations for the Interior Police and Discipline of the Bowdoin Cadets.* Brunswick, ME: J. Griffin, 1872. In Chamberlain Papers.

———. Thomas Brackett Reed Papers.

———. Trustees Records, Bowdoin College, 1854–1906.

Brunswick Record (ME).

Brunswick Telegraph (ME).

Bunker, Benjamin. *Bunker's Textbook of Political Deviltry.* Waterville, ME: Kennebec Democrat, 1880.

Calhoun, Charles C. *A Small College in Maine: Two Hundred Years of Bowdoin.* Brunswick, ME: Bowdoin College, 1993.

Calkins, Chris M. *The Final Bivouac: The Surrender Parade at Appomattox and the Disbanding of the Armies.* Lynchburg, VA: H. E. Howard, 1988.

Campbell, Joseph. *The Hero With a Thousand Faces.* New York: MJF Books, 1949.

Casey, Silas. *Infantry Tactics.* 3 vols. New York: D. Van Nostrand, 1862.

Catton, Bruce. *U.S. Grant and the American Military Tradition.* Boston: Little, Brown & Co., 1954.

Celebration of the Decennial Anniversary of the Founding of New Sweden, Maine, July 23, 1880. Portland, ME: B. Thurston & Co., 1881.

Chamberlain Association of America. *Joshua Chamberlain: A Sketch.* 1906.

———. *Joshua Lawrence Chamberlain Supplement: The Twelve Days at Augusta, 1880.* Smith & Sale, Printers, 1906.

Chamberlain, Joshua L. (JLC) *Address . . . at the Dedication of the Maine Monuments on the Battlefield of Gettysburg, October 3, 1893.* Augusta, ME: Maine Farmers Almanac Press, 1895.

———. Addresses as governor to the Maine legislature, 1867–70. In *Public Documents of Maine* for those years. See Maine.

———. "Do It! That's How!" In *Bowdoin* 64 (Spring and Summer 1991): 3–15.

———. "Last Salute of the Army of Northern Virginia." *Southern Historical Society Papers* 32 (1904): 355–63.

———. Letters in collections at Bowdoin College Special Collections, Hawthorne-Longfellow Library; Library of Congress; Maine Historical Society; Maine State Archives; Maine State Museum; Yale University, Sterling Library; Rutherford B. Hayes Presidential Center.

———. "Maine, Her Place in History." Address delivered at the Centennial

Exposition, Philadelphia, 4 November 1876. As "Centennial Address," in *Public Documents*. Vol. 1. Maine: 1877.

———. "The New Education." Inaugural address upon becoming president of Bowdoin College. Chamberlain Papers, Bowdoin College Special Collections, Hawthorne-Longfellow Library.

———. *The Passing of the Armies*. New York: G. P. Putnam's Sons, 1915.

———. Remarks made at the dinner of the Chamberlain Association of America in Boston on September 8, 1898. Included in the report of the Association published in 1902.

———. Report of a speech 17 October 1888 nominating the former president Rutherford B. Hayes for commander in chief of the Military Order of the Loyal Legion of the United States. Rutherford B. Hayes Papers. Rutherford B. Hayes Presidential Center, Fremont, OH.

———. "Through Blood and Fire at Gettysburg." *Hearst's Magazine*. June 1913.

Chamberlain, Welton C. *Richard Chamberlain of Braintree, 1642: His Norman and English Ancestors and Descendants, 865–1991*. Pinckney, MI: Privately printed, 1991.

Charnwood, Baron Godfrey R. B. *Abraham Lincoln*. Garden City, NY: Garden City Publishing Co., 1917.

Cross, Robert M. "Joshua Lawrence Chamberlain." Chamberlain Papers. Bowdoin College Special Collections, Hawthorne-Longfellow Library.

Daily Eastern Argus, (Portland, ME).

Dedication of the Twentieth Maine Monuments at Gettysburg October 3, 1889. Waldoboro, ME: News Steam Job Print, 1891.

de Jomini, Baron Antoine H. *The Art of War*. London: Greenhill Books, 1992.

Desjardin, Thomas A. *Stand Firm Ye Boys from Maine*. Gettysburg: Thomas Publications, 1995.

D'Este, Carlo. *Patton: A Genius for War*. New York: HarperCollins, 1995.

Dingley, Edward Nelson. *The Life and Times of Nelson Dingley, Jr., by His Son, Edward Nelson Dingley*. Kalamazoo, MI: Ihling Bros. & Everord, 1902.

Dow, Neal. *The Reminiscences of Neal Dow*. Portland, ME: Evening Express Publishing Co., 1898.

Eckert, Ralph L. *John Brown Gordon: Soldier, Southerner, American*. Baton Rouge, LA: Louisiana State Univ. Press, 1989.

Farnsworth, Arthur L. "How Business is Transacted at Custom Houses." *Board of Trade Journal*, (Portland, ME) January 1904.

BIBLIOGRAPHY 205

Fessenden, Edwin A., ed. *The Fessenden Family in America.* Vol. 2. New York: Vestal, 1971.

Fessenden, Francis. *Life and Public Services of William Pitt Fessenden.* Vol. 2. Boston: Houghton Mifflin Co., 1907.

Foner, Eric. *Reconstruction: America's Unfinished Revolution, 1863–1877.* New York: Harper & Row, 1988.

———. *A Short History of Reconstruction 1863–1877.* New York: Harper & Row, 1990.

———. *Nothing But Freedom: Emancipation and Its Legacy.* Baton Rouge, LA: Louisiana State Univ. Press, 1983.

Gerrish, Theodore. *Army Life: A Private's Reminiscences of the Civil War.* Portland, ME: Hoyt, Fogg & Donham, 1882.

———. *Life in the World's Wonderland.* Biddeford, ME: Press of the Biddeford Journal, 1887. There is also another edition, np. nd.

Gordon, John B. "Last Days of the Confederacy." In *Modern Eloquence.* Vol. 8. New York: Modern Eloquence Corporation, 1923.

———. *Reminiscences of the Civil War.* New York: Charles Scribner's Sons, 1903.

Graham, John. "Month of Madness: Maine's Brush with Civil War." Master's thesis, Univ. of New Hampshire, 1981.

Grant, Ulysses S. *Personal Memoirs of U. S. Grant.* 2 vols. in 1. New York: Charles Webster & Co., 1894.

Hatch, Louis C., ed. *Maine, a History.* 1919. Reprint, with an introduction and bibliography by William B. Jordan Jr., Somersworth, NH: New Hampshire Publishing Co., 1974.

Helmreich, Ernst C. *Religion at Bowdoin College: A History.* Brunswick, ME: Bowdoin College, 1981.

Hendricks, L. A. "Despatch from HQ Fifth Army Corps Near Appomattox Court House April 9, 4 p.m." *New York Freeman's Journal and Catholic Register.* 22 April 1865.

Historical and Pictorial Review. National Guard of the State of Maine, 1939. Baton Rouge, LA: Army and Navy Publishing Co., 1939.

The Lewiston Journal (ME).

Jorgensen, Jay. "Holding the Right: The 137th New York at Gettysburg." *Gettysburg Magazine.* no. 15.

Judson, Amos M. *History of the Eighty-Third Regiment Pennsylvania Volunteers.* Erie, PA: B.F.H. Lynn, [1865]; set in new type, Dayton, OH: Morningside Books, 1986.

Kennebec Journal (Augusta, ME).

Kennedy, John F. *Profiles in Courage*. Memorial Edition. New York: Harper & Row, 1964.

Ladd, David L., and Audrey J., eds. *The Bachelder Papers: Gettysburg in Their Own Words*. Vol. 2. Dayton, OH; Morningside House, 1994.

Lister, Brian C. "Alonzo Garcelon, 1813–1906: The Man and His Times." Ph.D. diss., Univ. of Maine at Orono, 1975. Facsimile, University Microfilms International, Ann Arbor, MI, 1979.

Little, George T. Historical sketch in *General Catalogue of Bowdoin College and the Medical School of Maine, 1794–1894*. Brunswick, ME: Bowdoin College, 1894.

Machiavelli, Niccolo. *The Prince*. New York: New American Library of World Literature, 1952.

Maine State Archives. Correspondence and other records pertaining to the reunion of veterans at the fiftieth anniversary of the Battle of Gettysburg.

Maine, published documents. *Adjutant General's Report*, 1864–65. Vol. 1.

———. *Annual Register of Maine*, 1879–80 and 1880–81.

———. *Journal of the House of Representatives*. 1868 and 1869.

———. *Laws of Maine: Acts and Resolves of the 37th Legislature* (1858), *the 46th Legislature* (1867), and *the 47th Legislature* (1868).

———. *Maine at Gettysburg. Report of Maine Commissioners, 1898*.

———. *Maine Reports*. Vol. 54.

———. *Public Documents, Legislative*, 1868.

———. *Public Documents of Maine, being the Annual Reports of Various Public Officers and Institutions*, 1867–70, 1877, and 1880.

———. *Report of the Joint Select Committee to Inquire Into the Condition of the Election Returns of September 8, 1879*.

Maine Writers Research Club. *Just Maine Folks*. Lewiston, ME: Journal Printshop, 1924.

Marriner, Ernest C. *The History of Colby College*. Waterville, ME: Colby College Press, 1963.

McCall, Samuel W. *The Life of Thomas Brackett Reed*. Boston: Houghton Mifflin Co., 1914.

Medal of Honor Recipients, 1863–1963. Washington, DC: Government Printing Office, 1964.

Miller, Nathan. *Theodore Roosevelt, A Life*. New York: William Morrow & Co., 1992.

(MOLLUS) Military Order of the Loyal Legion of the United States, Commandery of the State of Maine. *In Memoriam, Joshua Lawrence Chamberlain*. Portland, ME: 1914.

Mundy, James H. *Second to None: The Story of the 2nd Maine Volunteer Infantry.* Scarborough, ME: Harp Publications, 1992.

Nesbitt, Mark. *Through Blood and Fire: Selected Civil War Papers of Major General Joshua Chamberlain.* Mechanicsburg, PA: Stackpole Books, 1996.

New York Times

Norton, Oliver W. *The Attack and Defense of Little Round Top.* Dayton, OH: Press of Morningside Bookshop, 1978.

Oates, William C. *The War Between the Union and the Confederacy.* Dayton, OH: Press of Morningside Bookshop, 1974.

Old York Historical and Imprint Society. *Two Hundred and Fiftieth Anniversary of the Town of York, Maine, 1652–1902.* York, ME: Privately printed, 1902.

Portland Daily Advertiser (ME).

Portland Sunday Telegram (ME).

Portland Evening Express (ME).

Pullen, John J. *The Twentieth Maine: A Volunteer Regiment in the Civil War.* Philadelphia: J. B. Lippincott Co., 1957.

Reilly, Wayne. "The Harris Horror." *Down East Magazine* 43 (November 1996): 64–77.

Reunions of the Twentieth Maine Regiment Association at Portland. Waldoboro, ME: Press of Samuel L. Miller, 1881.

Ring, Elizabeth. "Fannie Hardy Eckstrom: Maine Woods Historian." *The New England Journal* 26 (March 1953): 45–64.

Roberts, Kenneth L. "Don't Say That About Maine." *The Saturday Evening Post*, 1948; Portland, ME: Anthoensen Press, 1986.

———. *Trending Into Maine.* 2nd ed. Garden City, NY: Doubleday, Doran & Co., 1944.

Schriver, Edward. "Reluctant Hangman: The State of Maine and Capital Punishment, 1820–1887." *The New England Quarterly:* 63 (June 1990): 271–87.

Shaara, Michael. *The Killer Angels.* New York: David McKay Co., 1974.

Sherman, Sylvia J. "Chamberlain Days." Lectures presented for the Pejepscot Historical Society, 16 August 1996 and 15 August 1997.

Simon, John Y., ed. *The Papers of Ulysses S. Grant.* Vol. 15. Cardondale: Southern Illinois Univ. Press, 1980.

Smith, Mrs. Winfield. Interview by Elizabeth D. Copeland. In Chamberlain Papers, Pejepscot Historical Society, Brunswick, ME.

Spear, Ellis. *The Civil War Recollections of General Ellis Spear.* Orono: Univ. of Maine Press, 1997.

Story of New Sweden as told at the Quarter Centennial Celebration, June 25, 1895. Portland, ME: Loring, Short & Harmon, 1896.

Styple, William B., ed. *With a Flash of His Sword: The Writings of Major Holman S. Melcher, 20th Maine Infantry*. Kearny, NJ: Belle Grove Publishing Co., 1994.

The Times Record (Brunswick, ME).

The Transcript (Portland, ME).

Trulock, Alice R. *In the Hands of Providence*. Chapel Hill: Univ. of North Carolina Press, 1992.

U.S. Army. *FM 22-100: Military Leadership*. Washington, DC: Headquarters Department of the Army, 1983 and 1990.

U.S. Treasury Department. *Customs Regulations of the United States*. Washington, DC: Government Printing Office, 1892.

Wallace, Willard M. *Soul of the Lion: A Biography of General Joshua L. Chamberlain*. New York: Thomas Nelson & Sons, 1960.

Wells, Walter. *Provisional Report Upon the Water-Power of Maine*. Augusta, ME: Stevens & Sayward, Printers to the State, 1868.

———. *The Water-Power of Maine*. Augusta, ME: Sprague, Owens & Nash, Printers to the State, 1869.

Whig & Courier (Bangor, ME).

Williams, Charles R., ed. *Diary and Letters of Rutherford Birchard Hayes*. Columbus, OH: The Ohio State Archaeological and Historical Society, 1922–26.

———. *The Life of Rutherford Birchard Hayes*. Vol. 1. Boston: Houghton Mifflin Co., 1914.

Williams, T. Harry. *Hayes of the Twenty-Third: The Civil War Volunteer Officer*. New York: Alfred A. Knopf, 1965.

Index

(Numerals in bold typeface indicate an illustration.)